MORRISON HOTEL

PUBLISHERS	Joshua Frankel & Sridhar Reddy
CFO & GENERAL COUNSEL	Kevin Meek
SENIOR V.P.	Josh Bernstein
V.P., PUBLIC RELATIONS & MARKETING	Jeremy Atkins
V.P., DIGITAL	Anthony Lauletta
EDITORIAL COORDINATOR	Dominique Rosés
ARTIST LIAISON	Jess Lechtenberg
PRODUCTION DESIGN DIRECTOR	Courtney Menard
DESIGN DIRECTOR	Tyler Boss
SENIOR DIGITAL MARKETING ASSOCIATE	Rebecca Cicione

WORLDWIDE MANAGEMENT	Jeffrey Jampol for JAM, Inc.
ASSOCIATE MANAGER	Kenny Nemes for JAM, Inc.
THE DOORS ARCHIVIST	David Dutkowski
LEGAL	John Branca, David Byrnes and Penny Lambert at Ziffren, Brittenham LLP

Special Thanks to Jesse Nicita & John Logan

MORRISON HOTEL

Written by .... Leah Moore

Lettered by ... Justin Birch

Edited by ... Rantz Hoseley

Cover Art by ... Chris Hunt

www.thedoors.com

DOORS PROPERTY, LLC

Morrison Hotel came along at the perfect time for The Doors. Jim was on trial for the Miami incident, so we couldn't do any touring. We had finished our most difficult album to make, The Soft Parade - it was a lot of work because we were trying to keep up with The Beatles and decided to bring in a string section and horns. It came out great with "Touch Me" topping the charts, but it just took forever to make. Morrison would get bored and go out drinking, so it was impossible to get a good vocal until the following day.

Morrison Hotel was going to be the opposite. We decided to have fun, and keep it simple and bluesy... Thus - "Roadhouse Blues", "Peace Frog", "Maggie M'Gill", and "The Spy"... some of my favorites. Also, the album cover was really fun to shoot. Ray was driving around in downtown L.A. and discovered the Morrison Hotel. Rooms $2.50 a night! So, we got our buddy Henry Diltz to come down and take pictures of us at the hotel. It turned out to be one of the most iconic album covers of all time.

I'm hoping our new graphic novel captures all of these things, and that the readers will be right there with us in spirit!

Robby Krieger, Los Angeles, 2020

Intro
Roadhouse Blues

Artist . . . . Tony Parker
Colorist . . . Aladdin Collar

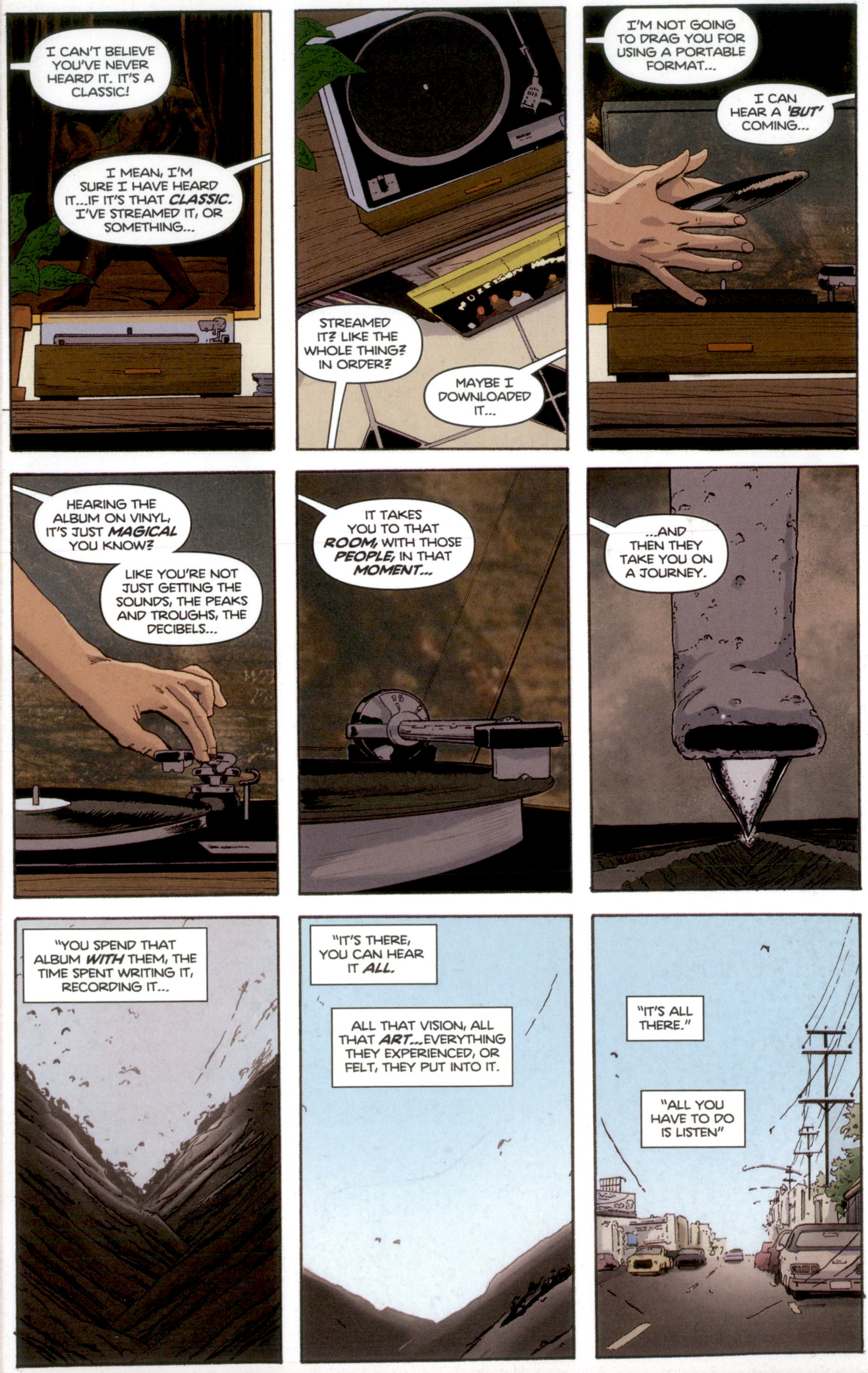

I CAN'T BELIEVE YOU'VE NEVER HEARD IT. IT'S A CLASSIC!
I MEAN, I'M SURE I HAVE HEARD IT...IF IT'S THAT CLASSIC. I'VE STREAMED IT, OR SOMETHING...
STREAMED IT? LIKE THE WHOLE THING? IN ORDER?
MAYBE I DOWNLOADED IT...
I'M NOT GOING TO DRAG YOU FOR USING A PORTABLE FORMAT...
I CAN HEAR A 'BUT' COMING...
HEARING THE ALBUM ON VINYL, IT'S JUST MAGICAL YOU KNOW?
LIKE YOU'RE NOT JUST GETTING THE SOUNDS, THE PEAKS AND TROUGHS, THE DECIBELS...
IT TAKES YOU TO THAT ROOM, WITH THOSE PEOPLE, IN THAT MOMENT...
...AND THEN THEY TAKE YOU ON A JOURNEY.
"YOU SPEND THAT ALBUM WITH THEM, THE TIME SPENT WRITING IT, RECORDING IT...
"IT'S THERE, YOU CAN HEAR IT ALL.
ALL THAT VISION, ALL THAT ART...EVERYTHING THEY EXPERIENCED, OR FELT, THEY PUT INTO IT.
"IT'S ALL THERE."
"ALL YOU HAVE TO DO IS LISTEN"

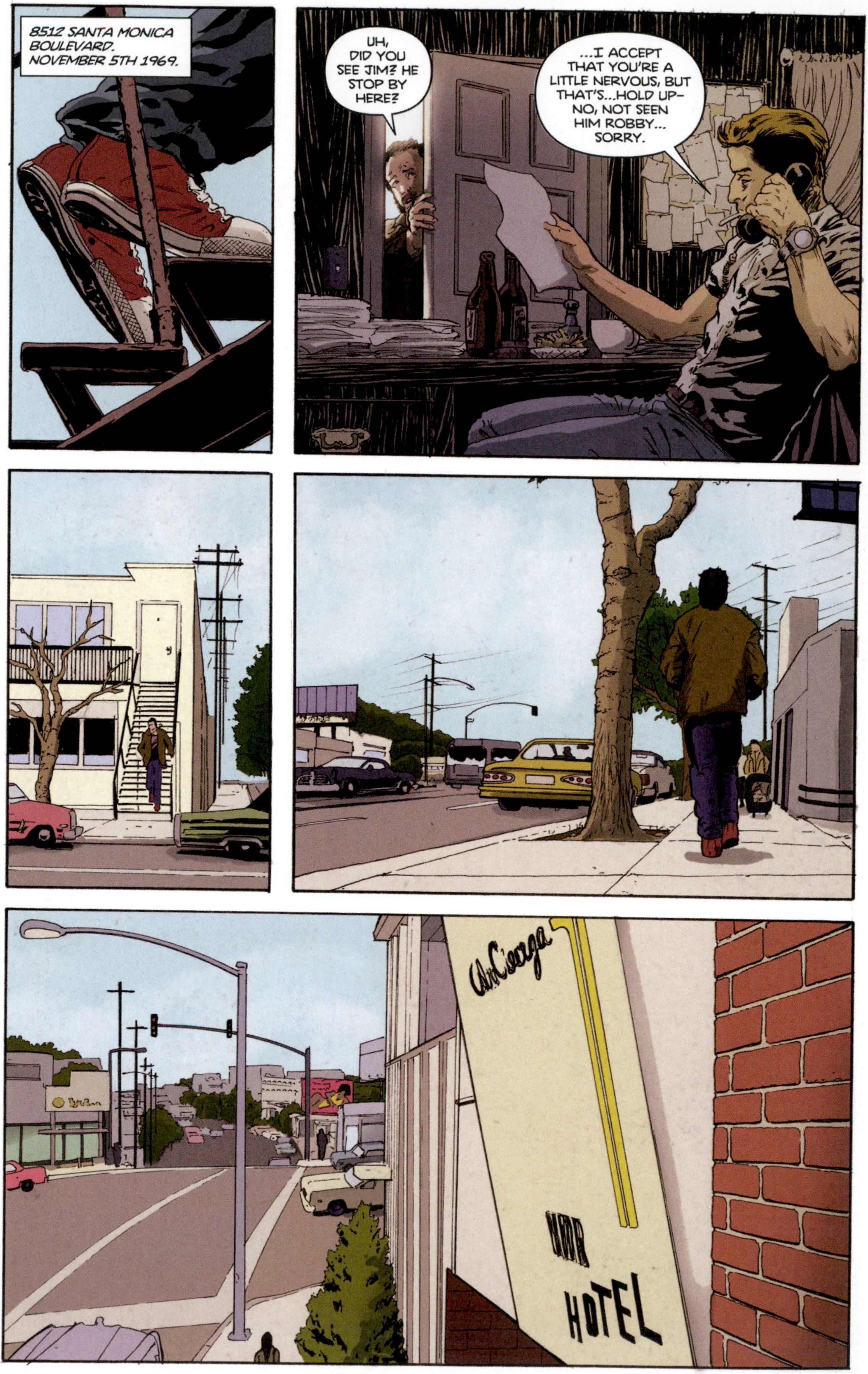
8512 SANTA MONICA BOULEVARD. NOVEMBER 5TH 1969.
UH, DID YOU SEE JIM? HE STOP BY HERE?
...I ACCEPT THAT YOU'RE A LITTLE NERVOUS, BUT THAT'S...HOLD UP– NO, NOT SEEN HIM ROBBY... SORRY.
HOTEL

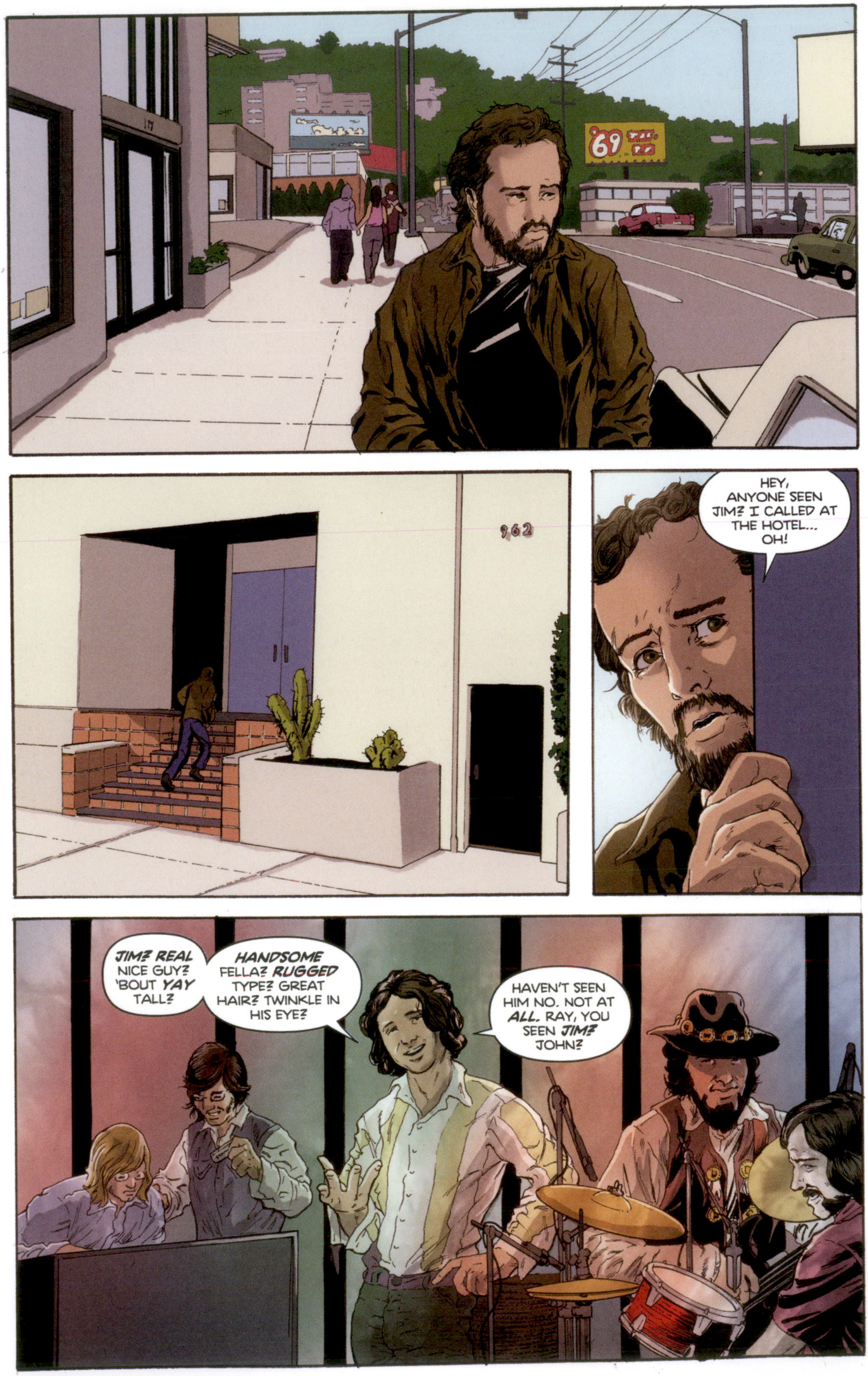

'69
962
HEY, ANYONE SEEN JIM? I CALLED AT THE HOTEL... OH!
JIM? REAL NICE GUY? 'BOUT YAY TALL?
HANDSOME FELLA? RUGGED TYPE? GREAT HAIR? TWINKLE IN HIS EYE?
HAVEN'T SEEN HIM NO. NOT AT ALL. RAY, YOU SEEN JIM? JOHN?

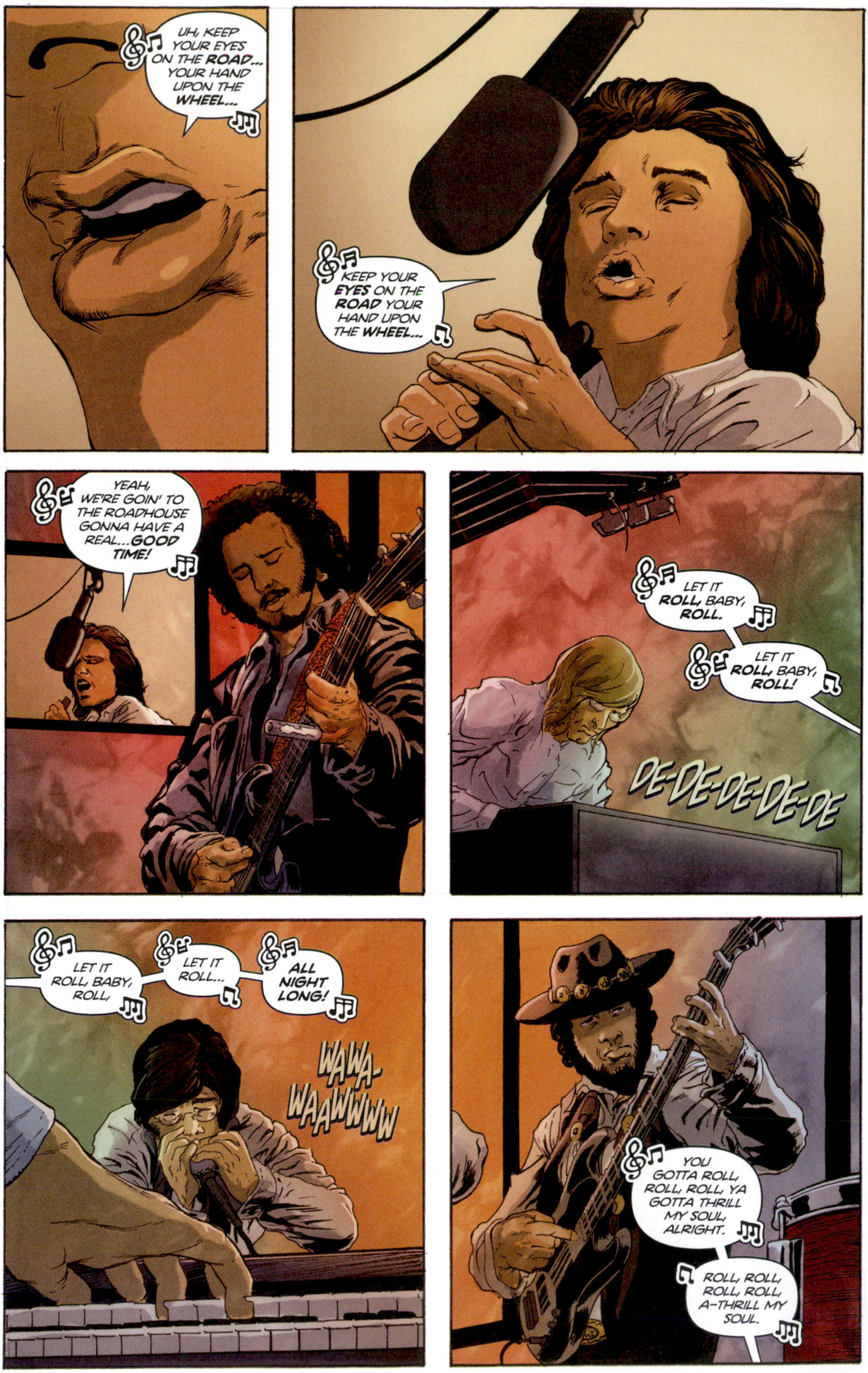
UH, KEEP YOUR EYES ON THE ROAD... YOUR HAND UPON THE WHEEL...
KEEP YOUR EYES ON THE ROAD YOUR HAND UPON THE WHEEL...
YEAH, WE'RE GOIN' TO THE ROADHOUSE GONNA HAVE A REAL...GOOD TIME!
LET IT ROLL, BABY, ROLL.
LET IT ROLL, BABY, ROLL!
DE-DE-DE-DE-DE
LET IT ROLL, BABY, ROLL,
LET IT ROLL...
ALL NIGHT LONG!
WAWA-WAAWWWW
YOU GOTTA ROLL, ROLL, ROLL, YA GOTTA THRILL MY SOUL, ALRIGHT.
ROLL, ROLL, ROLL, ROLL, A-THRILL MY SOUL.

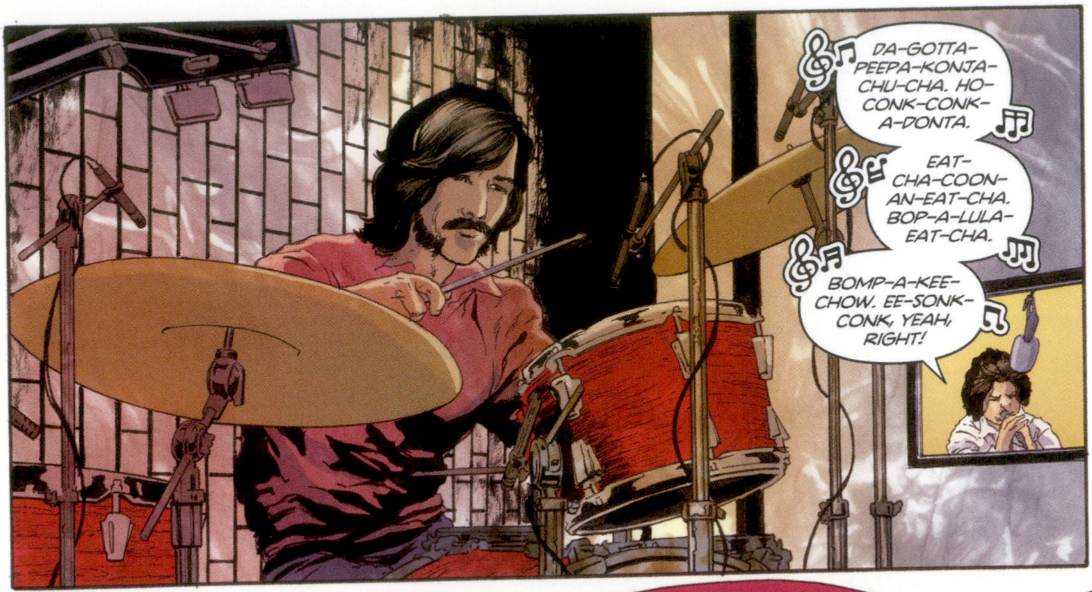
DA-GOTTA-PEEPA-KONJA-CHU-CHA. HO-CONK-CONK-A-DONTA.
EAT-CHA-COON-AN-EAT-CHA. BOP-A-LULA-EAT-CHA.
BOMP-A-KEE-CHOW. EE-SONK-CONK, YEAH, RIGHT!

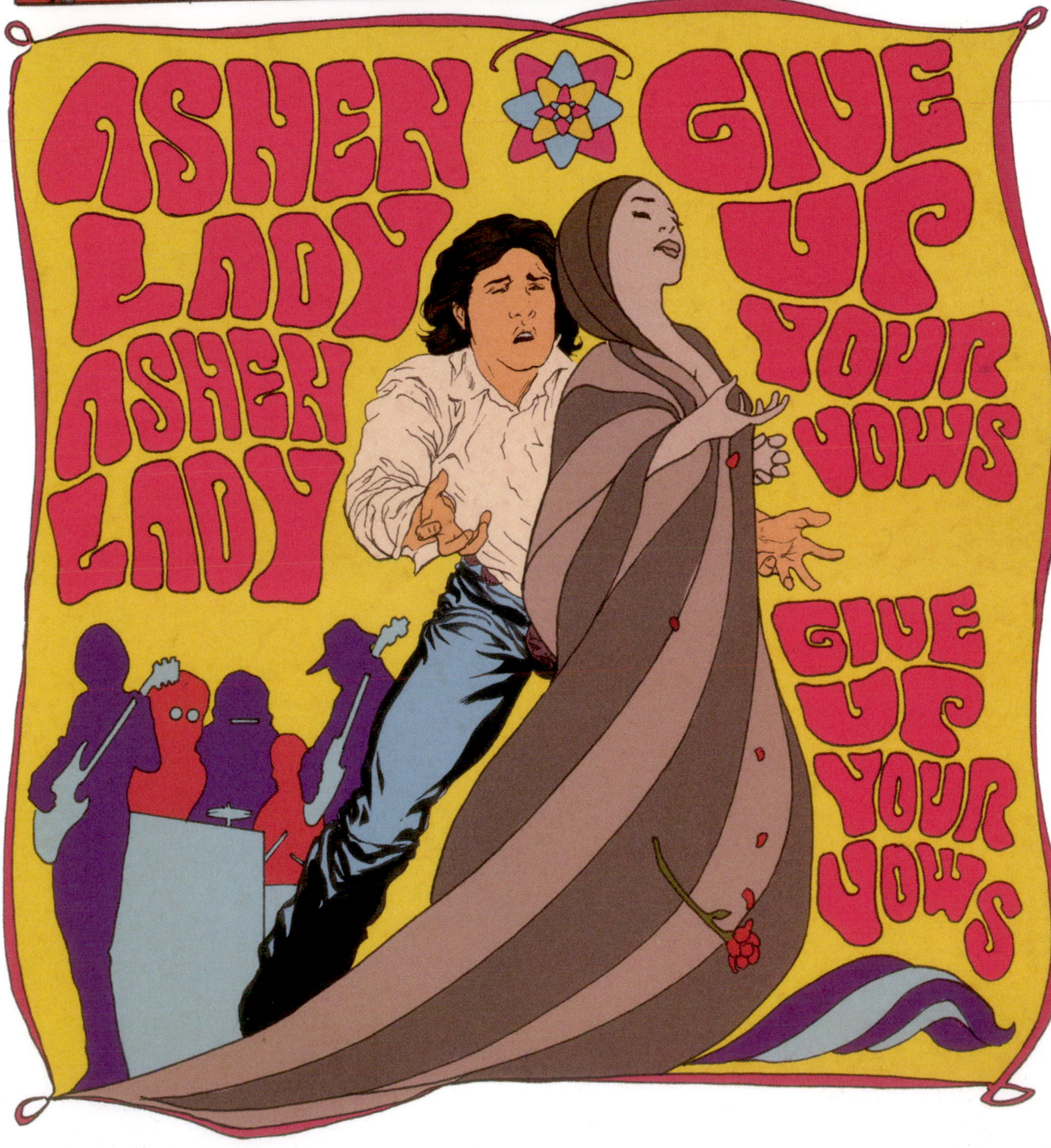
ASHEN LADY ASHEN LADY
GIVE UP YOUR VOWS
GIVE UP YOUR VOWS

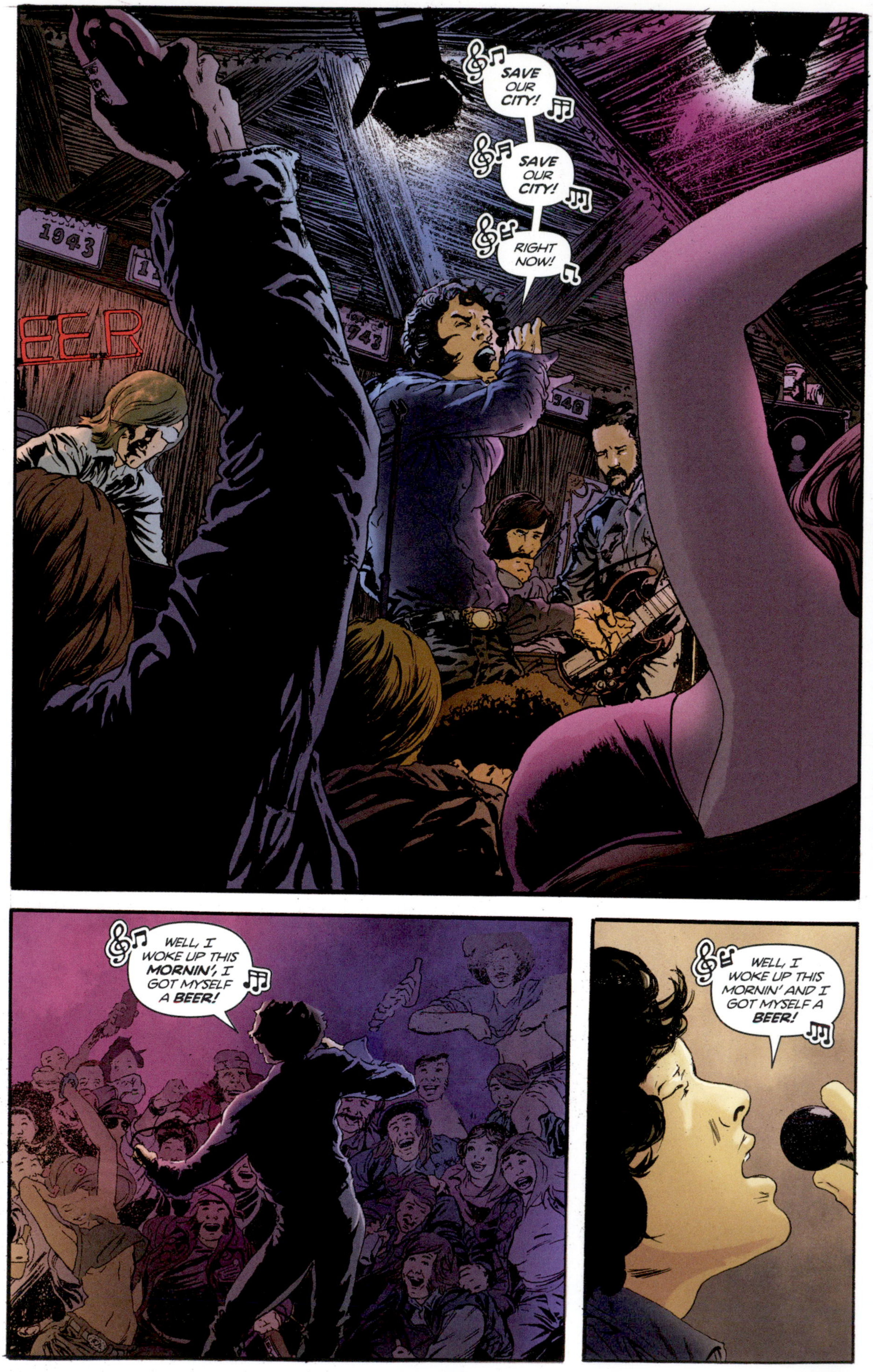
SAVE OUR CITY!
SAVE OUR CITY!
RIGHT NOW!
WELL, I WOKE UP THIS **MORNIN'**, I GOT MYSELF A **BEER!**
WELL, I WOKE UP THIS MORNIN' AND I GOT MYSELF A **BEER!**

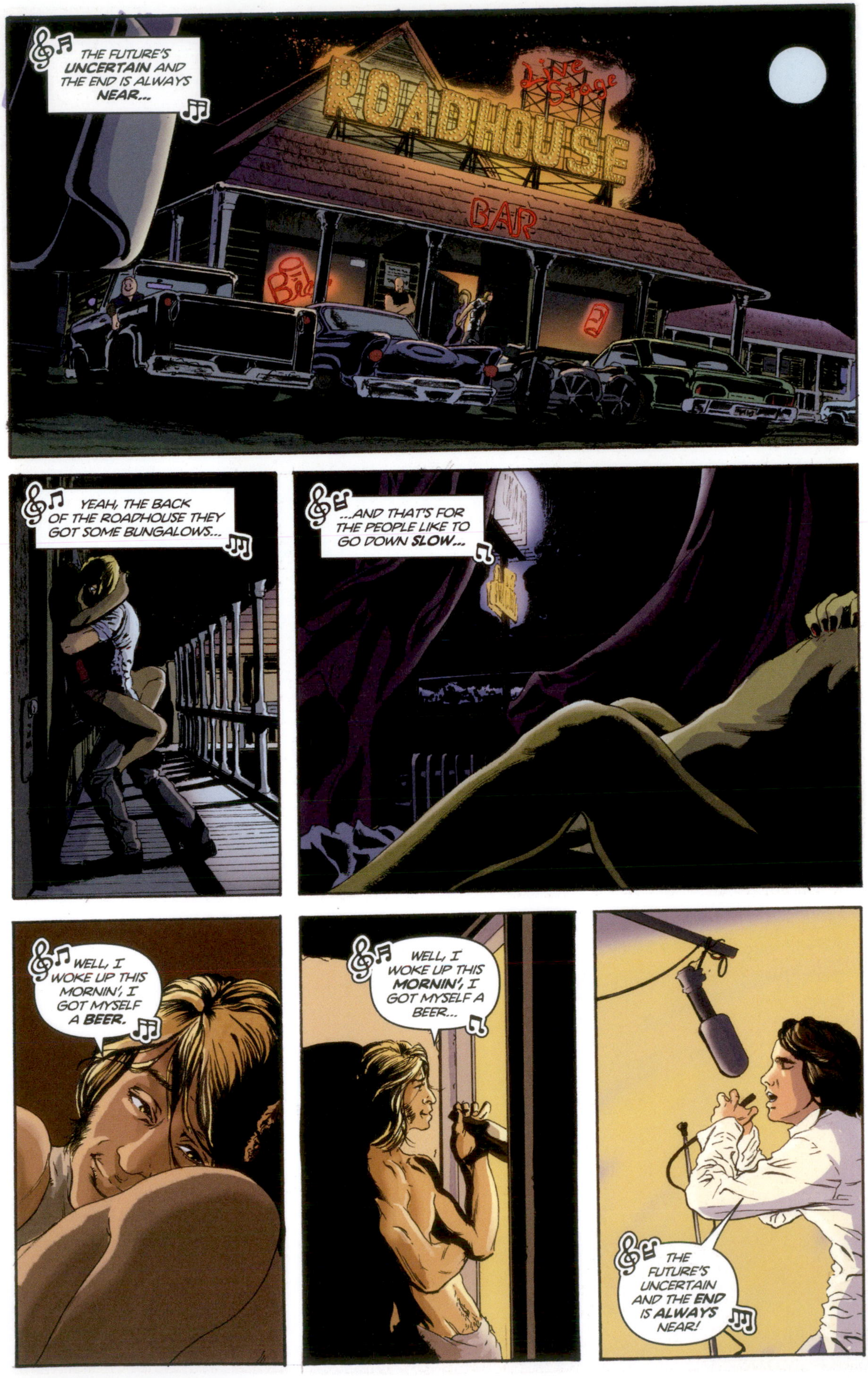
THE FUTURE'S UNCERTAIN AND THE END IS ALWAYS NEAR...
ROADHOUSE
Live Stage
BAR
YEAH, THE BACK OF THE ROADHOUSE THEY GOT SOME BUNGALOWS...
...AND THAT'S FOR THE PEOPLE LIKE TO GO DOWN SLOW...
WELL, I WOKE UP THIS MORNIN', I GOT MYSELF A BEER.
WELL, I WOKE UP THIS MORNIN', I GOT MYSELF A BEER...
THE FUTURE'S UNCERTAIN AND THE END IS ALWAYS NEAR!

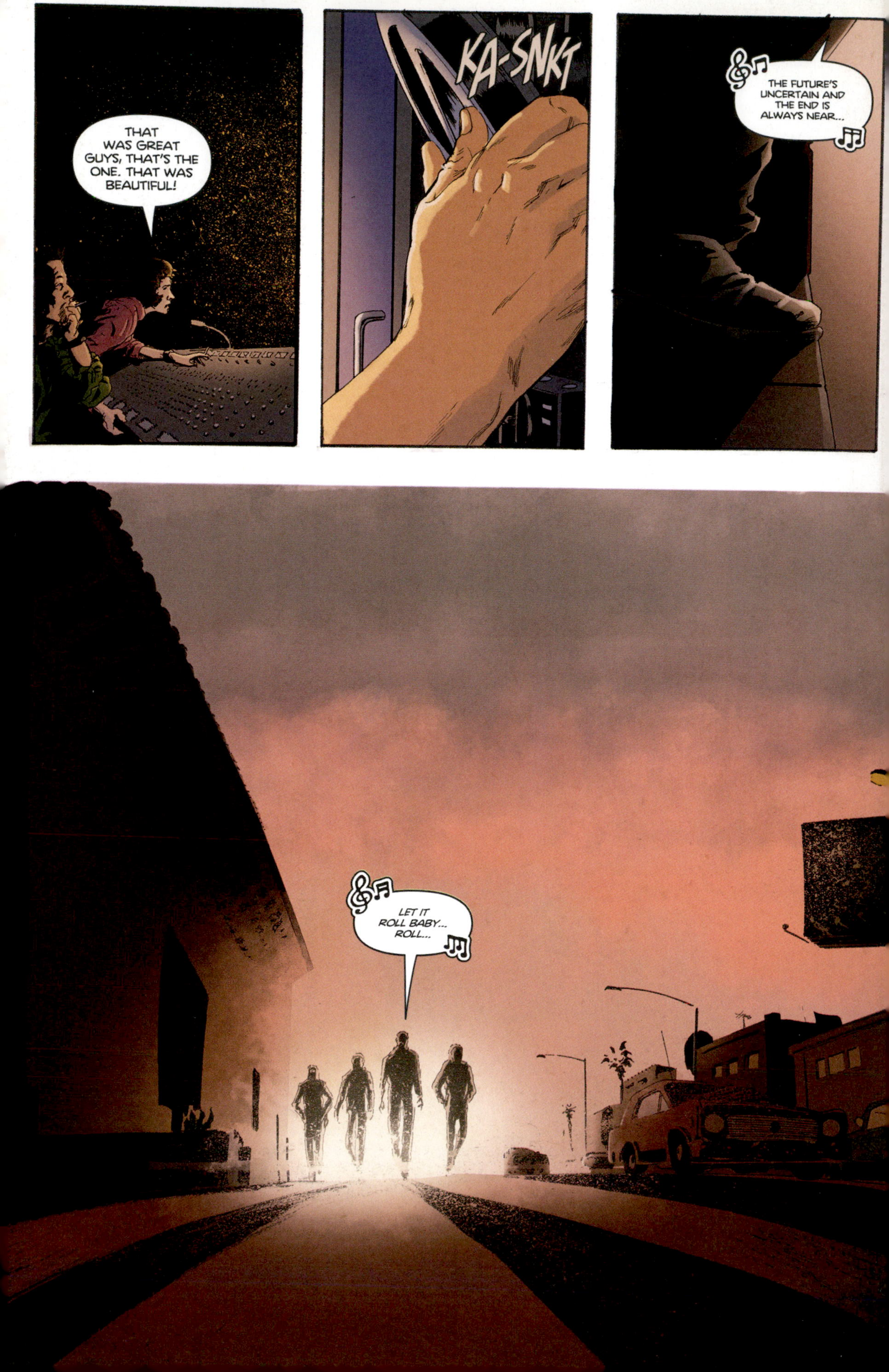
THAT WAS GREAT GUYS, THAT'S THE ONE. THAT WAS BEAUTIFUL!
KA-SNKT
THE FUTURE'S UNCERTAIN AND THE END IS ALWAYS NEAR...
LET IT ROLL BABY... ROLL...

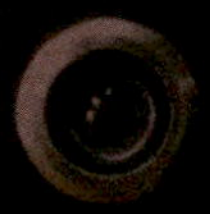

Interlude - Miami

Artist . . . John Pearson

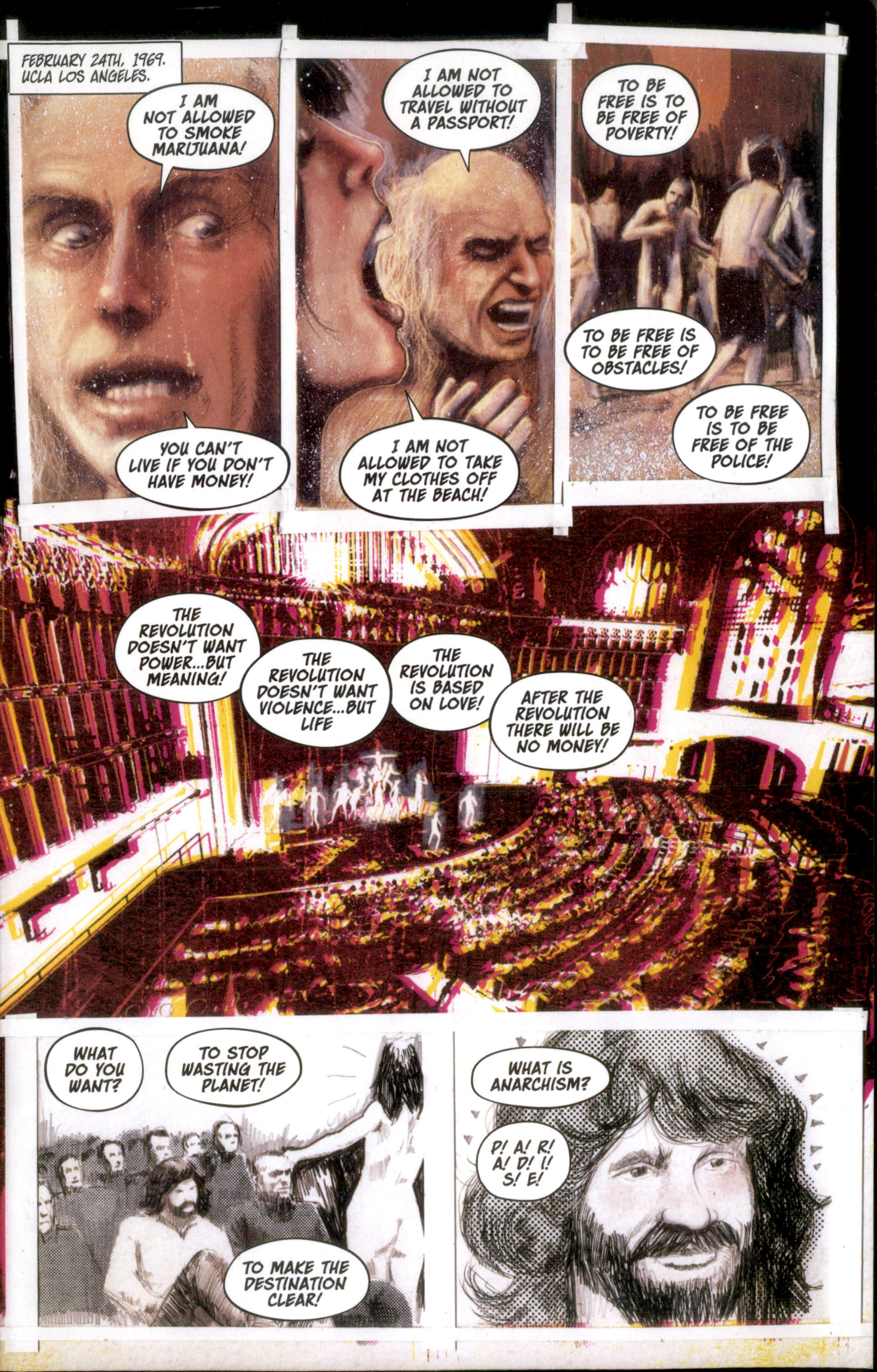
FEBRUARY 24TH, 1969. UCLA LOS ANGELES.
I AM NOT ALLOWED TO SMOKE MARIJUANA!
YOU CAN'T LIVE IF YOU DON'T HAVE MONEY!
I AM NOT ALLOWED TO TRAVEL WITHOUT A PASSPORT!
I AM NOT ALLOWED TO TAKE MY CLOTHES OFF AT THE BEACH!
TO BE FREE IS TO BE FREE OF POVERTY!
TO BE FREE IS TO BE FREE OF OBSTACLES!
TO BE FREE IS TO BE FREE OF THE POLICE!
THE REVOLUTION DOESN'T WANT POWER...BUT MEANING!
THE REVOLUTION DOESN'T WANT VIOLENCE...BUT LIFE
THE REVOLUTION IS BASED ON LOVE!
AFTER THE REVOLUTION THERE WILL BE NO MONEY!
WHAT DO YOU WANT?
TO STOP WASTING THE PLANET!
TO MAKE THE DESTINATION CLEAR!
WHAT IS ANARCHISM?
P! A! R! A! D! I! S! E!

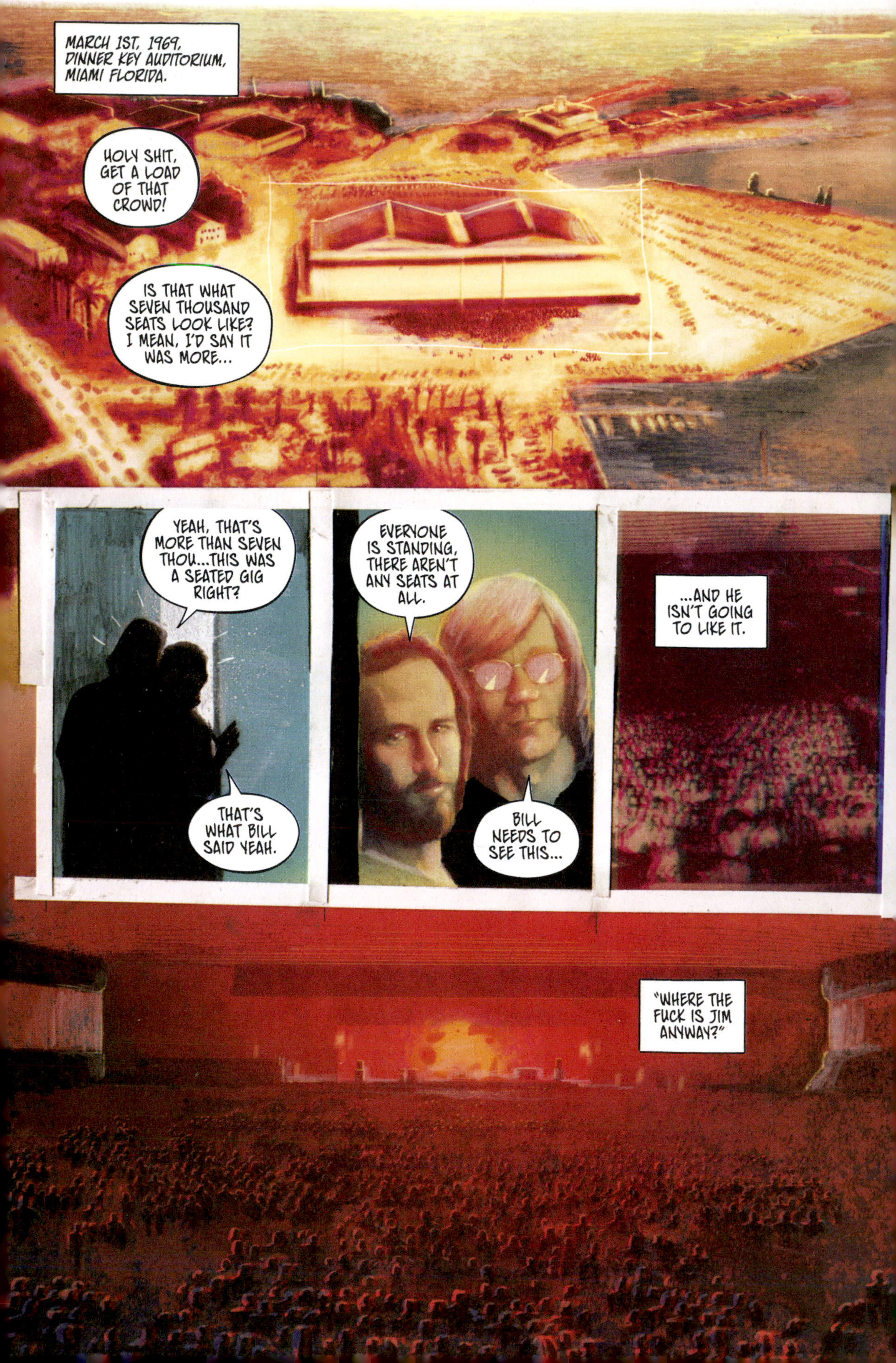
MARCH 1ST, 1969, DINNER KEY AUDITORIUM, MIAMI FLORIDA.
HOLY SHIT, GET A LOAD OF THAT CROWD!
IS THAT WHAT SEVEN THOUSAND SEATS LOOK LIKE? I MEAN, I'D SAY IT WAS MORE...
YEAH, THAT'S MORE THAN SEVEN THOU...THIS WAS A SEATED GIG RIGHT?
THAT'S WHAT BILL SAID YEAH.
EVERYONE IS STANDING, THERE AREN'T ANY SEATS AT ALL.
BILL NEEDS TO SEE THIS...
...AND HE ISN'T GOING TO LIKE IT.
"WHERE THE FUCK IS JIM ANYWAY?"

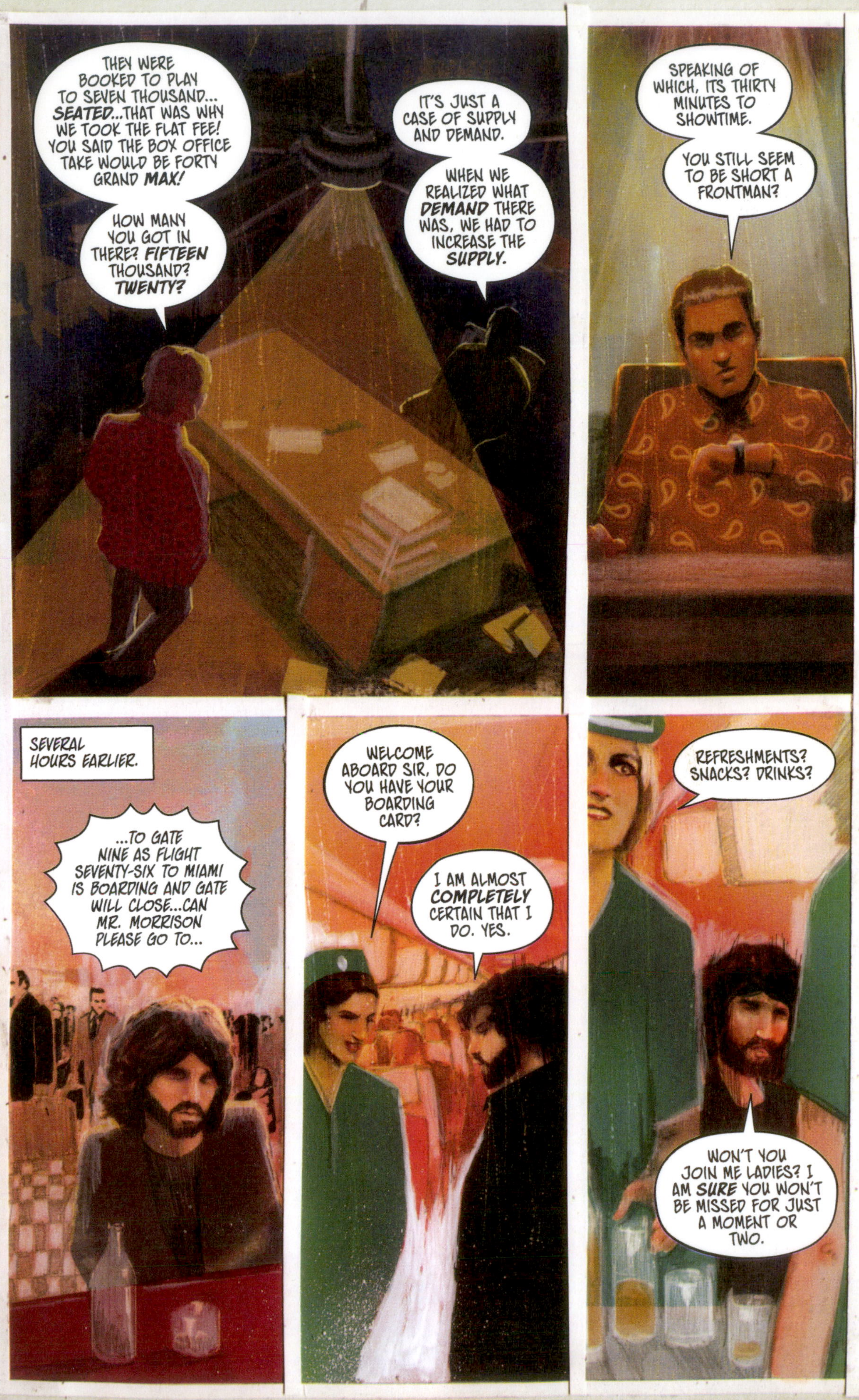
THEY WERE BOOKED TO PLAY TO SEVEN THOUSAND... **SEATED**...THAT WAS WHY WE TOOK THE FLAT FEE! YOU SAID THE BOX OFFICE TAKE WOULD BE FORTY GRAND **MAX!**
HOW MANY YOU GOT IN THERE? **FIFTEEN** THOUSAND? **TWENTY?**
IT'S JUST A CASE OF SUPPLY AND DEMAND.
WHEN WE REALIZED WHAT **DEMAND** THERE WAS, WE HAD TO INCREASE THE **SUPPLY.**
SPEAKING OF WHICH, ITS THIRTY MINUTES TO SHOWTIME.
YOU STILL SEEM TO BE SHORT A FRONTMAN?
SEVERAL HOURS EARLIER.
...TO GATE NINE AS FLIGHT SEVENTY-SIX TO MIAMI IS BOARDING AND GATE WILL CLOSE...CAN MR. MORRISON PLEASE GO TO...
WELCOME ABOARD SIR, DO YOU HAVE YOUR BOARDING CARD?
I AM ALMOST **COMPLETELY** CERTAIN THAT I DO. YES.
REFRESHMENTS? SNACKS? DRINKS?
WON'T YOU JOIN ME LADIES? I AM **SURE** YOU WON'T BE MISSED FOR JUST A MOMENT OR TWO.

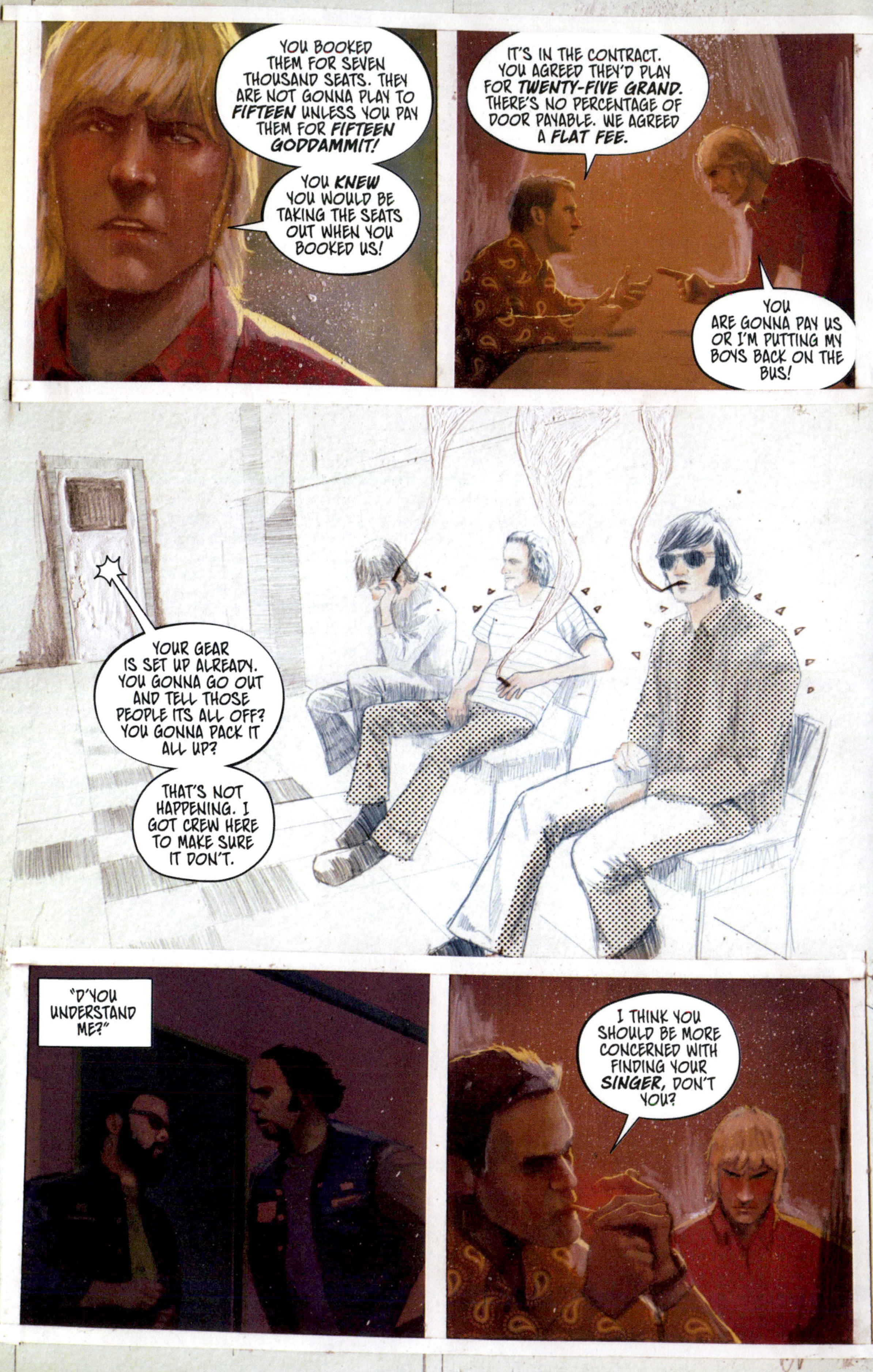
YOU BOOKED THEM FOR SEVEN THOUSAND SEATS. THEY ARE NOT GONNA PLAY TO FIFTEEN UNLESS YOU PAY THEM FOR FIFTEEN GODDAMMIT!
YOU KNEW YOU WOULD BE TAKING THE SEATS OUT WHEN YOU BOOKED US!
IT'S IN THE CONTRACT. YOU AGREED THEY'D PLAY FOR TWENTY-FIVE GRAND. THERE'S NO PERCENTAGE OF DOOR PAYABLE. WE AGREED A FLAT FEE.
YOU ARE GONNA PAY US OR I'M PUTTING MY BOYS BACK ON THE BUS!
YOUR GEAR IS SET UP ALREADY. YOU GONNA GO OUT AND TELL THOSE PEOPLE ITS ALL OFF? YOU GONNA PACK IT ALL UP?
THAT'S NOT HAPPENING. I GOT CREW HERE TO MAKE SURE IT DON'T.
"D'YOU UNDERSTAND ME?"
I THINK YOU SHOULD BE MORE CONCERNED WITH FINDING YOUR SINGER, DON'T YOU?

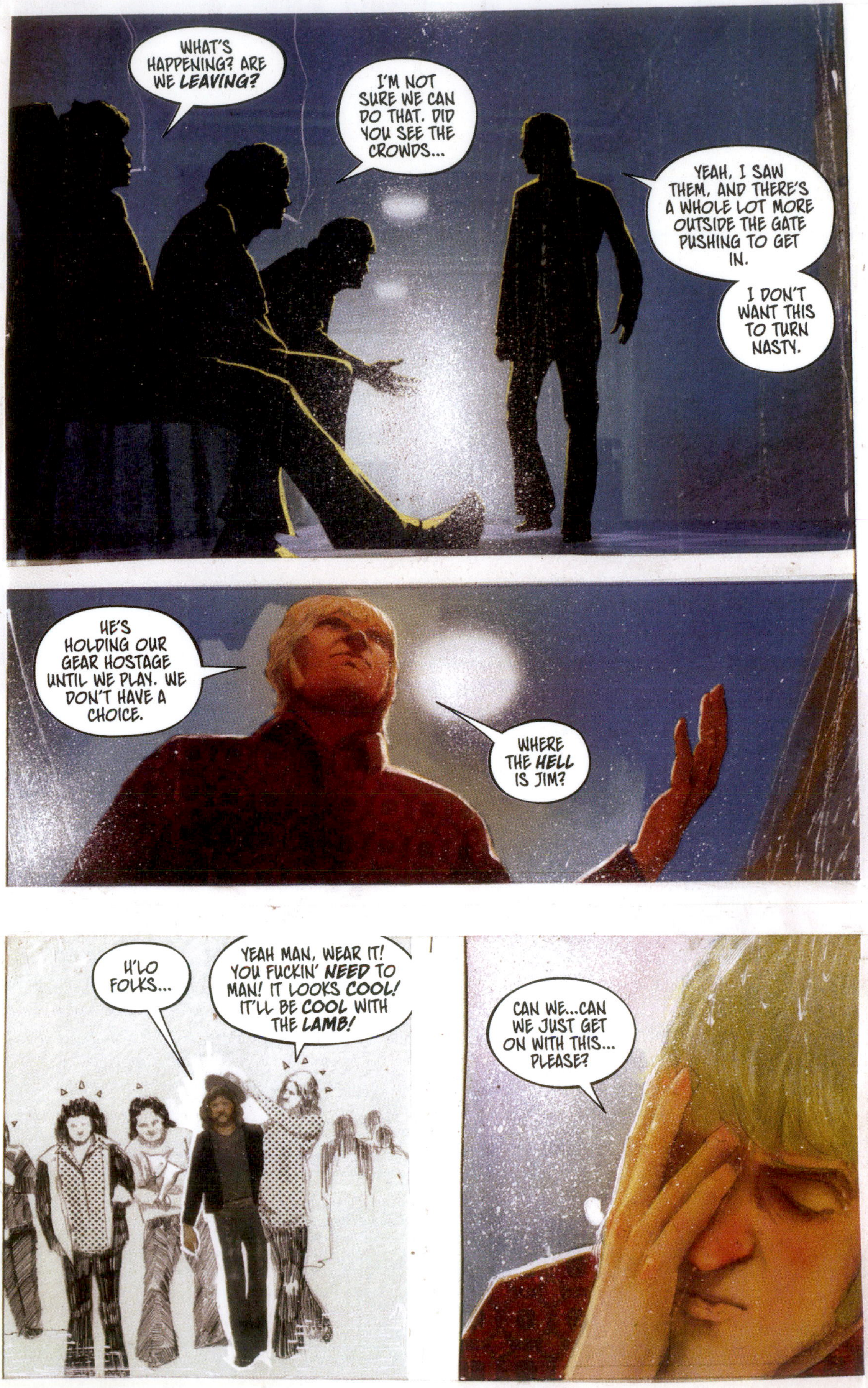
WHAT'S HAPPENING? ARE WE LEAVING?
I'M NOT SURE WE CAN DO THAT. DID YOU SEE THE CROWDS...
YEAH, I SAW THEM, AND THERE'S A WHOLE LOT MORE OUTSIDE THE GATE PUSHING TO GET IN.
I DON'T WANT THIS TO TURN NASTY.
HE'S HOLDING OUR GEAR HOSTAGE UNTIL WE PLAY. WE DON'T HAVE A CHOICE.
WHERE THE HELL IS JIM?
H'LO FOLKS...
YEAH MAN, WEAR IT! YOU FUCKIN' NEED TO MAN! IT LOOKS COOL! IT'LL BE COOL WITH THE LAMB!
CAN WE...CAN WE JUST GET ON WITH THIS... PLEASE?

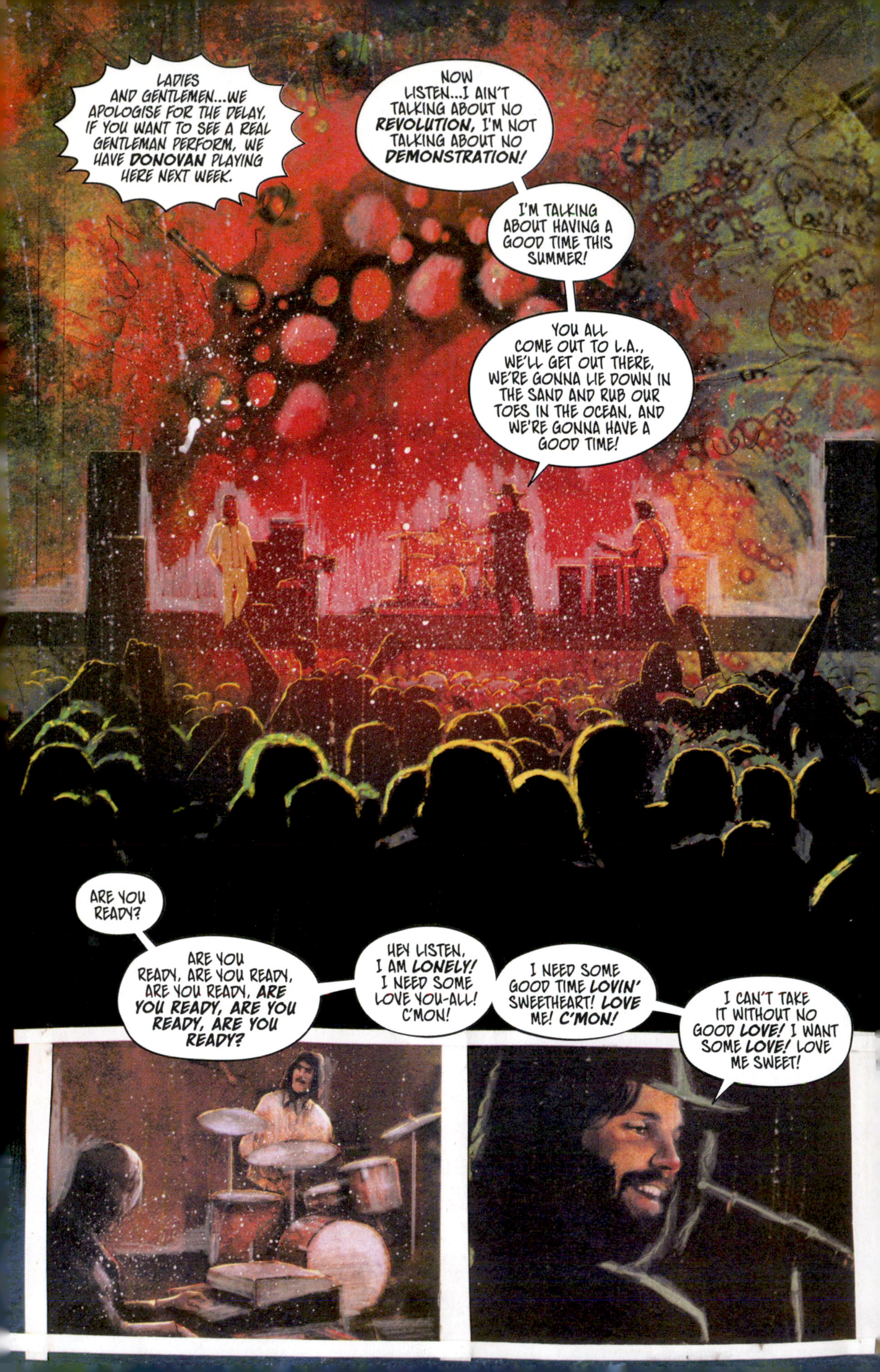
LADIES AND GENTLEMEN...WE APOLOGISE FOR THE DELAY. IF YOU WANT TO SEE A REAL GENTLEMAN PERFORM, WE HAVE **DONOVAN** PLAYING HERE NEXT WEEK.
NOW LISTEN...I AIN'T TALKING ABOUT NO **REVOLUTION,** I'M NOT TALKING ABOUT NO **DEMONSTRATION!**
I'M TALKING ABOUT HAVING A GOOD TIME THIS SUMMER!
YOU ALL COME OUT TO L.A., WE'LL GET OUT THERE, WE'RE GONNA LIE DOWN IN THE SAND AND RUB OUR TOES IN THE OCEAN, AND WE'RE GONNA HAVE A GOOD TIME!
ARE YOU READY?
ARE YOU READY, ARE YOU READY, ARE YOU READY, **ARE YOU READY, ARE YOU READY, ARE YOU READY?**
HEY LISTEN, I AM **LONELY!** I NEED SOME LOVE YOU-ALL! C'MON!
I NEED SOME GOOD TIME **LOVIN'** SWEETHEART! **LOVE** ME! **C'MON!**
I CAN'T TAKE IT WITHOUT NO GOOD **LOVE!** I WANT SOME **LOVE!** LOVE ME SWEET!

AIN'T NOBODY GONNA *LOVE* MY ASS? COME ON!

I *NEED* YA! I *LOVE* YA!

THERE'S SO *MANY* OF YOU OUT THERE, NOBODY'S GONNA *LOVE* ME SWEETHEART? COME ON! I *NEED* IT!

HEY THERE'S A BUNCH OF PEOPLE BACK THERE I DIDN'T EVEN *NOTICE!*

HEY, HOW ABOUT FIFTY OR SIXTY OF YOU PEOPLE COME ON UP HERE AND *LOVE* MY ASS?

FIVE TO ONE BABY, ONE IN FIVE...NO-ONE HERE GETS OUT ALIVE...

YOU GET YOURS; I'LL GET MINE...

GONNA MAKE IT BABY IF WE *TRY!* YEAH COME ON!

THE OLD GET OLD AND THE YOUNG GET STRONGER,

MAY TAKE A WEEK AND IT MAY TAKE LONGER...

THEY GOT THE GUNS, BUT, WE GOT THE NUMBERS...

...GONNA WIN, YEAH, WE'RE TAKING OVER!

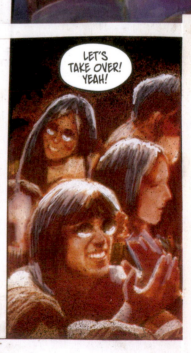

LET'S TAKE OVER! YEAH!

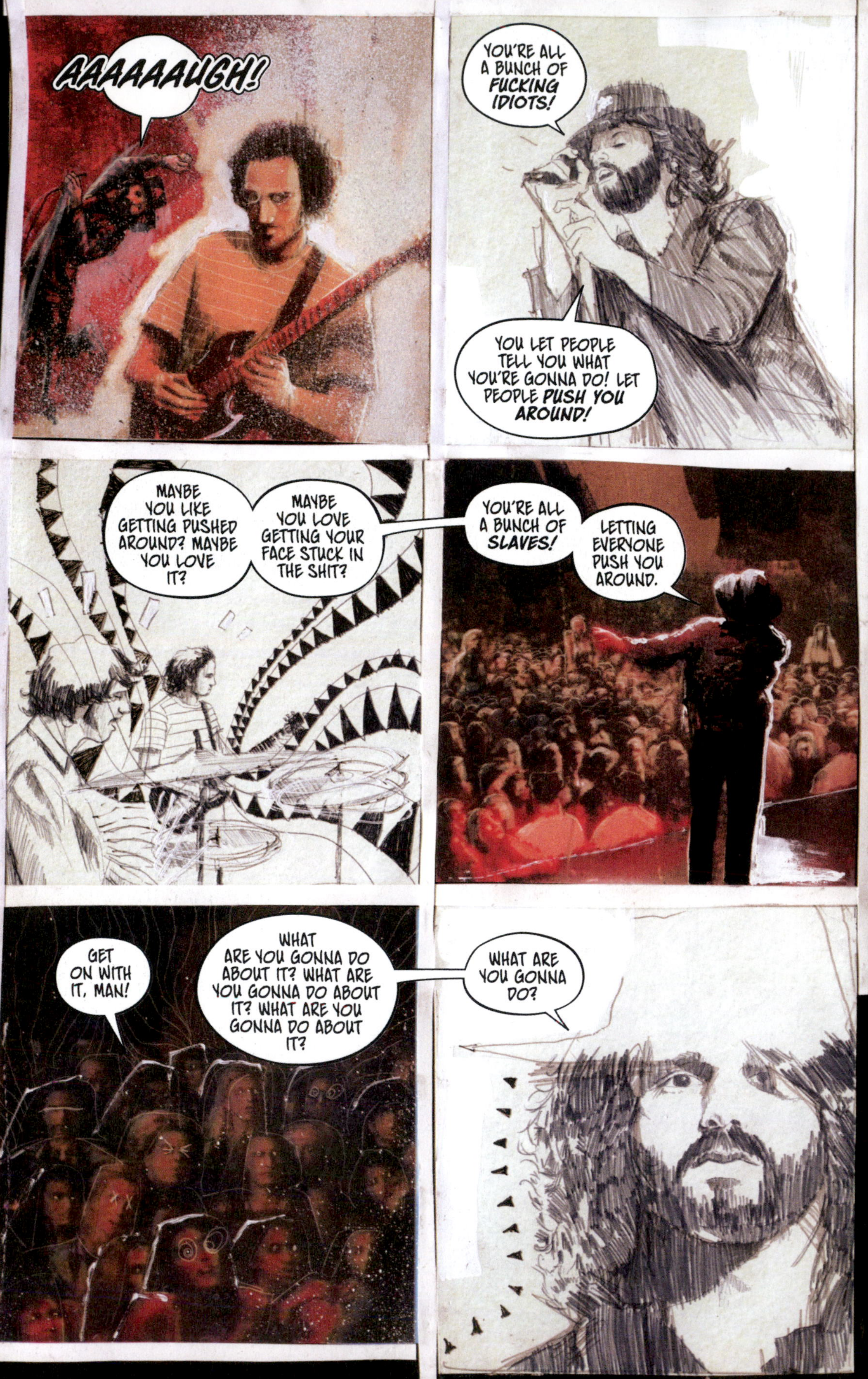
AAAAAAUGH!
YOU'RE ALL A BUNCH OF FUCKING IDIOTS!
YOU LET PEOPLE TELL YOU WHAT YOU'RE GONNA DO! LET PEOPLE PUSH YOU AROUND!
MAYBE YOU LIKE GETTING PUSHED AROUND? MAYBE YOU LOVE IT?
MAYBE YOU LOVE GETTING YOUR FACE STUCK IN THE SHIT?
YOU'RE ALL A BUNCH OF SLAVES!
LETTING EVERYONE PUSH YOU AROUND.
GET ON WITH IT, MAN!
WHAT ARE YOU GONNA DO ABOUT IT? WHAT ARE YOU GONNA DO ABOUT IT? WHAT ARE YOU GONNA DO ABOUT IT?
WHAT ARE YOU GONNA DO?

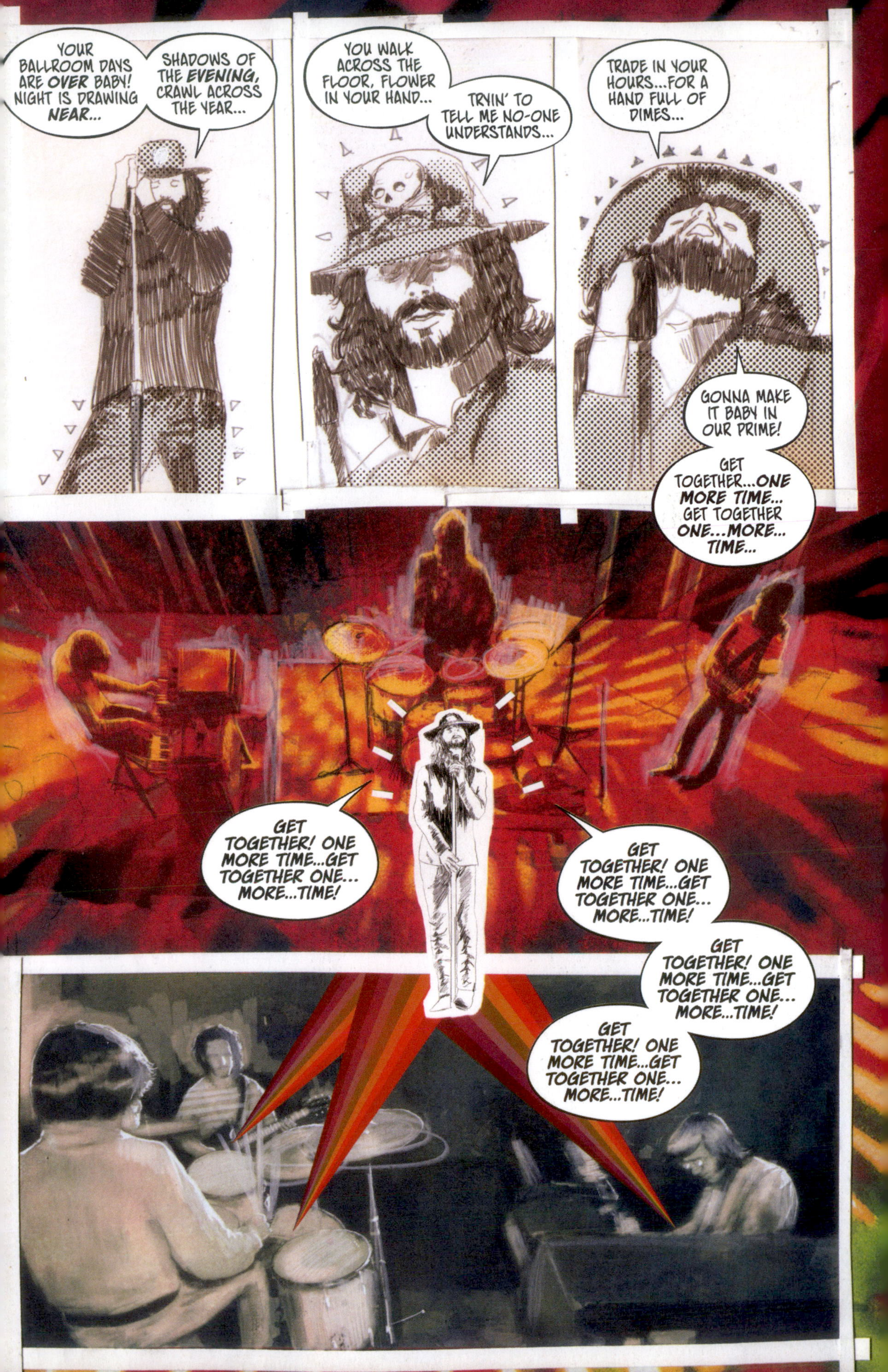
YOUR BALLROOM DAYS ARE **OVER** BABY! NIGHT IS DRAWING **NEAR**...
SHADOWS OF THE ***EVENING***, CRAWL ACROSS THE YEAR...
YOU WALK ACROSS THE FLOOR, FLOWER IN YOUR HAND...
TRYIN' TO TELL ME NO-ONE UNDERSTANDS...
TRADE IN YOUR HOURS...FOR A HAND FULL OF DIMES...
GONNA MAKE IT BABY IN OUR PRIME!
GET TOGETHER...***ONE MORE TIME...*** GET TOGETHER ***ONE...MORE... TIME...***
GET TOGETHER! ONE MORE TIME...GET TOGETHER ONE... MORE...TIME!
GET TOGETHER! ONE MORE TIME...GET TOGETHER ONE... MORE...TIME!
GET TOGETHER! ONE MORE TIME...GET TOGETHER ONE... MORE...TIME!
GET TOGETHER! ONE MORE TIME...GET TOGETHER ONE... MORE...TIME!

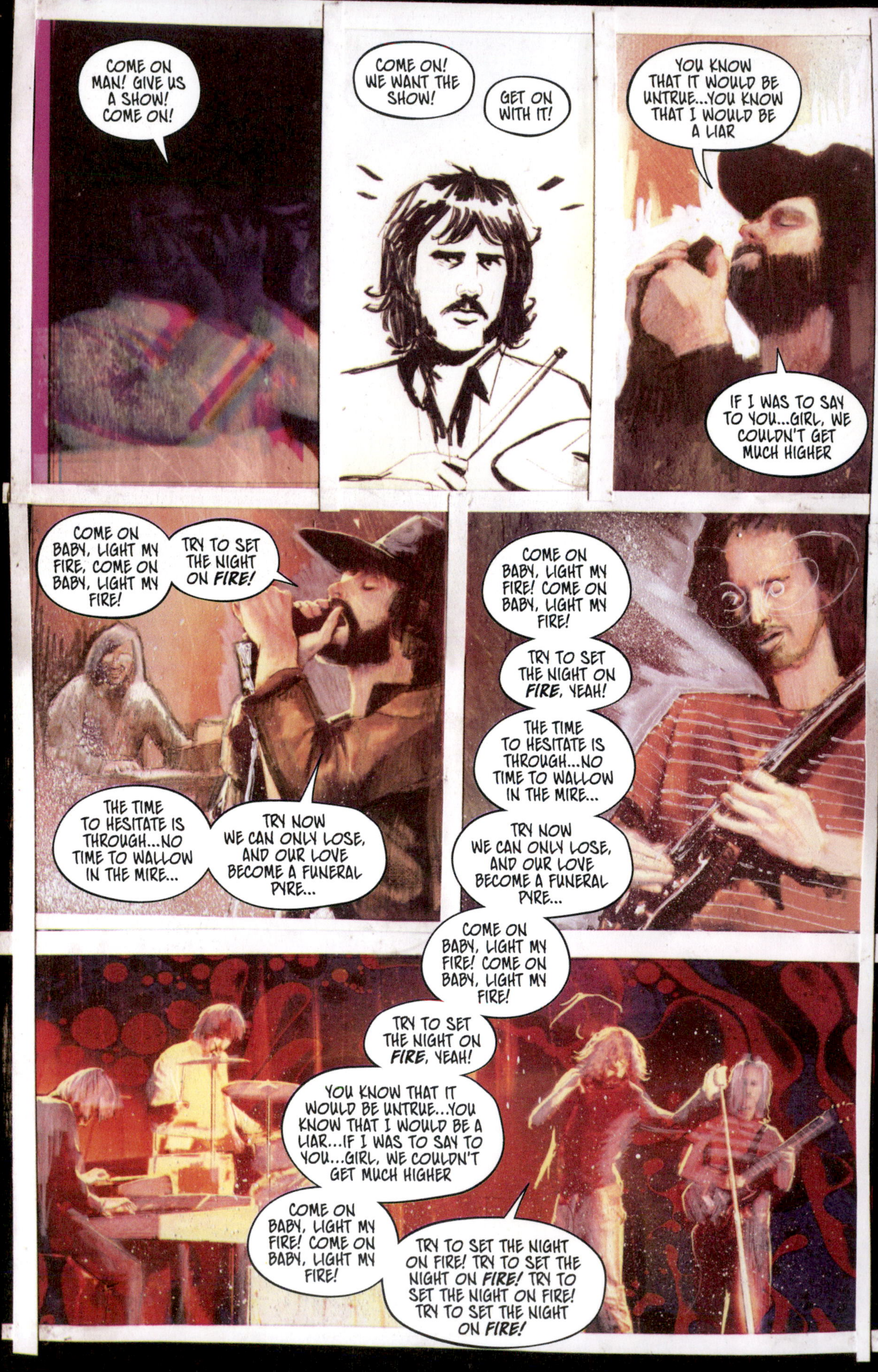
COME ON MAN! GIVE US A SHOW! COME ON!
COME ON! WE WANT THE SHOW!
GET ON WITH IT!
YOU KNOW THAT IT WOULD BE UNTRUE...YOU KNOW THAT I WOULD BE A LIAR
IF I WAS TO SAY TO YOU...GIRL, WE COULDN'T GET MUCH HIGHER
COME ON BABY, LIGHT MY FIRE, COME ON BABY, LIGHT MY FIRE!
TRY TO SET THE NIGHT ON *FIRE!*
THE TIME TO HESITATE IS THROUGH...NO TIME TO WALLOW IN THE MIRE...
TRY NOW WE CAN ONLY LOSE, AND OUR LOVE BECOME A FUNERAL PYRE...
COME ON BABY, LIGHT MY FIRE! COME ON BABY, LIGHT MY FIRE!
TRY TO SET THE NIGHT ON *FIRE*, YEAH!
THE TIME TO HESITATE IS THROUGH...NO TIME TO WALLOW IN THE MIRE...
TRY NOW WE CAN ONLY LOSE, AND OUR LOVE BECOME A FUNERAL PYRE...
COME ON BABY, LIGHT MY FIRE! COME ON BABY, LIGHT MY FIRE!
TRY TO SET THE NIGHT ON *FIRE*, YEAH!
YOU KNOW THAT IT WOULD BE UNTRUE...YOU KNOW THAT I WOULD BE A LIAR...IF I WAS TO SAY TO YOU...GIRL, WE COULDN'T GET MUCH HIGHER
COME ON BABY, LIGHT MY FIRE! COME ON BABY, LIGHT MY FIRE!
TRY TO SET THE NIGHT ON FIRE! TRY TO SET THE NIGHT ON *FIRE!* TRY TO SET THE NIGHT ON FIRE! TRY TO SET THE NIGHT ON *FIRE!*

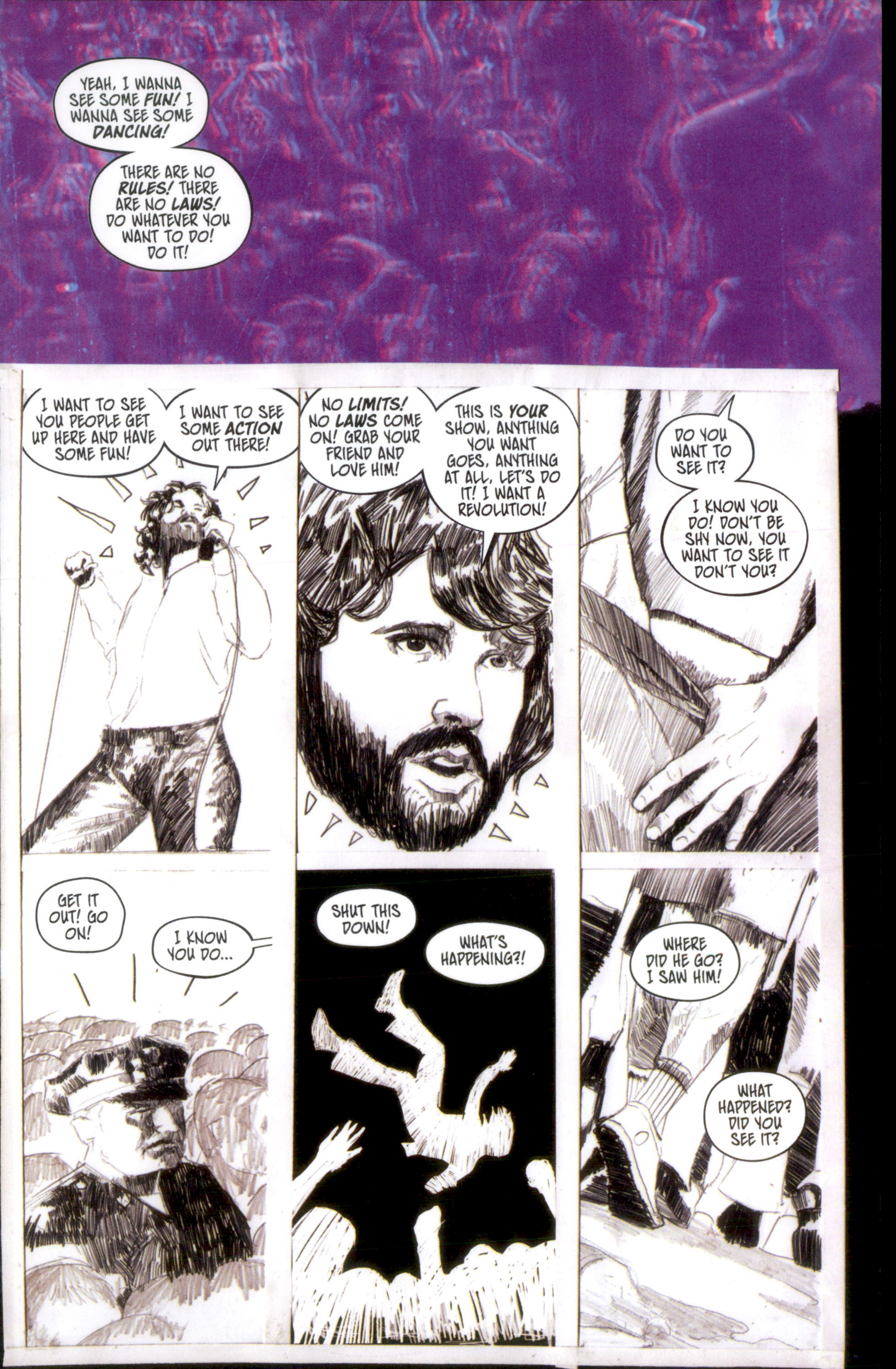
YEAH, I WANNA SEE SOME FUN! I WANNA SEE SOME DANCING!
THERE ARE NO RULES! THERE ARE NO LAWS! DO WHATEVER YOU WANT TO DO! DO IT!
I WANT TO SEE YOU PEOPLE GET UP HERE AND HAVE SOME FUN!
I WANT TO SEE SOME ACTION OUT THERE!
NO LIMITS! NO LAWS COME ON! GRAB YOUR FRIEND AND LOVE HIM!
THIS IS YOUR SHOW, ANYTHING YOU WANT GOES, ANYTHING AT ALL, LET'S DO IT! I WANT A REVOLUTION!
DO YOU WANT TO SEE IT?
I KNOW YOU DO! DON'T BE SHY NOW, YOU WANT TO SEE IT DON'T YOU?
GET IT OUT! GO ON!
I KNOW YOU DO...
SHUT THIS DOWN!
WHAT'S HAPPENING?!
WHERE DID HE GO? I SAW HIM!
WHAT HAPPENED? DID YOU SEE IT?

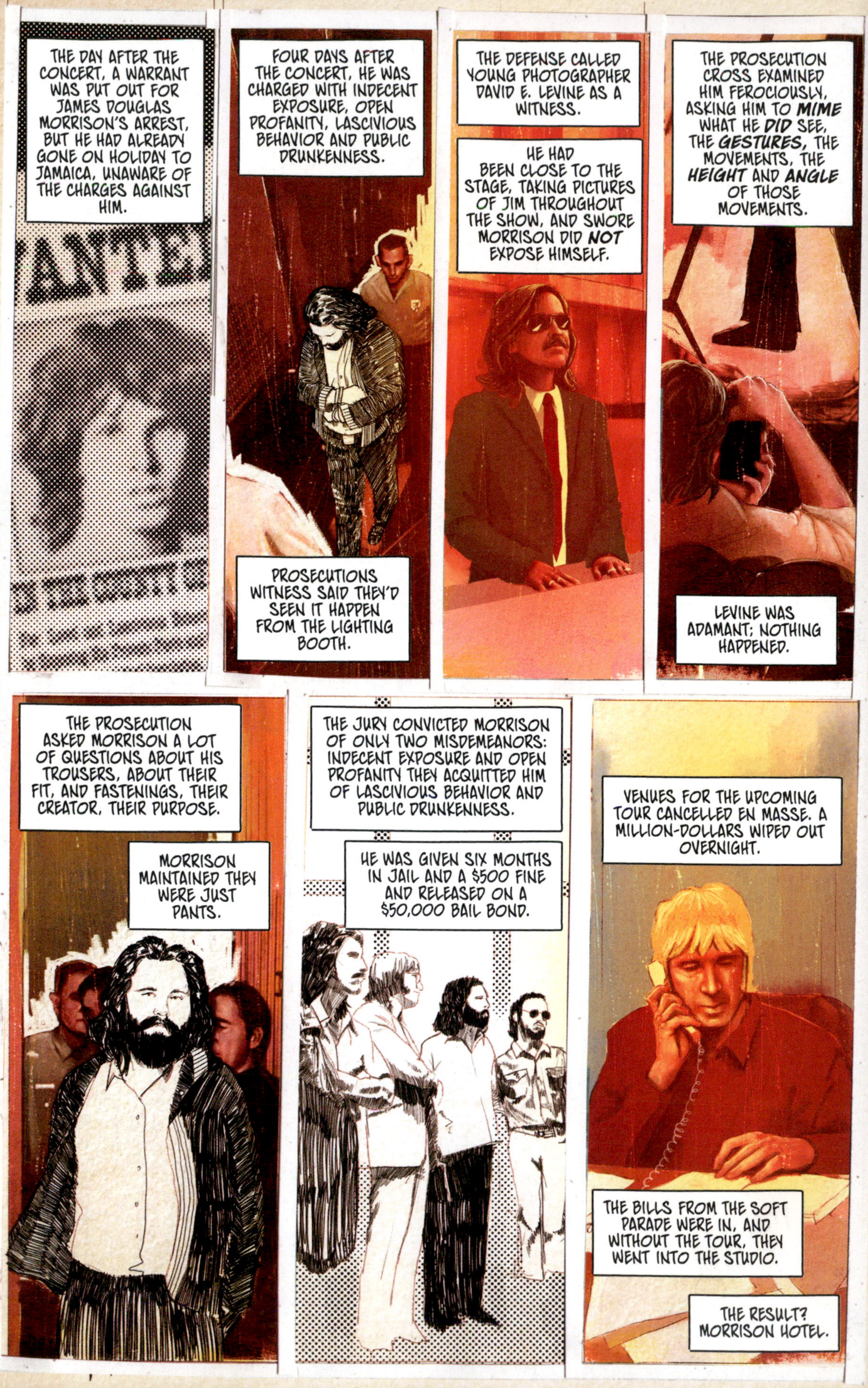
THE DAY AFTER THE CONCERT, A WARRANT WAS PUT OUT FOR JAMES DOUGLAS MORRISON'S ARREST, BUT HE HAD ALREADY GONE ON HOLIDAY TO JAMAICA, UNAWARE OF THE CHARGES AGAINST HIM.
FOUR DAYS AFTER THE CONCERT, HE WAS CHARGED WITH INDECENT EXPOSURE, OPEN PROFANITY, LASCIVIOUS BEHAVIOR AND PUBLIC DRUNKENNESS.
PROSECUTIONS WITNESS SAID THEY'D SEEN IT HAPPEN FROM THE LIGHTING BOOTH.
THE DEFENSE CALLED YOUNG PHOTOGRAPHER DAVID E. LEVINE AS A WITNESS.
HE HAD BEEN CLOSE TO THE STAGE, TAKING PICTURES OF JIM THROUGHOUT THE SHOW, AND SWORE MORRISON DID **NOT** EXPOSE HIMSELF.
THE PROSECUTION CROSS EXAMINED HIM FEROCIOUSLY, ASKING HIM TO **MIME** WHAT HE **DID** SEE, THE **GESTURES**, THE MOVEMENTS, THE **HEIGHT** AND **ANGLE** OF THOSE MOVEMENTS.
LEVINE WAS ADAMANT; NOTHING HAPPENED.
THE PROSECUTION ASKED MORRISON A LOT OF QUESTIONS ABOUT HIS TROUSERS, ABOUT THEIR FIT, AND FASTENINGS, THEIR CREATOR, THEIR PURPOSE.
MORRISON MAINTAINED THEY WERE JUST PANTS.
THE JURY CONVICTED MORRISON OF ONLY TWO MISDEMEANORS: INDECENT EXPOSURE AND OPEN PROFANITY THEY ACQUITTED HIM OF LASCIVIOUS BEHAVIOR AND PUBLIC DRUNKENNESS.
HE WAS GIVEN SIX MONTHS IN JAIL AND A $500 FINE AND RELEASED ON A $50,000 BAIL BOND.
VENUES FOR THE UPCOMING TOUR CANCELLED EN MASSE. A MILLION-DOLLARS WIPED OUT OVERNIGHT.
THE BILLS FROM THE SOFT PARADE WERE IN, AND WITHOUT THE TOUR, THEY WENT INTO THE STUDIO.
THE RESULT? MORRISON HOTEL.

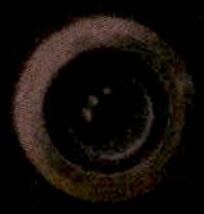

Waiting for the Sun

Artist . . . Mike Oeming
Colorist . . . Taki Soma

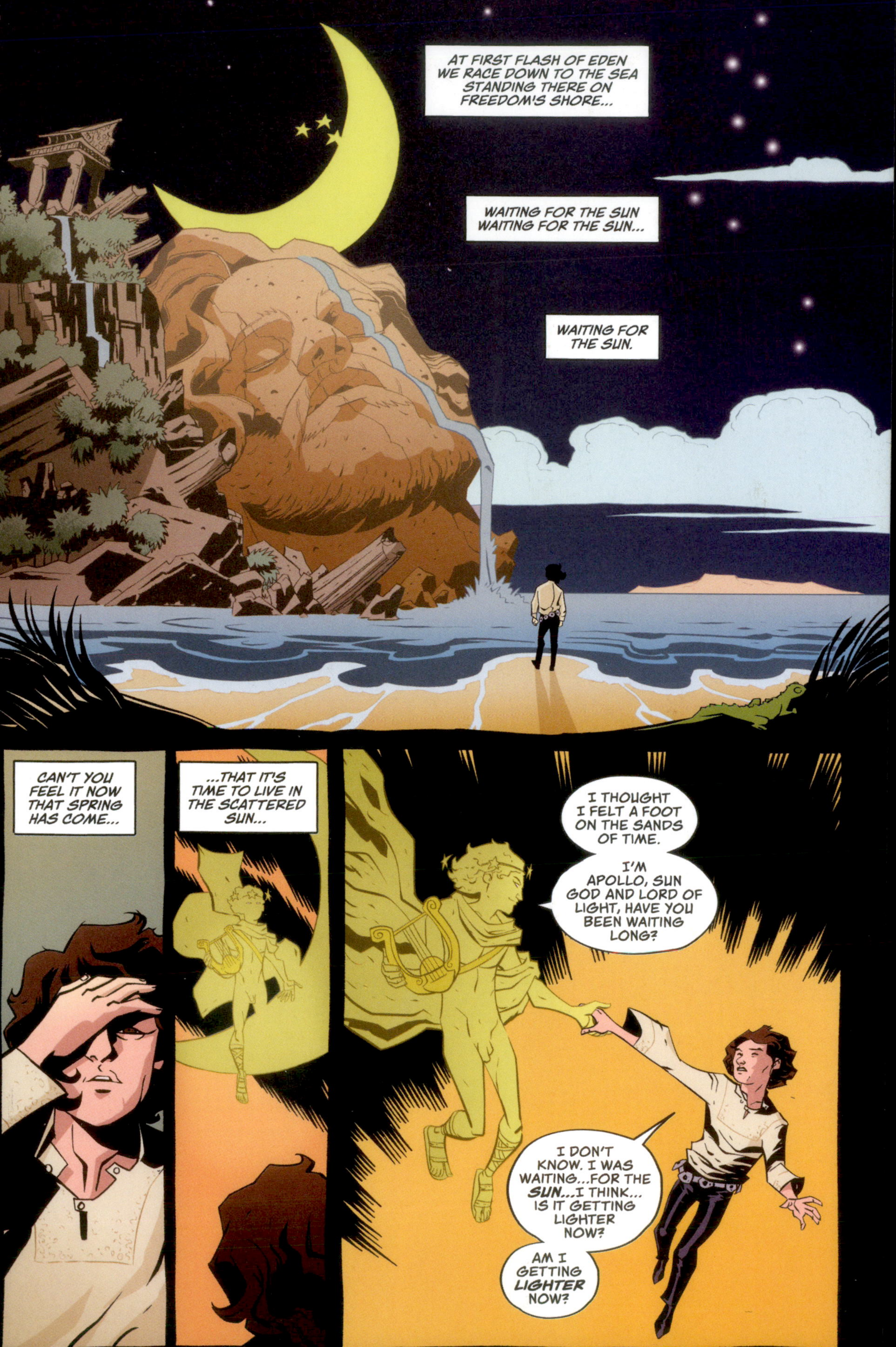
AT FIRST FLASH OF EDEN WE RACE DOWN TO THE SEA STANDING THERE ON FREEDOM'S SHORE...
WAITING FOR THE SUN WAITING FOR THE SUN...
WAITING FOR THE SUN.
CAN'T YOU FEEL IT NOW THAT SPRING HAS COME...
...THAT IT'S TIME TO LIVE IN THE SCATTERED SUN...
I THOUGHT I FELT A FOOT ON THE SANDS OF TIME.
I'M APOLLO, SUN GOD AND LORD OF LIGHT, HAVE YOU BEEN WAITING LONG?
I DON'T KNOW. I WAS WAITING...FOR THE SUN...I THINK... IS IT GETTING LIGHTER NOW?
AM I GETTING LIGHTER NOW?

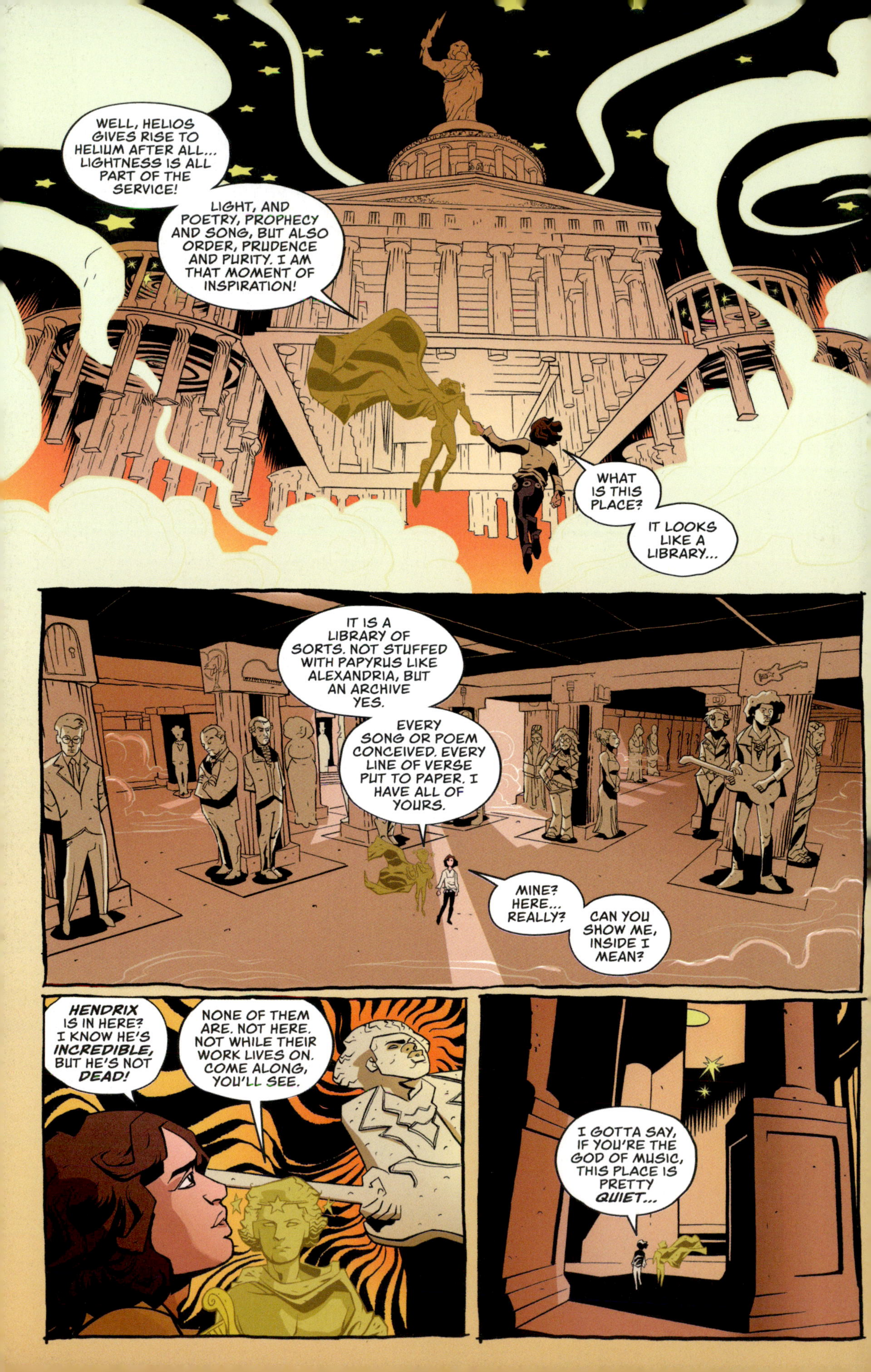
WELL, HELIOS GIVES RISE TO HELIUM AFTER ALL... LIGHTNESS IS ALL PART OF THE SERVICE!
LIGHT, AND POETRY, PROPHECY AND SONG, BUT ALSO ORDER, PRUDENCE AND PURITY. I AM THAT MOMENT OF INSPIRATION!
WHAT IS THIS PLACE?
IT LOOKS LIKE A LIBRARY...
IT IS A LIBRARY OF SORTS. NOT STUFFED WITH PAPYRUS LIKE ALEXANDRIA, BUT AN ARCHIVE YES.
EVERY SONG OR POEM CONCEIVED. EVERY LINE OF VERSE PUT TO PAPER. I HAVE ALL OF YOURS.
MINE? HERE... REALLY?
CAN YOU SHOW ME, INSIDE I MEAN?
HENDRIX IS IN HERE? I KNOW HE'S *INCREDIBLE,* BUT HE'S NOT *DEAD!*
NONE OF THEM ARE. NOT HERE. NOT WHILE THEIR WORK LIVES ON. COME ALONG, YOU'LL SEE.
I GOTTA SAY, IF YOU'RE THE GOD OF MUSIC, THIS PLACE IS PRETTY *QUIET...*

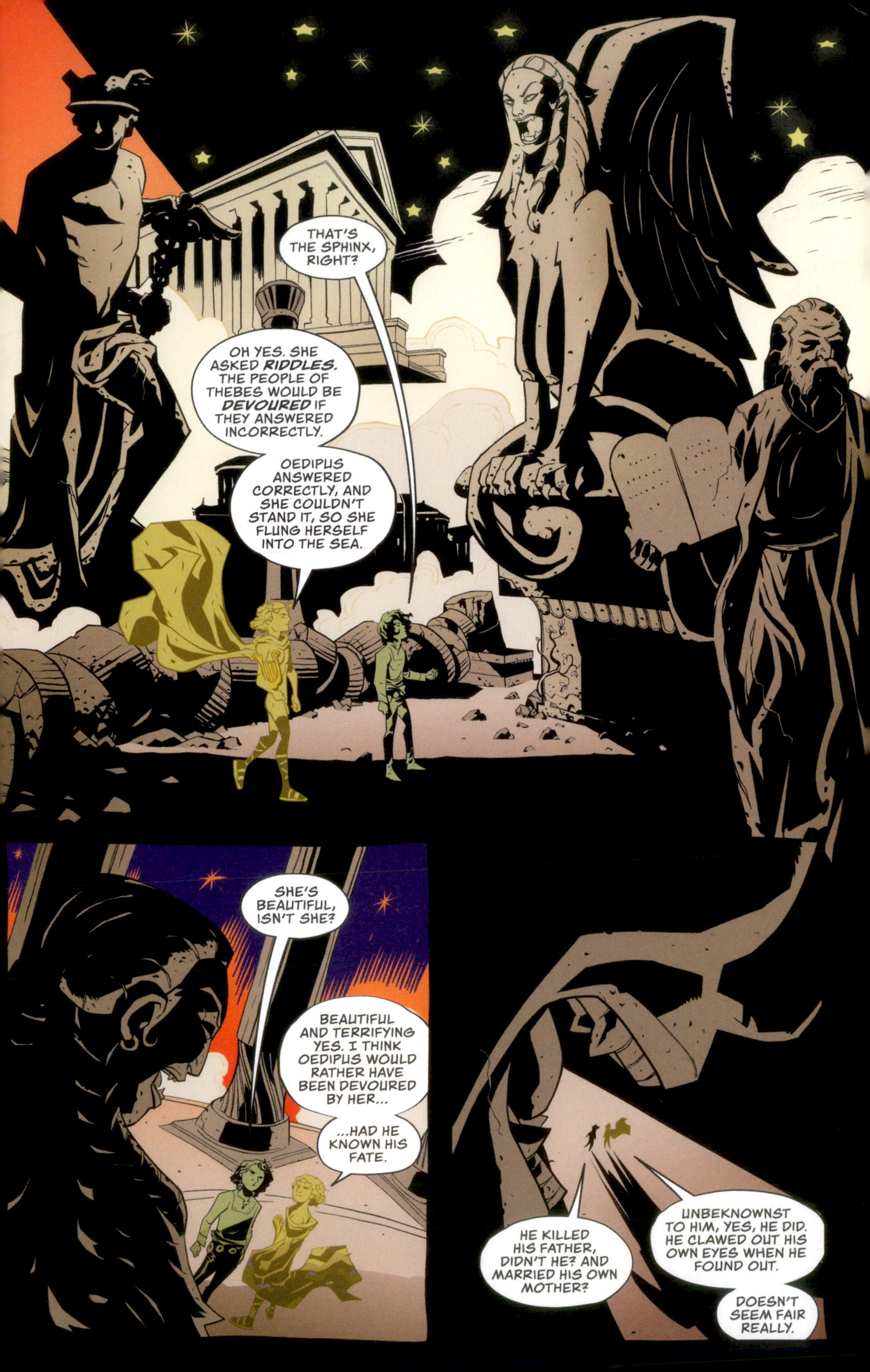
THAT'S THE SPHINX, RIGHT?
OH YES. SHE ASKED RIDDLES. THE PEOPLE OF THEBES WOULD BE DEVOURED IF THEY ANSWERED INCORRECTLY.
OEDIPUS ANSWERED CORRECTLY, AND SHE COULDN'T STAND IT, SO SHE FLUNG HERSELF INTO THE SEA.
SHE'S BEAUTIFUL, ISN'T SHE?
BEAUTIFUL AND TERRIFYING YES. I THINK OEDIPUS WOULD RATHER HAVE BEEN DEVOURED BY HER...
...HAD HE KNOWN HIS FATE.
HE KILLED HIS FATHER, DIDN'T HE? AND MARRIED HIS OWN MOTHER?
UNBEKNOWNST TO HIM, YES, HE DID. HE CLAWED OUT HIS OWN EYES WHEN HE FOUND OUT.
DOESN'T SEEM FAIR REALLY.

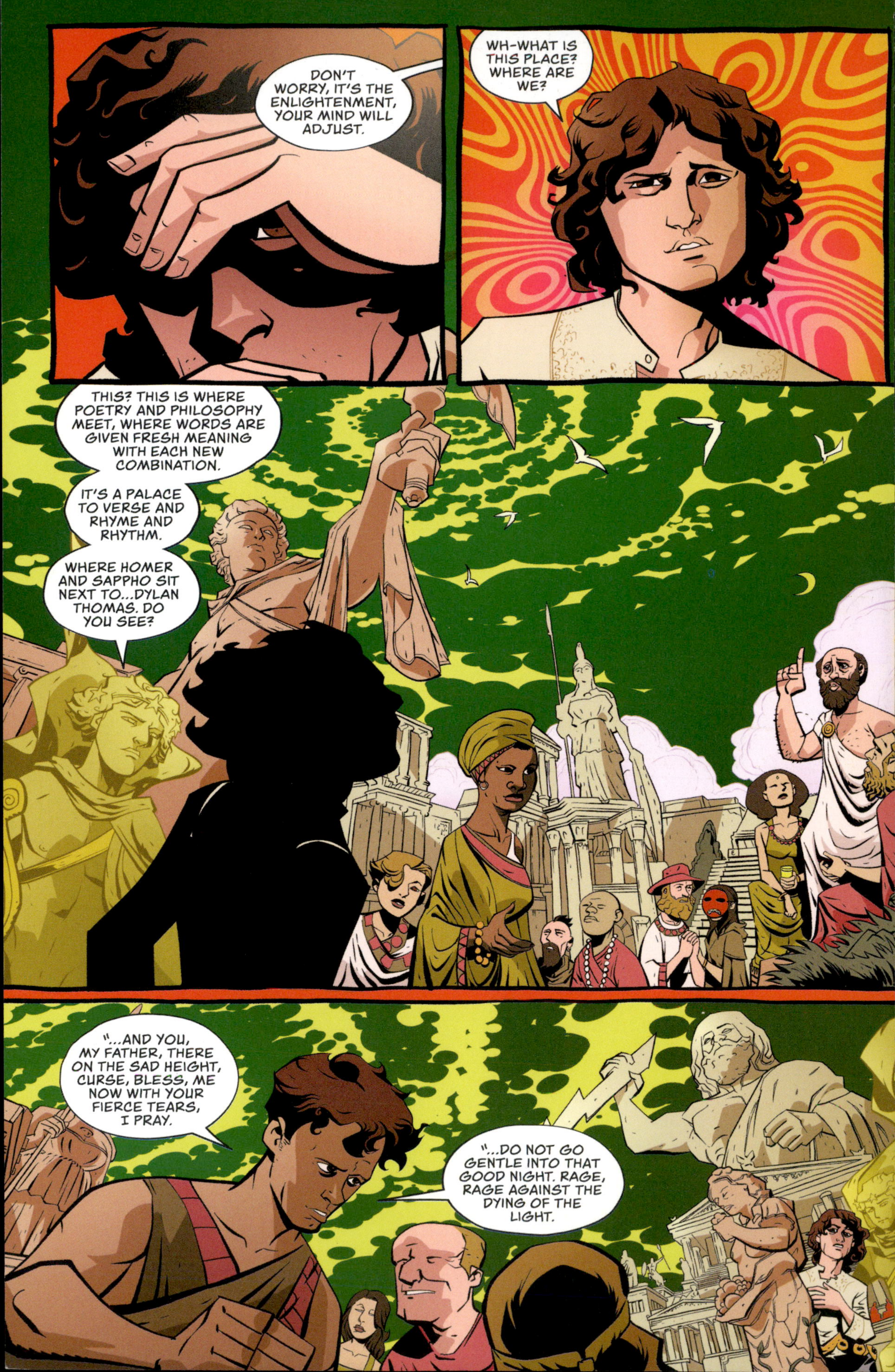
DON'T WORRY, IT'S THE ENLIGHTENMENT, YOUR MIND WILL ADJUST.
WH-WHAT IS THIS PLACE? WHERE ARE WE?
THIS? THIS IS WHERE POETRY AND PHILOSOPHY MEET, WHERE WORDS ARE GIVEN FRESH MEANING WITH EACH NEW COMBINATION.
IT'S A PALACE TO VERSE AND RHYME AND RHYTHM.
WHERE HOMER AND SAPPHO SIT NEXT TO...DYLAN THOMAS. DO YOU SEE?
"...AND YOU, MY FATHER, THERE ON THE SAD HEIGHT, CURSE, BLESS, ME NOW WITH YOUR FIERCE TEARS, I PRAY.
"...DO NOT GO GENTLE INTO THAT GOOD NIGHT. RAGE, RAGE AGAINST THE DYING OF THE LIGHT.

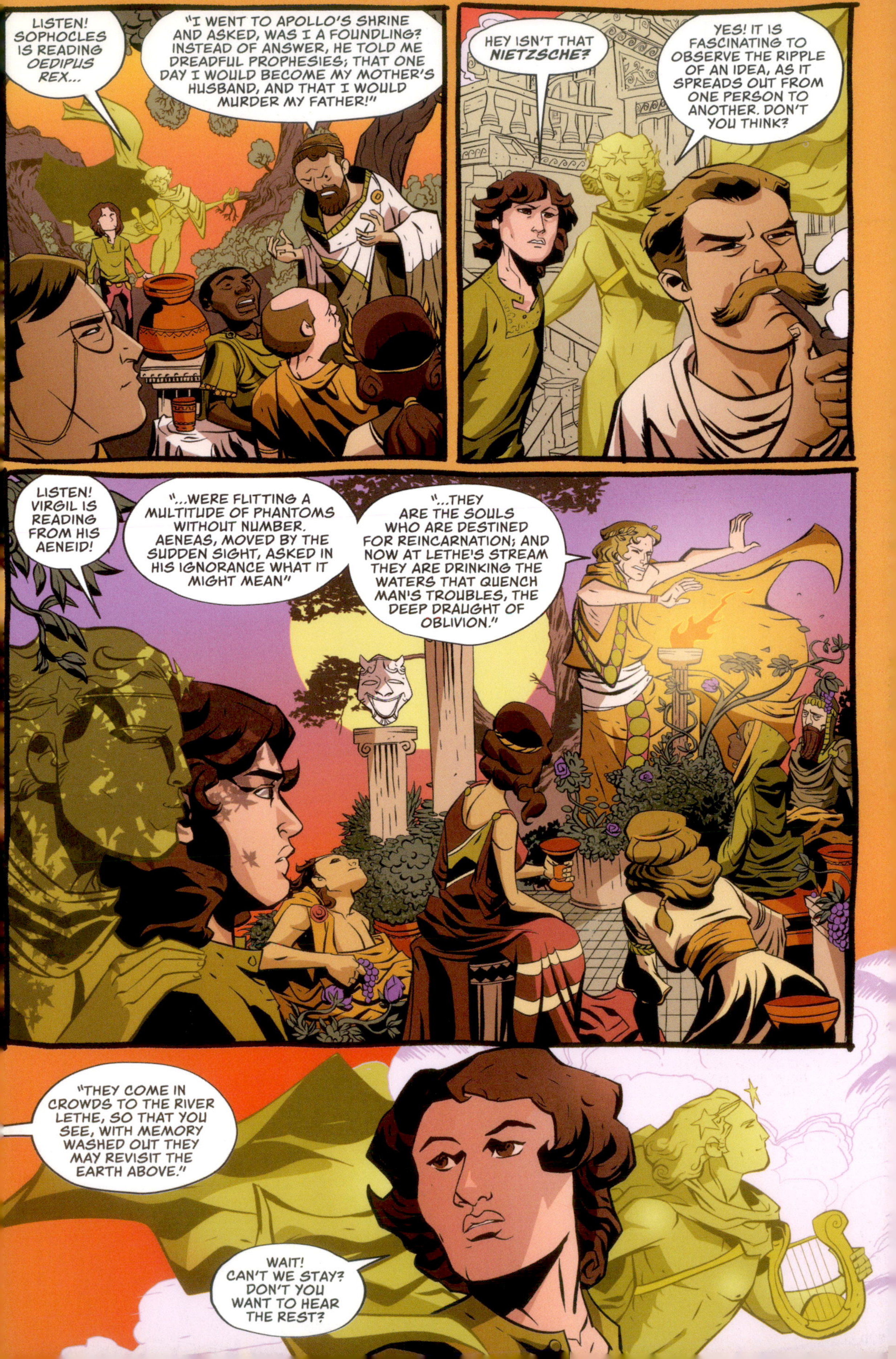
LISTEN! SOPHOCLES IS READING *OEDIPUS REX*...
"I WENT TO APOLLO'S SHRINE AND ASKED, WAS I A FOUNDLING? INSTEAD OF ANSWER, HE TOLD ME DREADFUL PROPHESIES; THAT ONE DAY I WOULD BECOME MY MOTHER'S HUSBAND, AND THAT I WOULD MURDER MY FATHER!"
HEY ISN'T THAT *NIETZSCHE?*
YES! IT IS FASCINATING TO OBSERVE THE RIPPLE OF AN IDEA, AS IT SPREADS OUT FROM ONE PERSON TO ANOTHER. DON'T YOU THINK?
LISTEN! VIRGIL IS READING FROM HIS AENEID!
"...WERE FLITTING A MULTITUDE OF PHANTOMS WITHOUT NUMBER. AENEAS, MOVED BY THE SUDDEN SIGHT, ASKED IN HIS IGNORANCE WHAT IT MIGHT MEAN"
"...THEY ARE THE SOULS WHO ARE DESTINED FOR REINCARNATION; AND NOW AT LETHE'S STREAM THEY ARE DRINKING THE WATERS THAT QUENCH MAN'S TROUBLES, THE DEEP DRAUGHT OF OBLIVION."
"THEY COME IN CROWDS TO THE RIVER LETHE, SO THAT YOU SEE, WITH MEMORY WASHED OUT THEY MAY REVISIT THE EARTH ABOVE."
WAIT! CAN'T WE STAY? DON'T YOU WANT TO HEAR THE REST?

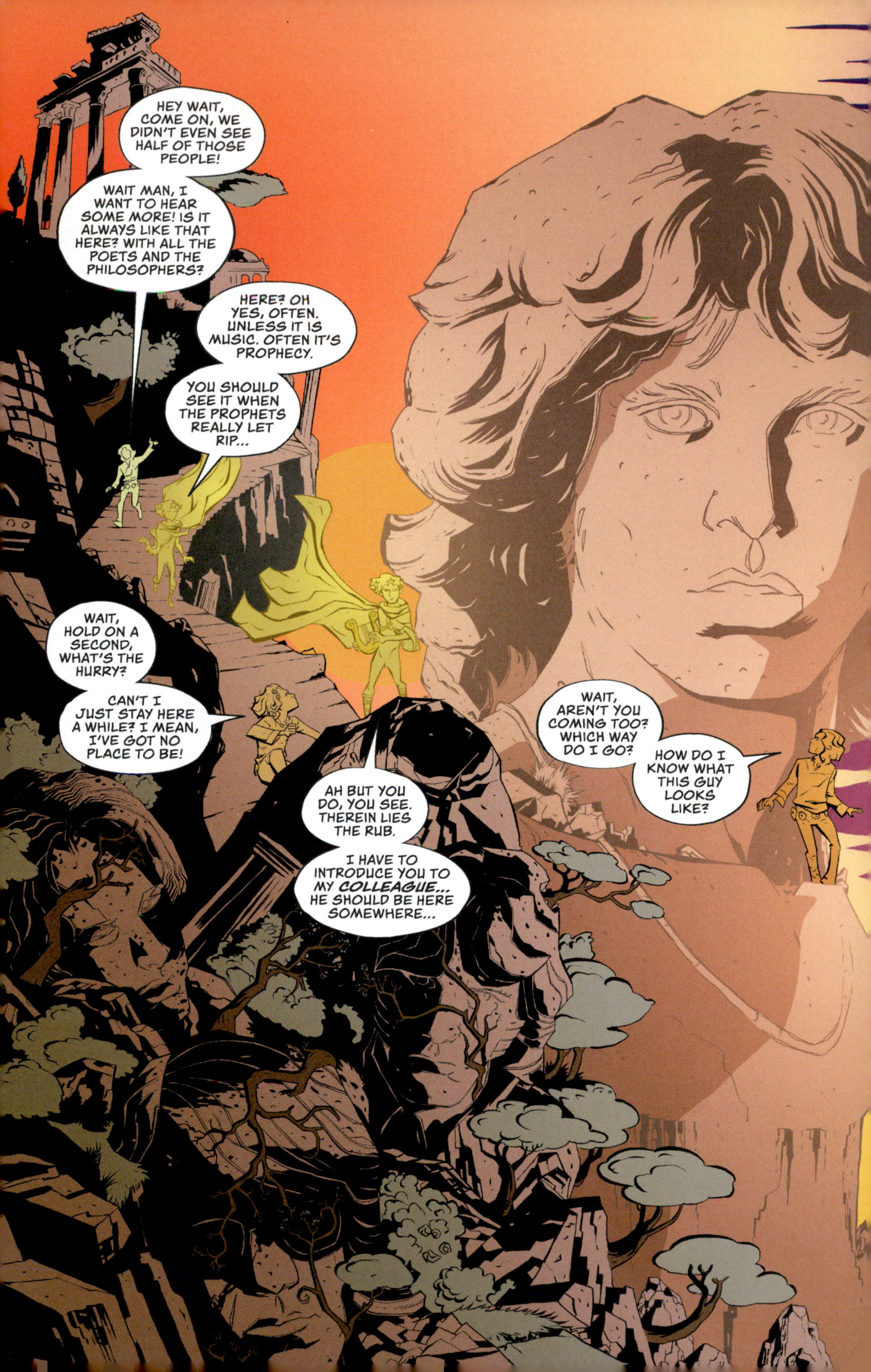
HEY WAIT, COME ON, WE DIDN'T EVEN SEE HALF OF THOSE PEOPLE!
WAIT MAN, I WANT TO HEAR SOME MORE! IS IT ALWAYS LIKE THAT HERE? WITH ALL THE POETS AND THE PHILOSOPHERS?
HERE? OH YES, OFTEN. UNLESS IT IS MUSIC. OFTEN IT'S PROPHECY.
YOU SHOULD SEE IT WHEN THE PROPHETS REALLY LET RIP...
WAIT, HOLD ON A SECOND, WHAT'S THE HURRY?
CAN'T I JUST STAY HERE A WHILE? I MEAN, I'VE GOT NO PLACE TO BE!
AH BUT YOU DO, YOU SEE. THEREIN LIES THE RUB.
I HAVE TO INTRODUCE YOU TO MY ***COLLEAGUE...*** HE SHOULD BE HERE SOMEWHERE...
WAIT, AREN'T YOU COMING TOO? WHICH WAY DO I GO?
HOW DO I KNOW WHAT THIS GUY LOOKS LIKE?

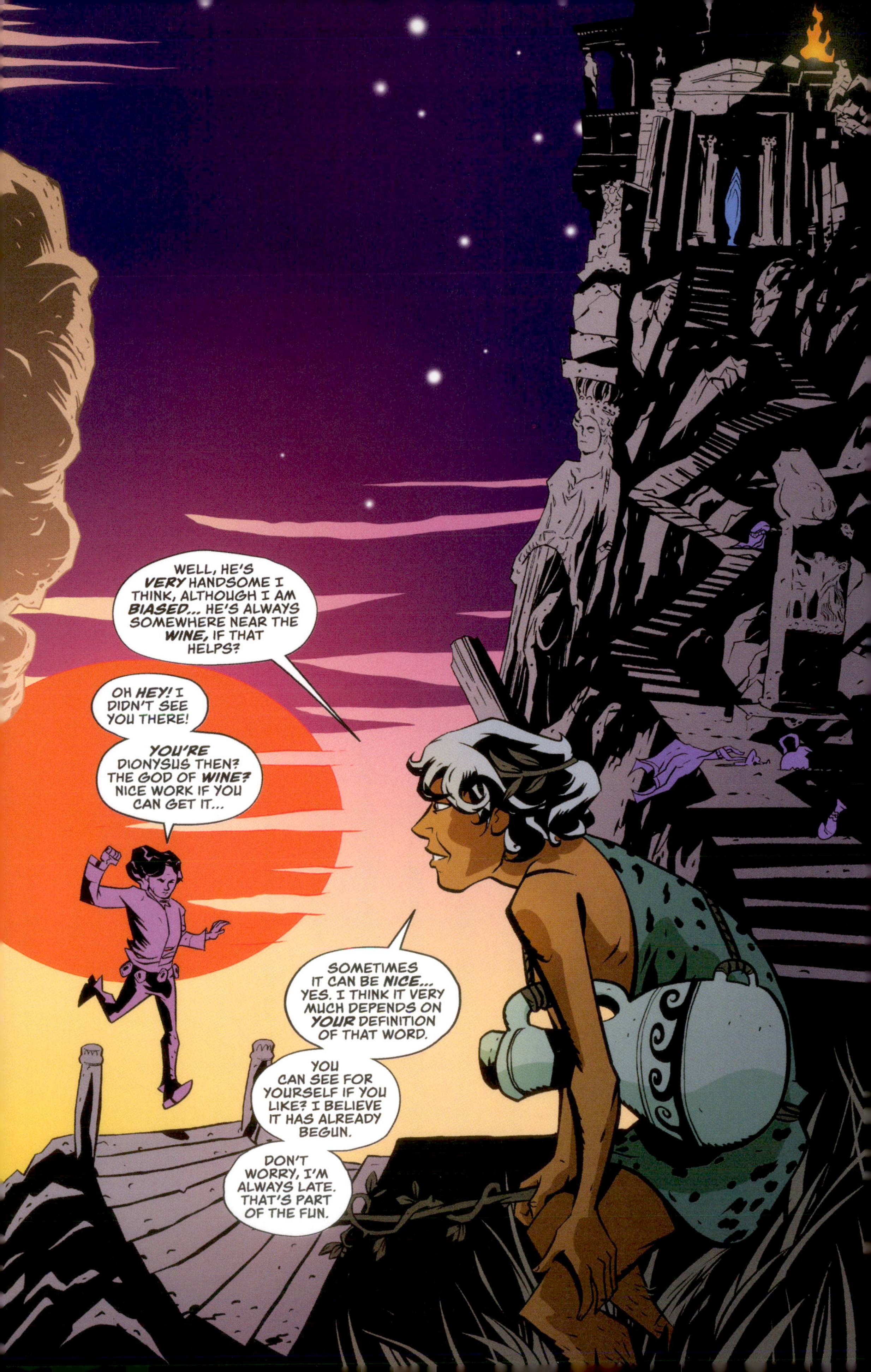

WELL, HE'S VERY HANDSOME I THINK, ALTHOUGH I AM BIASED... HE'S ALWAYS SOMEWHERE NEAR THE WINE, IF THAT HELPS?
OH HEY! I DIDN'T SEE YOU THERE!
YOU'RE DIONYSUS THEN? THE GOD OF WINE? NICE WORK IF YOU CAN GET IT...
SOMETIMES IT CAN BE NICE... YES. I THINK IT VERY MUCH DEPENDS ON YOUR DEFINITION OF THAT WORD.
YOU CAN SEE FOR YOURSELF IF YOU LIKE? I BELIEVE IT HAS ALREADY BEGUN.
DON'T WORRY, I'M ALWAYS LATE. THAT'S PART OF THE FUN.

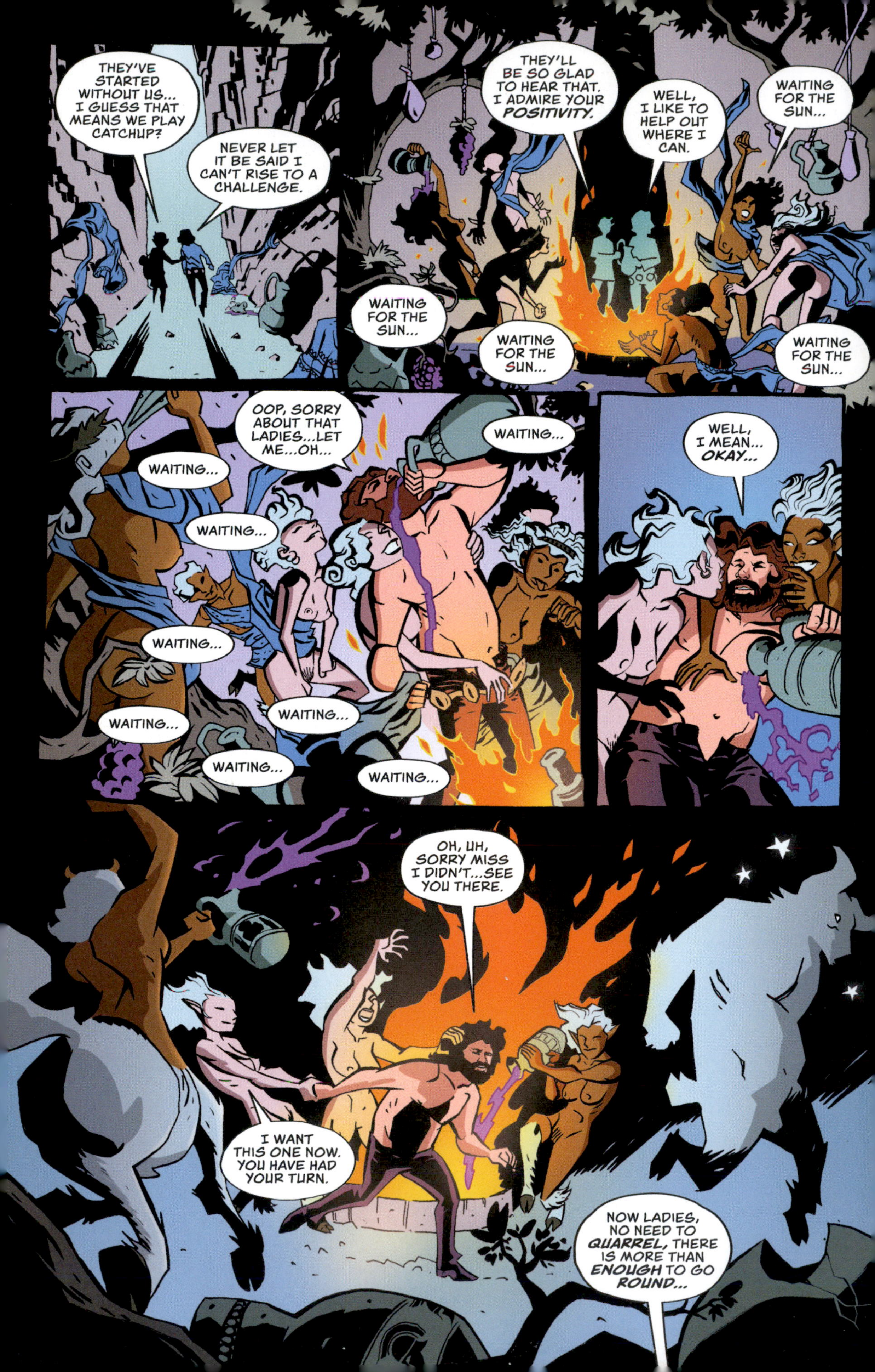
THEY'VE STARTED WITHOUT US... I GUESS THAT MEANS WE PLAY CATCHUP?
NEVER LET IT BE SAID I CAN'T RISE TO A CHALLENGE.
THEY'LL BE SO GLAD TO HEAR THAT. I ADMIRE YOUR POSITIVITY.
WELL, I LIKE TO HELP OUT WHERE I CAN.
WAITING FOR THE SUN...
WAITING FOR THE SUN...
WAITING FOR THE SUN...
WAITING FOR THE SUN...
OOP, SORRY ABOUT THAT LADIES...LET ME...OH...
WAITING...
WAITING...
WAITING...
WAITING...
WAITING...
WAITING...
WAITING...
WAITING...
WELL, I MEAN... OKAY...
OH, UH, SORRY MISS I DIDN'T...SEE YOU THERE.
I WANT THIS ONE NOW. YOU HAVE HAD YOUR TURN.
NOW LADIES, NO NEED TO QUARREL, THERE IS MORE THAN ENOUGH TO GO ROUND...

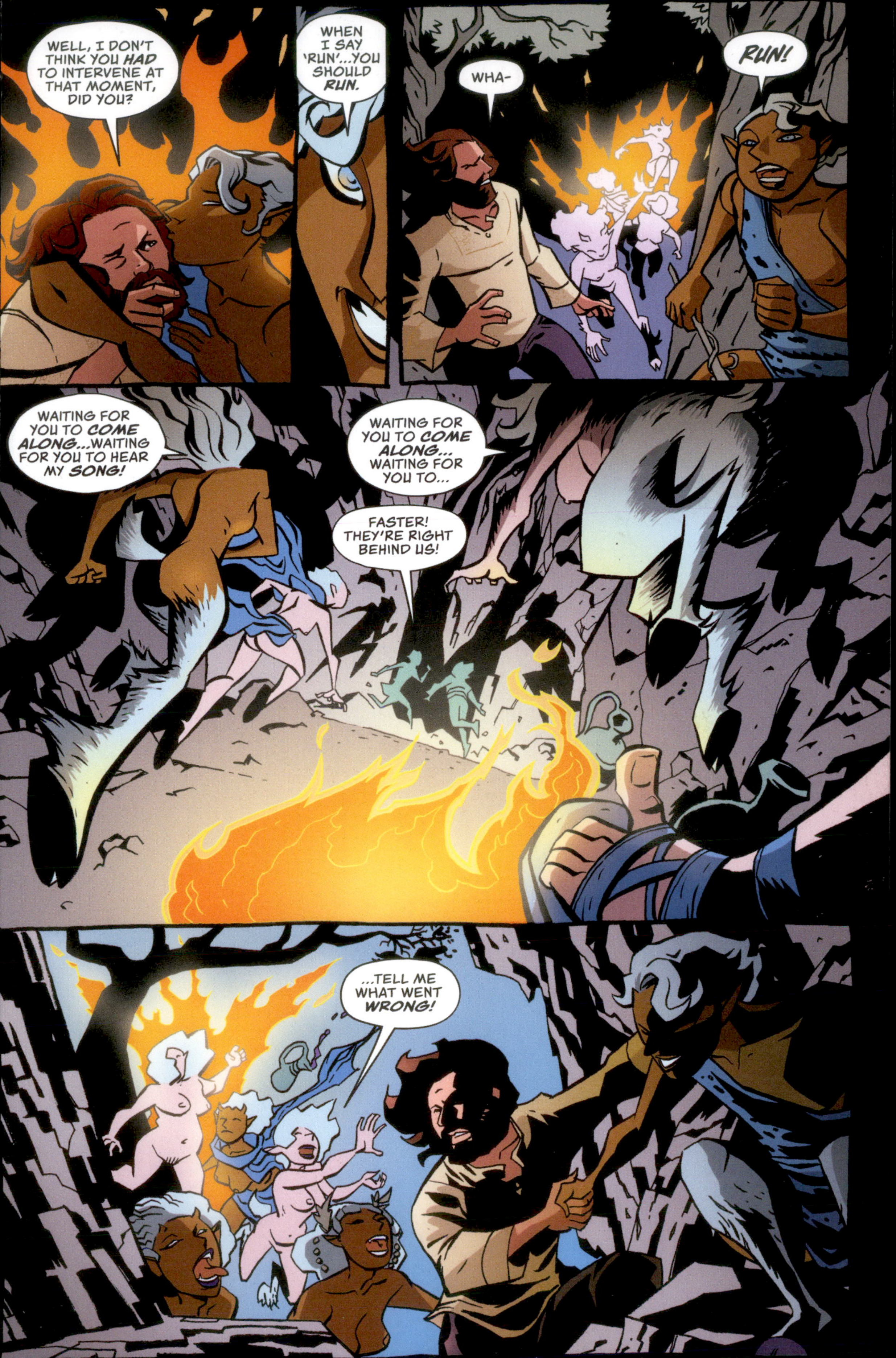
WELL, I DON'T THINK YOU HAD TO INTERVENE AT THAT MOMENT, DID YOU?
WHEN I SAY 'RUN'...YOU SHOULD RUN.
WHA-
RUN!
WAITING FOR YOU TO COME ALONG...WAITING FOR YOU TO HEAR MY SONG!
WAITING FOR YOU TO COME ALONG... WAITING FOR YOU TO...
FASTER! THEY'RE RIGHT BEHIND US!
...TELL ME WHAT WENT WRONG!

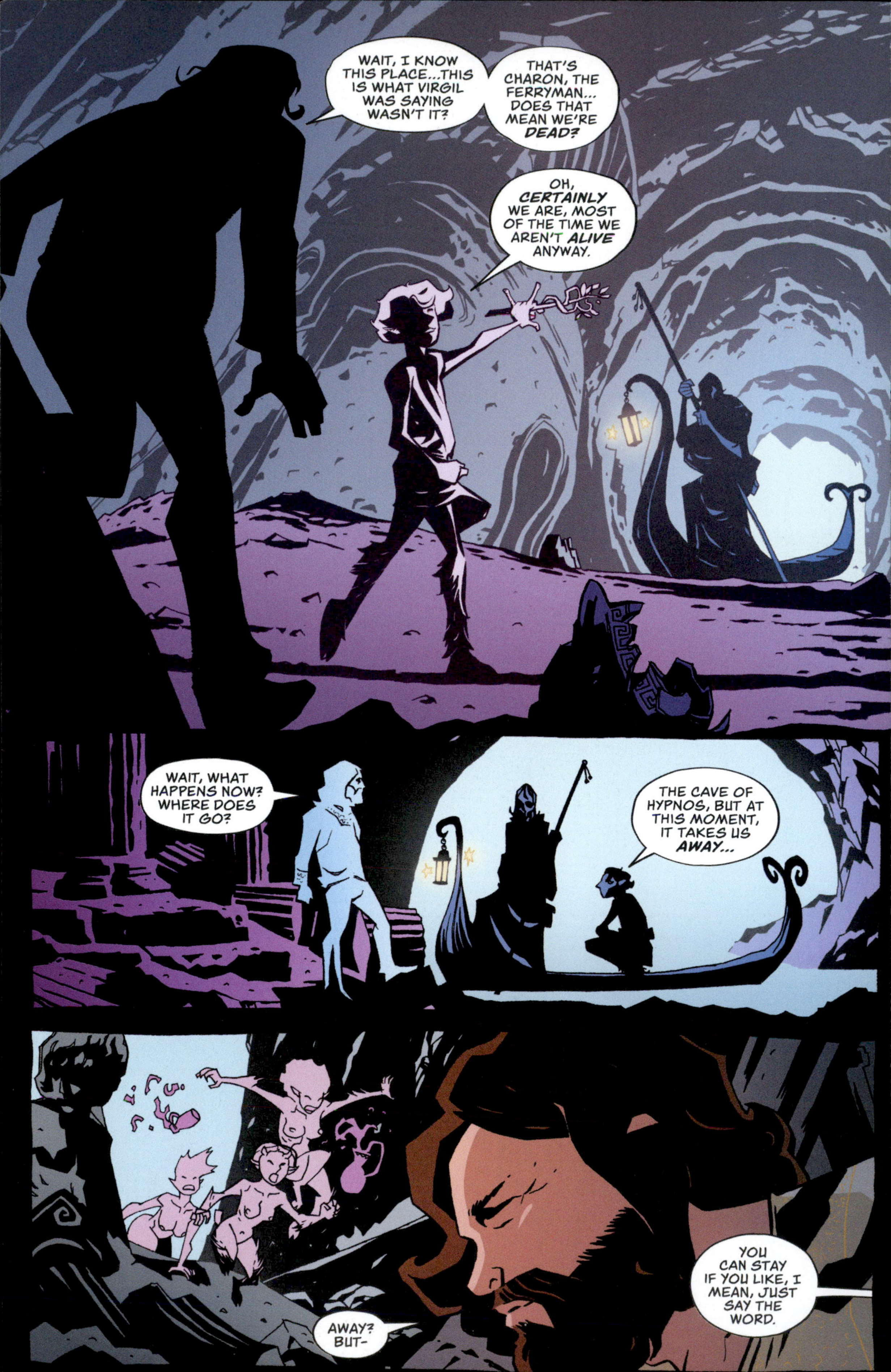
WAIT, I KNOW THIS PLACE...THIS IS WHAT VIRGIL WAS SAYING WASN'T IT?
THAT'S CHARON, THE FERRYMAN... DOES THAT MEAN WE'RE DEAD?
OH, CERTAINLY WE ARE, MOST OF THE TIME WE AREN'T ALIVE ANYWAY.
WAIT, WHAT HAPPENS NOW? WHERE DOES IT GO?
THE CAVE OF HYPNOS, BUT AT THIS MOMENT, IT TAKES US AWAY...
YOU CAN STAY IF YOU LIKE, I MEAN, JUST SAY THE WORD.
AWAY? BUT-

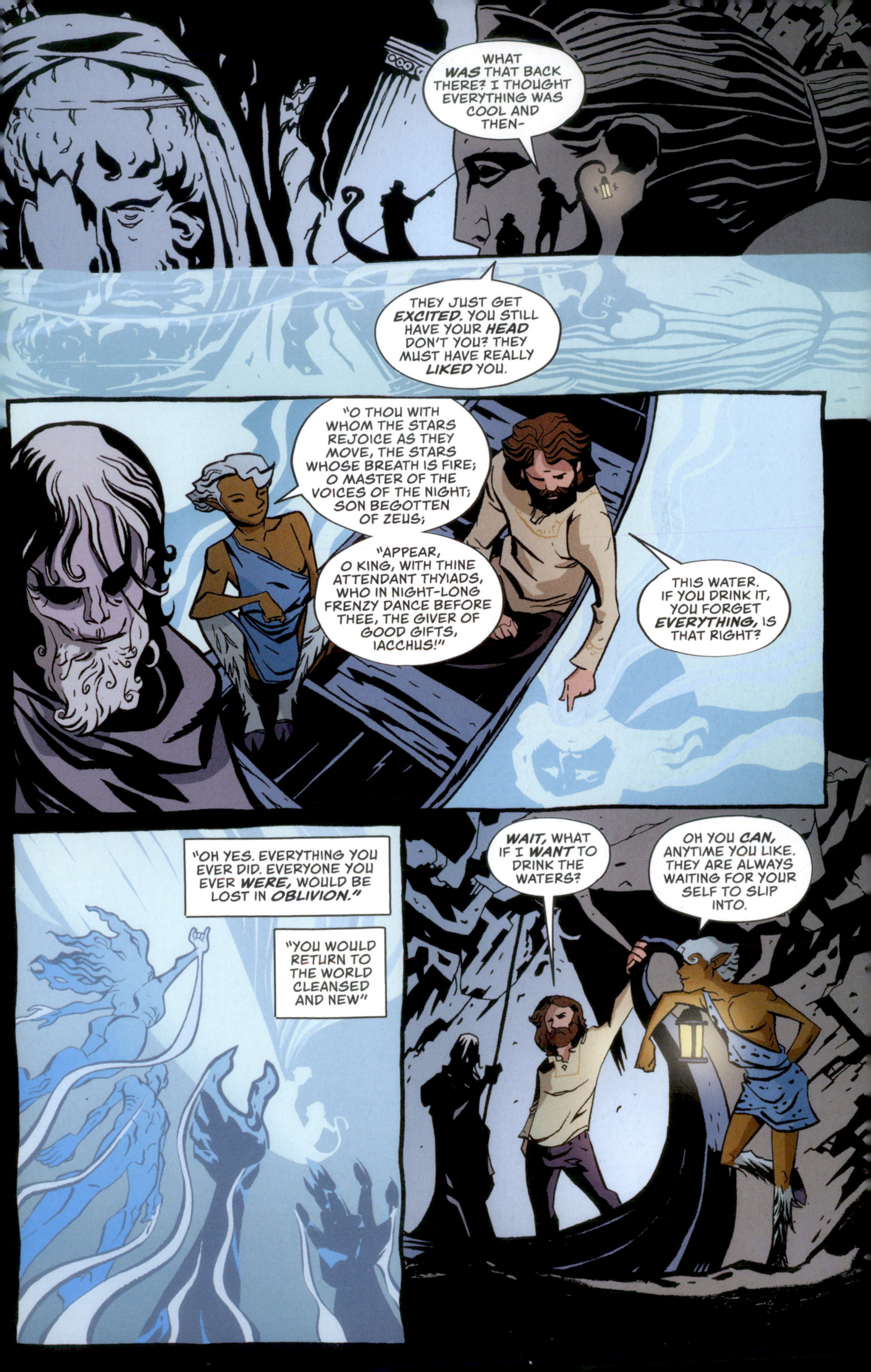
WHAT WAS THAT BACK THERE? I THOUGHT EVERYTHING WAS COOL AND THEN-
THEY JUST GET EXCITED. YOU STILL HAVE YOUR HEAD DON'T YOU? THEY MUST HAVE REALLY LIKED YOU.
"O THOU WITH WHOM THE STARS REJOICE AS THEY MOVE, THE STARS WHOSE BREATH IS FIRE; O MASTER OF THE VOICES OF THE NIGHT; SON BEGOTTEN OF ZEUS;
"APPEAR, O KING, WITH THINE ATTENDANT THYIADS, WHO IN NIGHT-LONG FRENZY DANCE BEFORE THEE, THE GIVER OF GOOD GIFTS, IACCHUS!"
THIS WATER. IF YOU DRINK IT, YOU FORGET EVERYTHING, IS THAT RIGHT?
"OH YES. EVERYTHING YOU EVER DID. EVERYONE YOU EVER WERE, WOULD BE LOST IN OBLIVION."
"YOU WOULD RETURN TO THE WORLD CLEANSED AND NEW"
WAIT, WHAT IF I WANT TO DRINK THE WATERS?
OH YOU CAN, ANYTIME YOU LIKE. THEY ARE ALWAYS WAITING FOR YOUR SELF TO SLIP INTO.

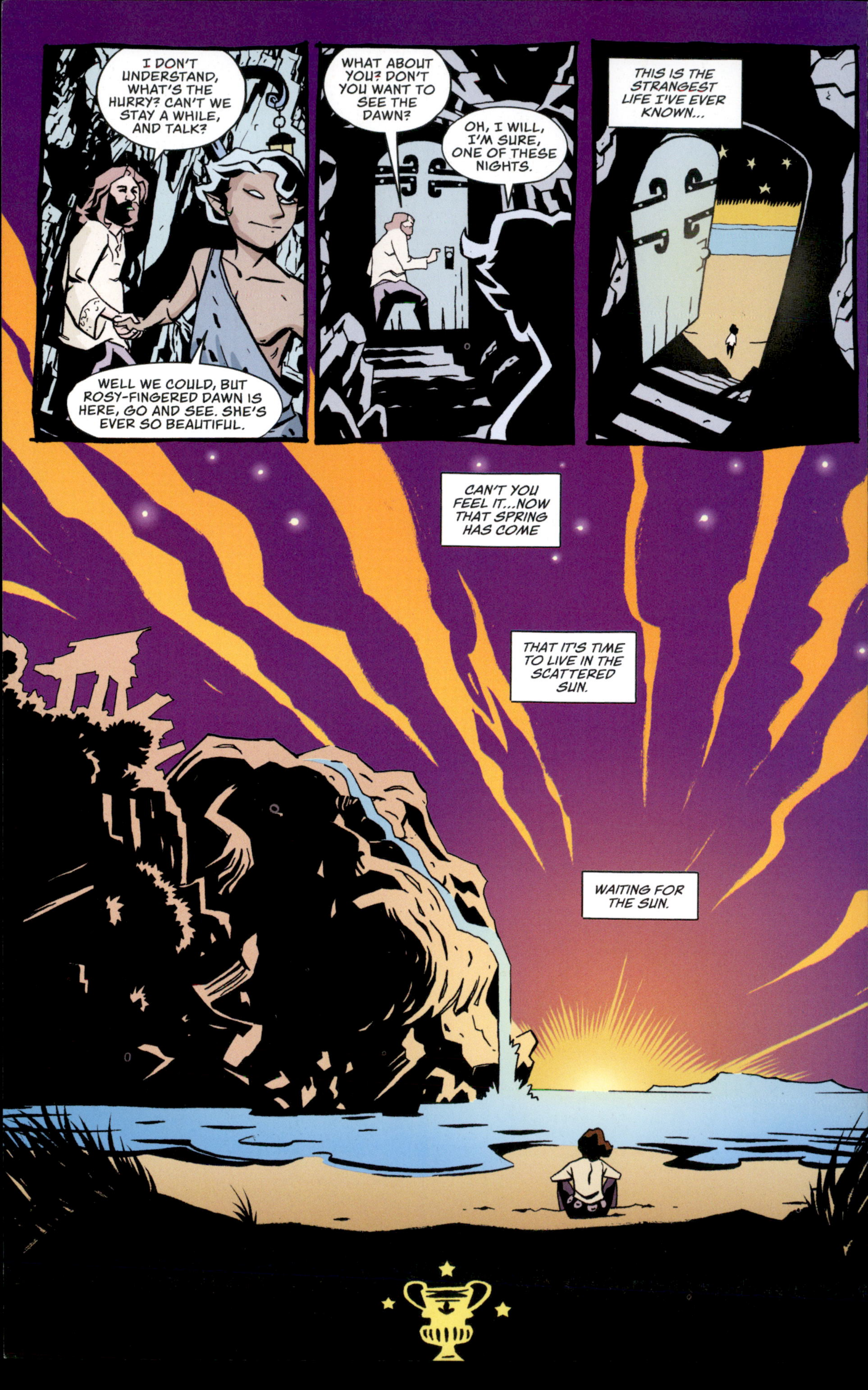
I DON'T UNDERSTAND, WHAT'S THE HURRY? CAN'T WE STAY A WHILE, AND TALK?
WELL WE COULD, BUT ROSY-FINGERED DAWN IS HERE, GO AND SEE. SHE'S EVER SO BEAUTIFUL.
WHAT ABOUT YOU? DON'T YOU WANT TO SEE THE DAWN?
OH, I WILL, I'M SURE, ONE OF THESE NIGHTS.
THIS IS THE STRANGEST LIFE I'VE EVER KNOWN...
CAN'T YOU FEEL IT...NOW THAT SPRING HAS COME
THAT IT'S TIME TO LIVE IN THE SCATTERED SUN.
WAITING FOR THE SUN.

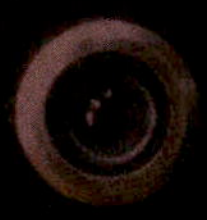

You Make Me Real

Artist . . . Marguerite Sauvage

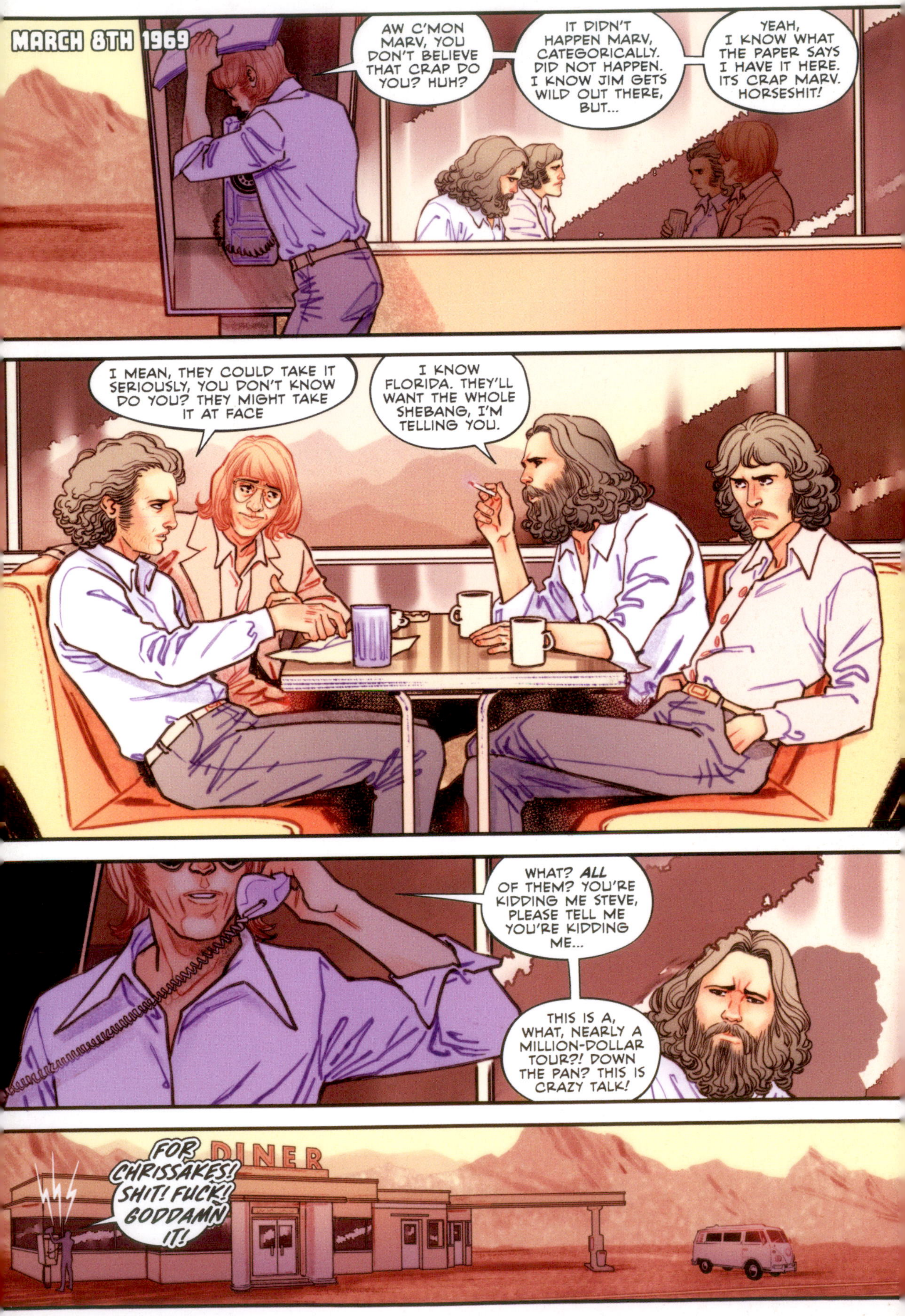
MARCH 8TH 1969
AW C'MON MARV, YOU DON'T BELIEVE THAT CRAP DO YOU? HUH?
IT DIDN'T HAPPEN MARV, CATEGORICALLY. DID NOT HAPPEN. I KNOW JIM GETS WILD OUT THERE, BUT...
YEAH, I KNOW WHAT THE PAPER SAYS I HAVE IT HERE. ITS CRAP MARV. HORSESHIT!
I MEAN, THEY COULD TAKE IT SERIOUSLY, YOU DON'T KNOW DO YOU? THEY MIGHT TAKE IT AT FACE
I KNOW FLORIDA. THEY'LL WANT THE WHOLE SHEBANG, I'M TELLING YOU.
WHAT? ALL OF THEM? YOU'RE KIDDING ME STEVE, PLEASE TELL ME YOU'RE KIDDING ME...
THIS IS A, WHAT, NEARLY A MILLION-DOLLAR TOUR?! DOWN THE PAN? THIS IS CRAZY TALK!
DINER
FOR CHRISSAKES! SHIT! FUCK! GODDAMN IT!

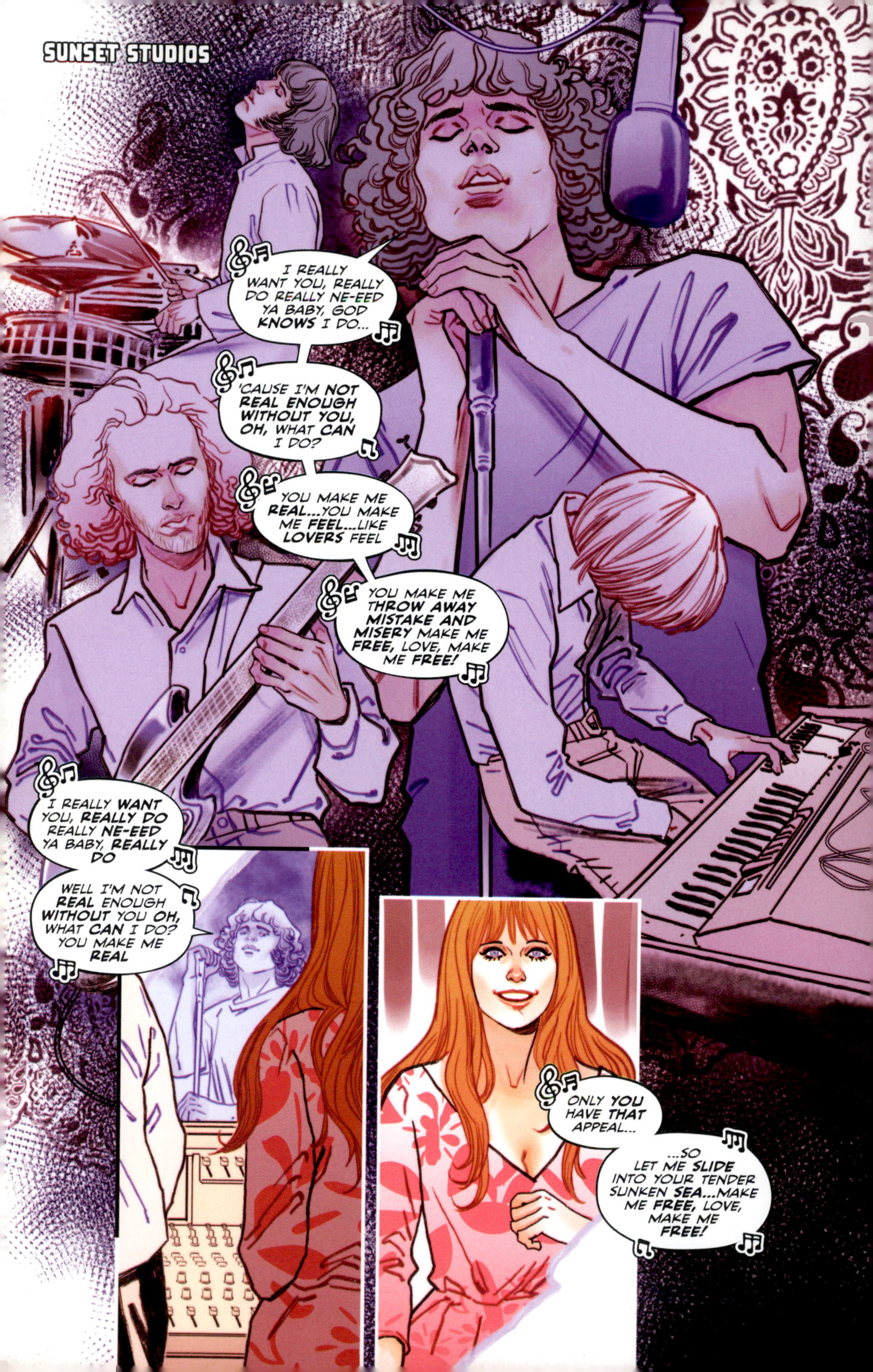
SUNSET STUDIOS
I REALLY WANT YOU, REALLY DO REALLY NE-EED YA BABY, GOD KNOWS I DO...
'CAUSE I'M NOT REAL ENOUGH WITHOUT YOU, OH, WHAT CAN I DO?
YOU MAKE ME REAL...YOU MAKE ME FEEL...LIKE LOVERS FEEL
YOU MAKE ME THROW AWAY MISTAKE AND MISERY MAKE ME FREE, LOVE, MAKE ME FREE!
I REALLY WANT YOU, REALLY DO REALLY NE-EED YA BABY, REALLY DO
WELL I'M NOT REAL ENOUGH WITHOUT YOU OH, WHAT CAN I DO? YOU MAKE ME REAL
ONLY YOU HAVE THAT APPEAL...
...SO LET ME SLIDE INTO YOUR TENDER SUNKEN SEA...MAKE ME FREE, LOVE, MAKE ME FREE!

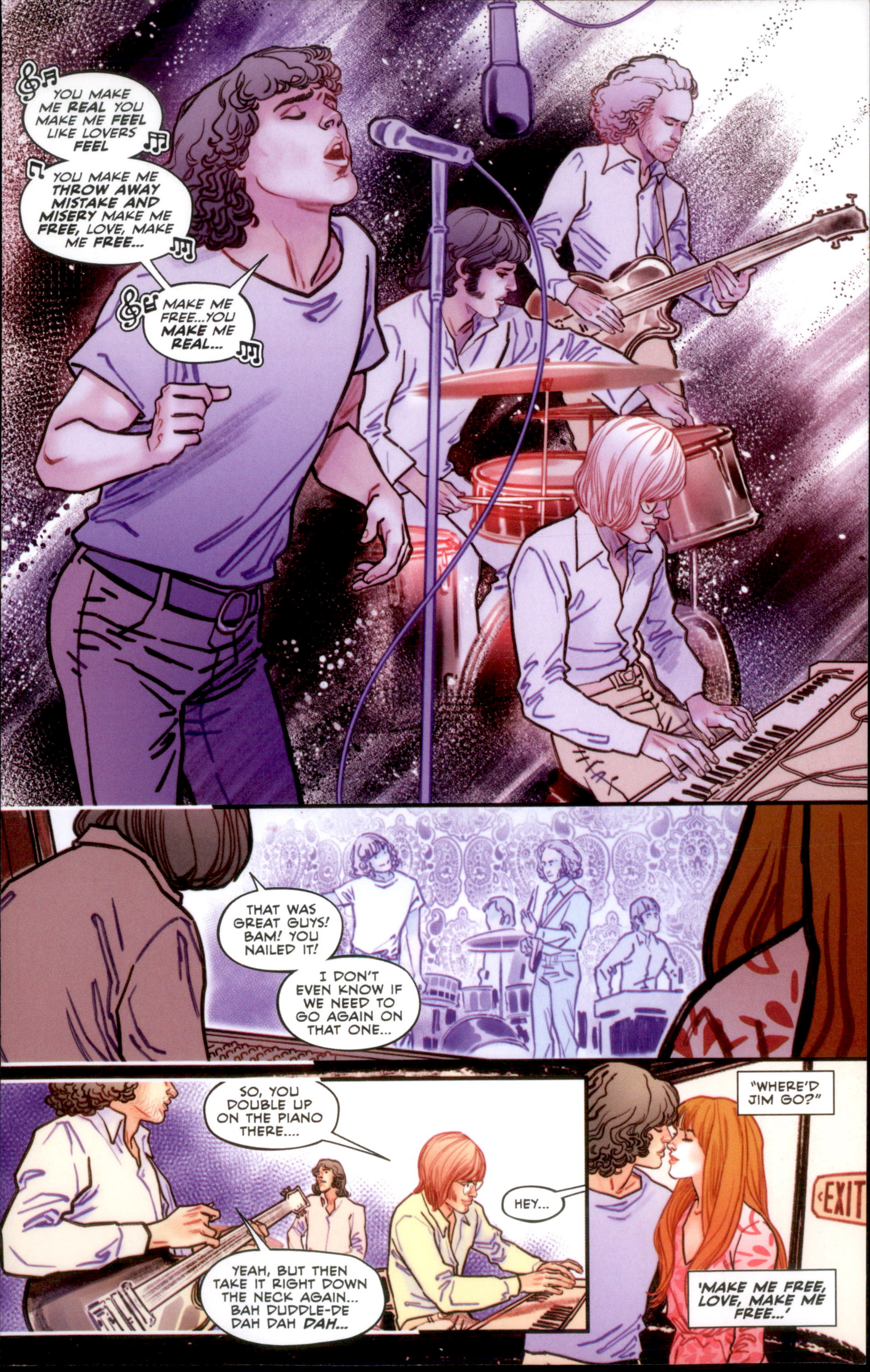
YOU MAKE ME REAL YOU MAKE ME FEEL LIKE LOVERS FEEL
YOU MAKE ME THROW AWAY MISTAKE AND MISERY MAKE ME FREE, LOVE, MAKE ME FREE...
MAKE ME FREE...YOU MAKE ME REAL...
THAT WAS GREAT GUYS! BAM! YOU NAILED IT!
I DON'T EVEN KNOW IF WE NEED TO GO AGAIN ON THAT ONE...
SO, YOU DOUBLE UP ON THE PIANO THERE....
YEAH, BUT THEN TAKE IT RIGHT DOWN THE NECK AGAIN... BAH DUDDLE-DE DAH DAH DAH...
HEY...
"WHERE'D JIM GO?"
EXIT
'MAKE ME FREE, LOVE, MAKE ME FREE...'

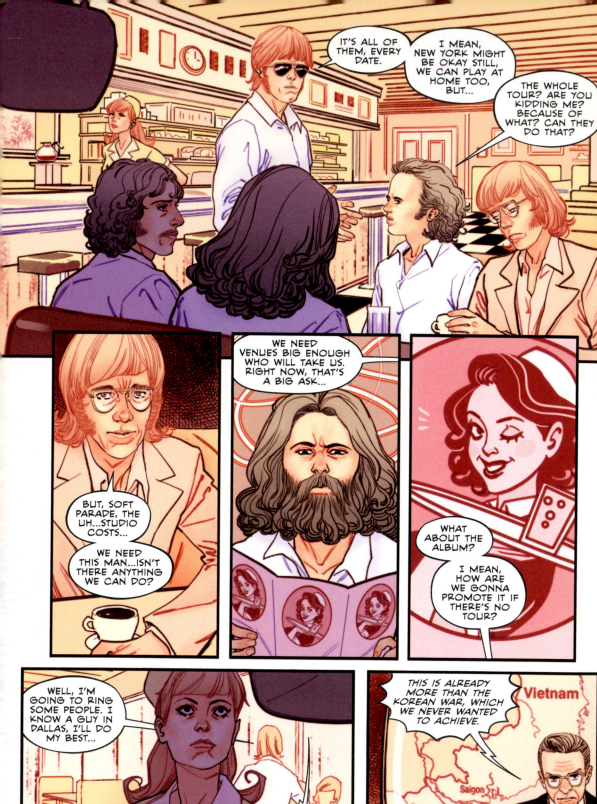

IT'S ALL OF THEM, EVERY DATE.

I MEAN, NEW YORK MIGHT BE OKAY STILL, WE CAN PLAY AT HOME TOO, BUT...

THE WHOLE TOUR? ARE YOU KIDDING ME? BECAUSE OF WHAT? CAN THEY DO THAT?

WE NEED VENUES BIG ENOUGH WHO WILL TAKE US. RIGHT NOW, THAT'S A BIG ASK...

BUT, SOFT PARADE, THE UH...STUDIO COSTS...

WE NEED THIS MAN...ISN'T THERE ANYTHING WE CAN DO?

WHAT ABOUT THE ALBUM?

I MEAN, HOW ARE WE GONNA PROMOTE IT IF THERE'S NO TOUR?

WELL, I'M GOING TO RING SOME PEOPLE. I KNOW A GUY IN DALLAS, I'LL DO MY BEST...

...DEPARTMENT OF DEFENSE REPORTED THAT AS OF THE FIRST OF MARCH, 32,376 MEN HAVE LOST THEIR LIVES IN VIETNAM.

THIS IS ALREADY MORE THAN THE KOREAN WAR, WHICH WE NEVER WANTED TO ACHIEVE.

Vietnam

Saigon

WE'RE GOING TO HAVE TO HUSTLE FELLAS, BUT YOU'RE NO STRANGERS TO THAT...

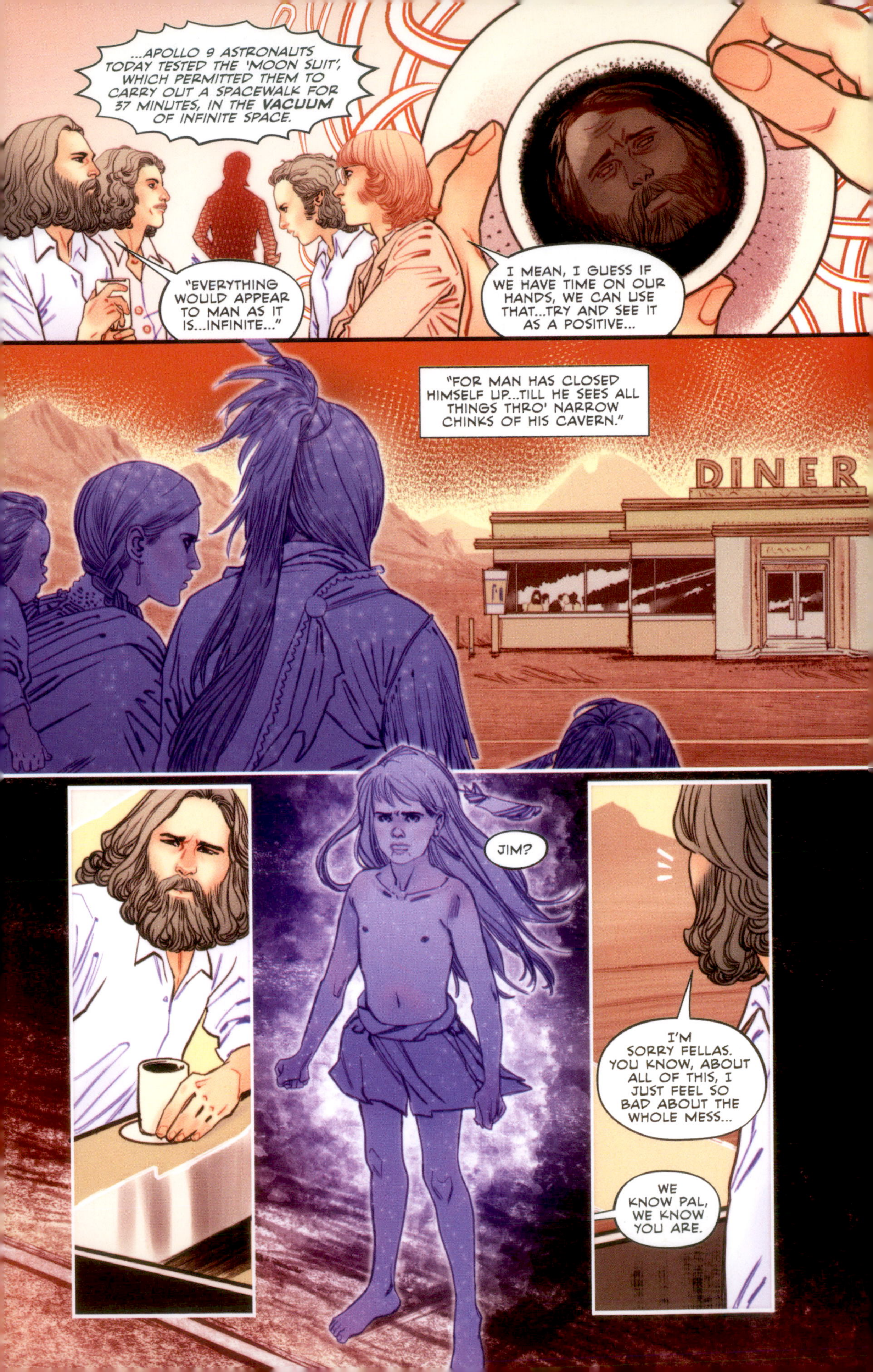
...APOLLO 9 ASTRONAUTS TODAY TESTED THE 'MOON SUIT', WHICH PERMITTED THEM TO CARRY OUT A SPACEWALK FOR 37 MINUTES, IN THE **VACUUM** OF INFINITE SPACE.
"EVERYTHING WOULD APPEAR TO MAN AS IT IS...INFINITE..."
I MEAN, I GUESS IF WE HAVE TIME ON OUR HANDS, WE CAN USE THAT...TRY AND SEE IT AS A POSITIVE...
"FOR MAN HAS CLOSED HIMSELF UP...TILL HE SEES ALL THINGS THRO' NARROW CHINKS OF HIS CAVERN."
DINER
JIM?
I'M SORRY FELLAS. YOU KNOW, ABOUT ALL OF THIS, I JUST FEEL SO BAD ABOUT THE WHOLE MESS...
WE KNOW PAL, WE KNOW YOU ARE.

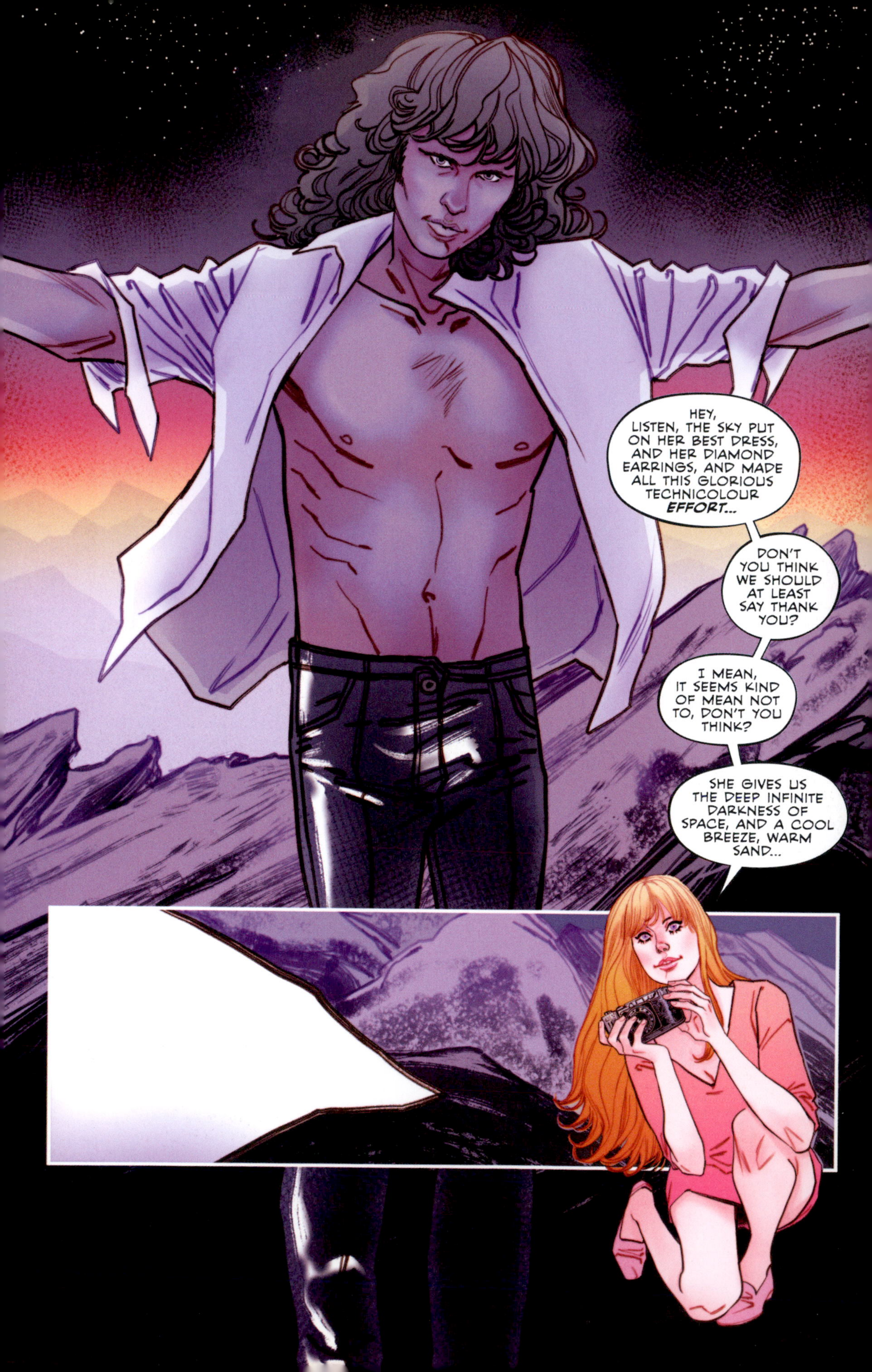
HEY, LISTEN, THE SKY PUT ON HER BEST DRESS, AND HER DIAMOND EARRINGS, AND MADE ALL THIS GLORIOUS TECHNICOLOUR *EFFORT*...
DON'T YOU THINK WE SHOULD AT LEAST SAY THANK YOU?
I MEAN, IT SEEMS KIND OF MEAN NOT TO, DON'T YOU THINK?
SHE GIVES US THE DEEP INFINITE DARKNESS OF SPACE, AND A COOL BREEZE, WARM SAND...

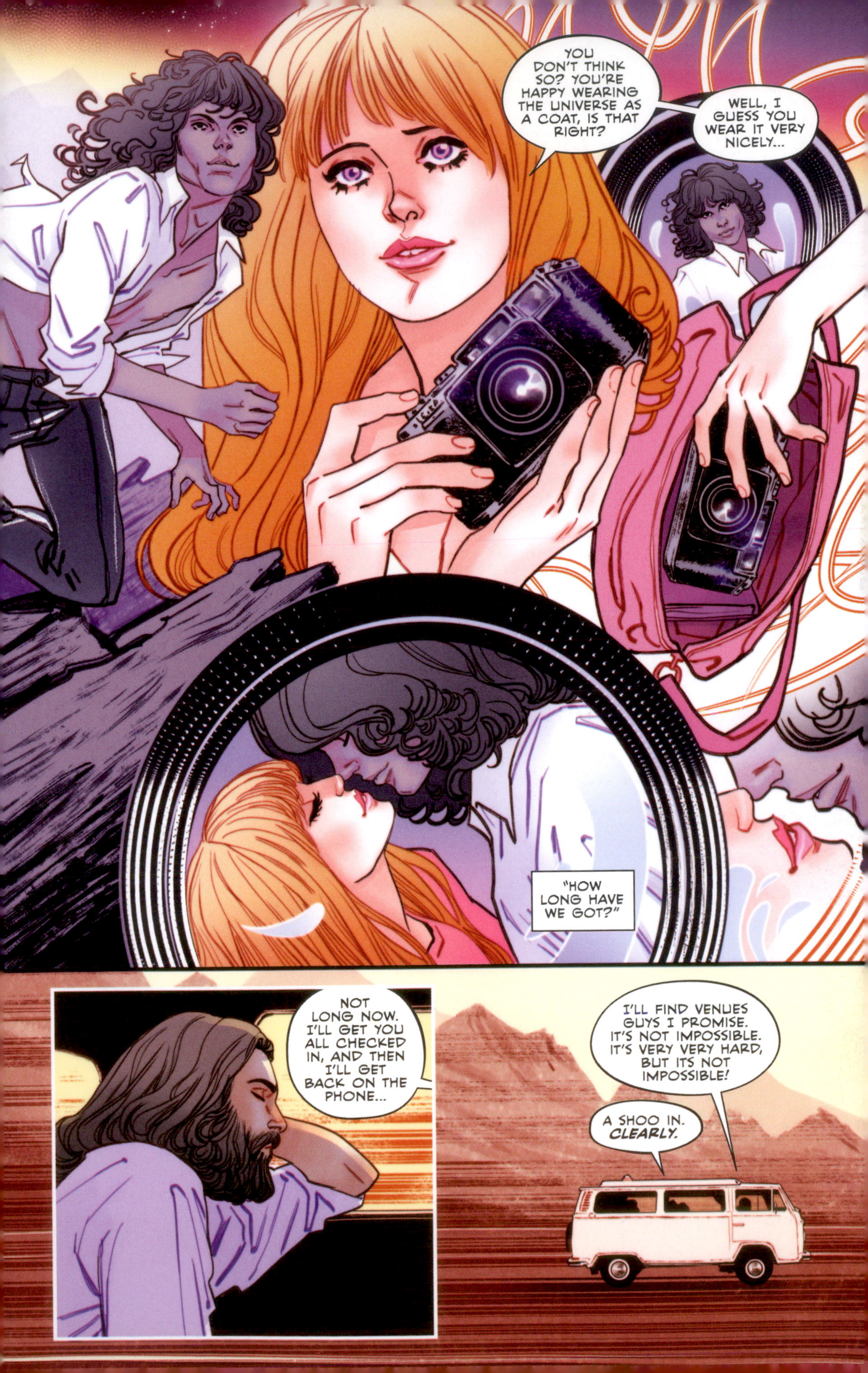
YOU DON'T THINK SO? YOU'RE HAPPY WEARING THE UNIVERSE AS A COAT, IS THAT RIGHT?
WELL, I GUESS YOU WEAR IT VERY NICELY...
"HOW LONG HAVE WE GOT?"
NOT LONG NOW. I'LL GET YOU ALL CHECKED IN, AND THEN I'LL GET BACK ON THE PHONE...
I'LL FIND VENUES GUYS I PROMISE. IT'S NOT IMPOSSIBLE. IT'S VERY VERY HARD, BUT ITS NOT IMPOSSIBLE!
A SHOO IN. *CLEARLY.*

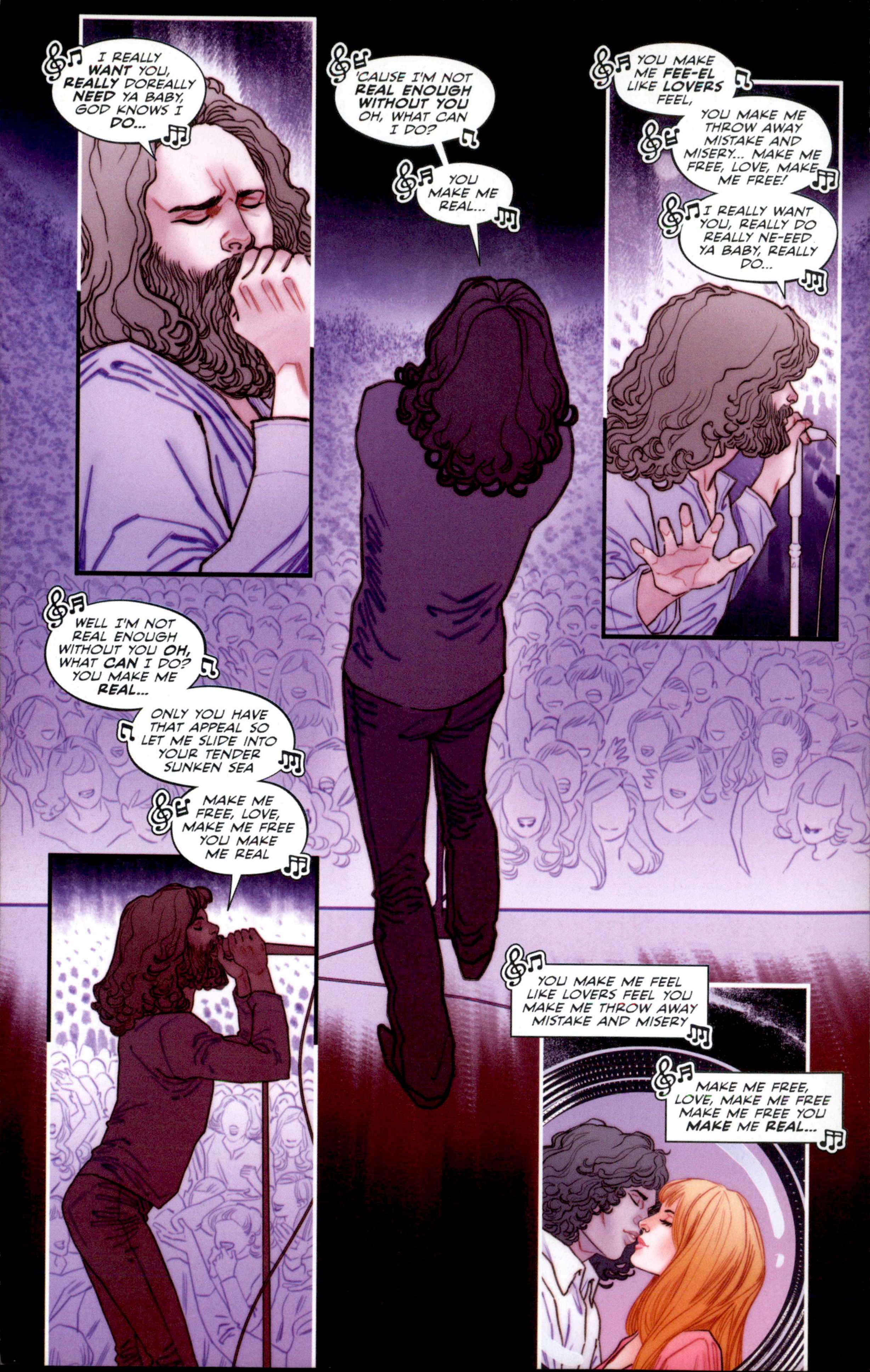
I REALLY WANT YOU, REALLY DOREALLY NEED YA BABY, GOD KNOWS I DO...
'CAUSE I'M NOT REAL ENOUGH WITHOUT YOU OH, WHAT CAN I DO?
YOU MAKE ME REAL...
YOU MAKE ME FEE-EL LIKE LOVERS FEEL,
YOU MAKE ME THROW AWAY MISTAKE AND MISERY... MAKE ME FREE, LOVE, MAKE ME FREE!
I REALLY WANT YOU, REALLY DO REALLY NE-EED YA BABY, REALLY DO...
WELL I'M NOT REAL ENOUGH WITHOUT YOU OH, WHAT CAN I DO? YOU MAKE ME REAL...
ONLY YOU HAVE THAT APPEAL SO LET ME SLIDE INTO YOUR TENDER SUNKEN SEA
MAKE ME FREE, LOVE, MAKE ME FREE YOU MAKE ME REAL
YOU MAKE ME FEEL LIKE LOVERS FEEL YOU MAKE ME THROW AWAY MISTAKE AND MISERY
MAKE ME FREE, LOVE, MAKE ME FREE MAKE ME FREE YOU MAKE ME REAL...

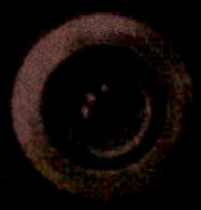

Peace Frog

Artist . . . Sebastián Piriz

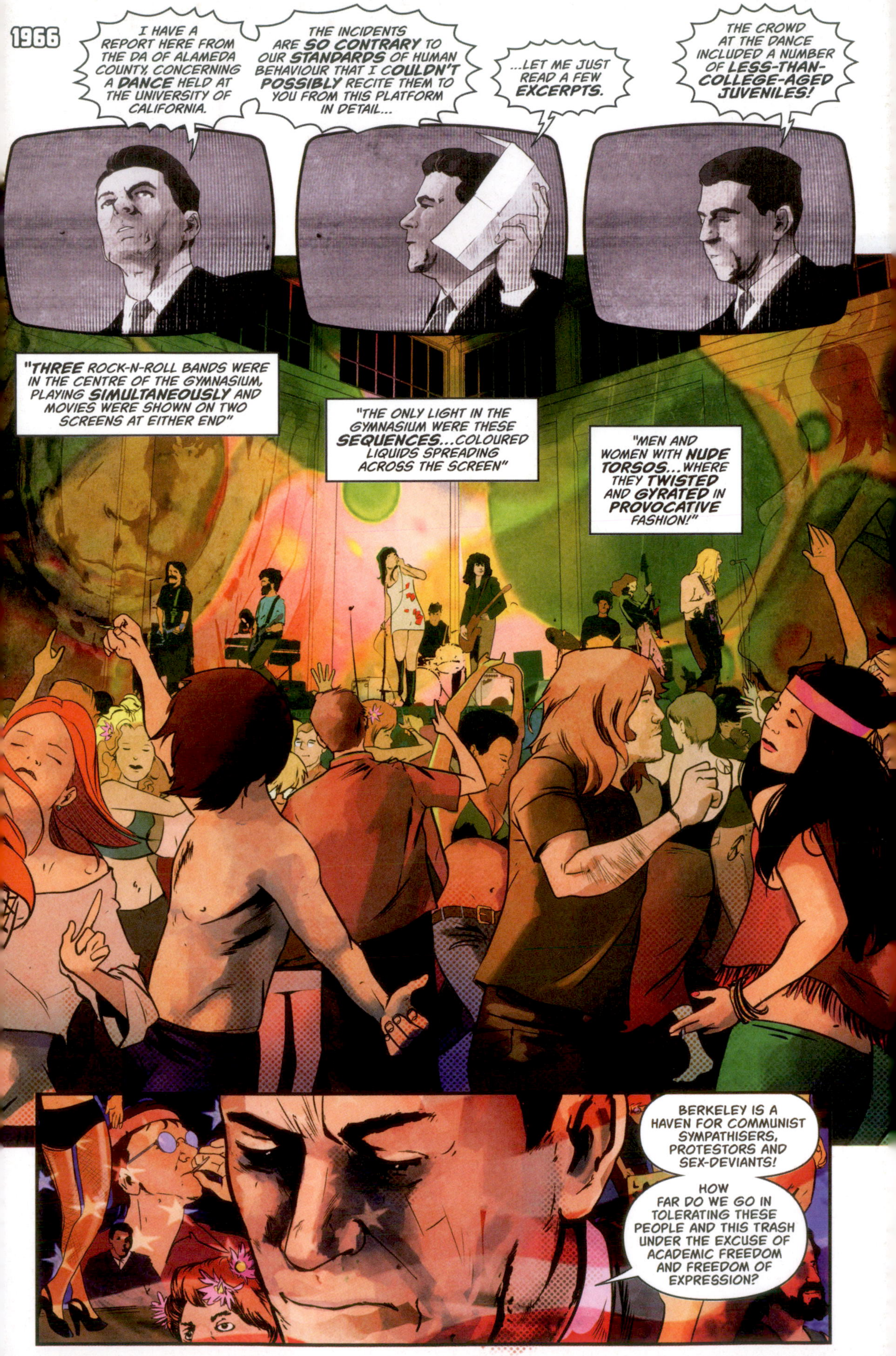
1966
I HAVE A REPORT HERE FROM THE DA OF ALAMEDA COUNTY, CONCERNING A DANCE HELD AT THE UNIVERSITY OF CALIFORNIA.
THE INCIDENTS ARE SO CONTRARY TO OUR STANDARDS OF HUMAN BEHAVIOUR THAT I COULDN'T POSSIBLY RECITE THEM TO YOU FROM THIS PLATFORM IN DETAIL...
...LET ME JUST READ A FEW EXCERPTS.
THE CROWD AT THE DANCE INCLUDED A NUMBER OF LESS-THAN-COLLEGE-AGED JUVENILES!
"THREE ROCK-N-ROLL BANDS WERE IN THE CENTRE OF THE GYMNASIUM, PLAYING SIMULTANEOUSLY AND MOVIES WERE SHOWN ON TWO SCREENS AT EITHER END"
"THE ONLY LIGHT IN THE GYMNASIUM WERE THESE SEQUENCES...COLOURED LIQUIDS SPREADING ACROSS THE SCREEN"
"MEN AND WOMEN WITH NUDE TORSOS...WHERE THEY TWISTED AND GYRATED IN PROVOCATIVE FASHION!"
BERKELEY IS A HAVEN FOR COMMUNIST SYMPATHISERS, PROTESTORS AND SEX-DEVIANTS!
HOW FAR DO WE GO IN TOLERATING THESE PEOPLE AND THIS TRASH UNDER THE EXCUSE OF ACADEMIC FREEDOM AND FREEDOM OF EXPRESSION?

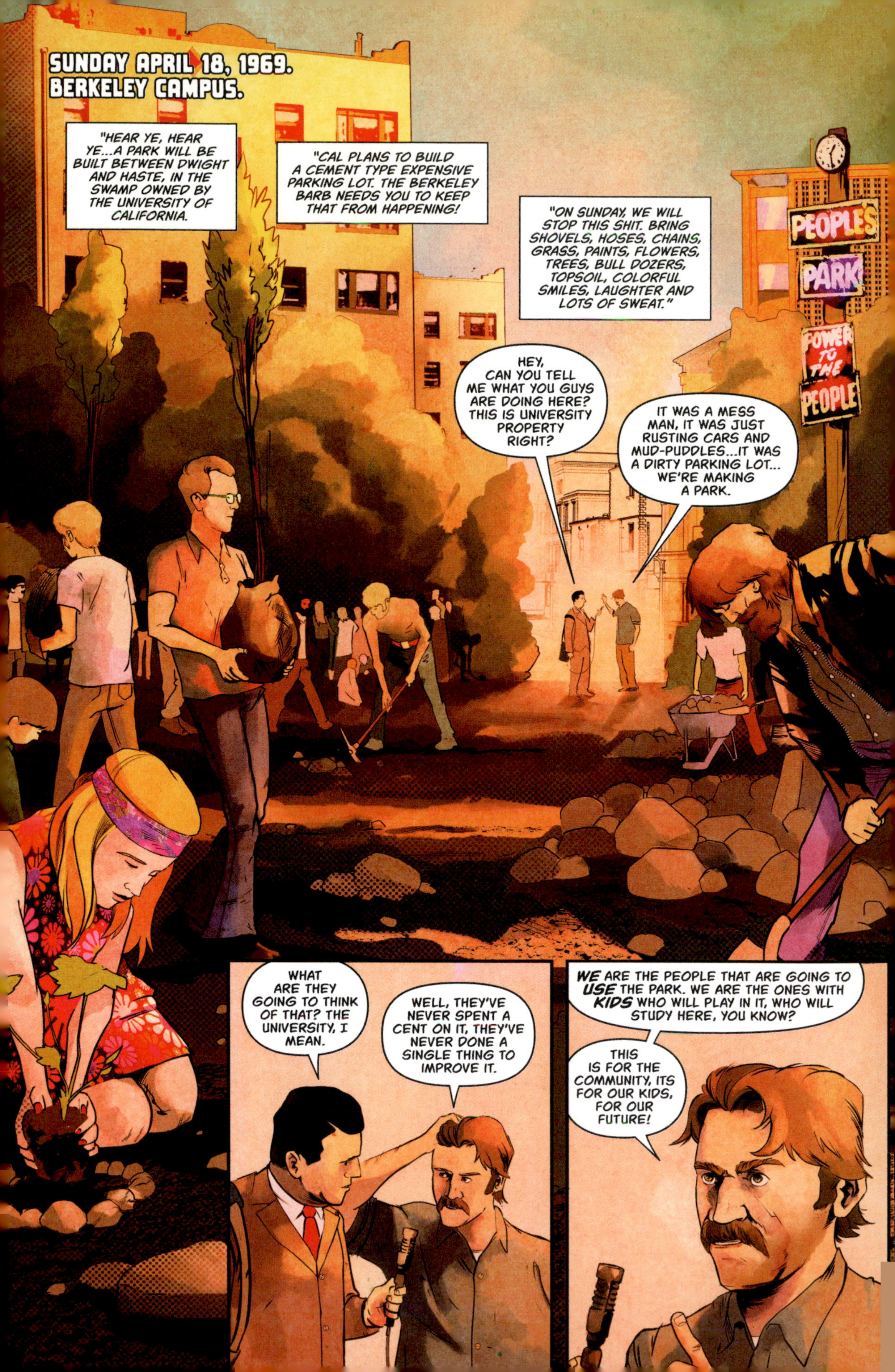
SUNDAY APRIL 18, 1969. BERKELEY CAMPUS.
"HEAR YE, HEAR YE...A PARK WILL BE BUILT BETWEEN DWIGHT AND HASTE, IN THE SWAMP OWNED BY THE UNIVERSITY OF CALIFORNIA.
"CAL PLANS TO BUILD A CEMENT TYPE EXPENSIVE PARKING LOT. THE BERKELEY BARB NEEDS YOU TO KEEP THAT FROM HAPPENING!
"ON SUNDAY, WE WILL STOP THIS SHIT. BRING SHOVELS, HOSES, CHAINS, GRASS, PAINTS, FLOWERS, TREES, BULL DOZERS, TOPSOIL, COLORFUL SMILES, LAUGHTER AND LOTS OF SWEAT."
PEOPLES PARK
POWER TO THE PEOPLE
HEY, CAN YOU TELL ME WHAT YOU GUYS ARE DOING HERE? THIS IS UNIVERSITY PROPERTY RIGHT?
IT WAS A MESS MAN, IT WAS JUST RUSTING CARS AND MUD-PUDDLES...IT WAS A DIRTY PARKING LOT... WE'RE MAKING A PARK.
WHAT ARE THEY GOING TO THINK OF THAT? THE UNIVERSITY, I MEAN.
WELL, THEY'VE NEVER SPENT A CENT ON IT, THEY'VE NEVER DONE A SINGLE THING TO IMPROVE IT.
WE ARE THE PEOPLE THAT ARE GOING TO USE THE PARK. WE ARE THE ONES WITH KIDS WHO WILL PLAY IN IT, WHO WILL STUDY HERE, YOU KNOW?
THIS IS FOR THE COMMUNITY, ITS FOR OUR KIDS, FOR OUR FUTURE!

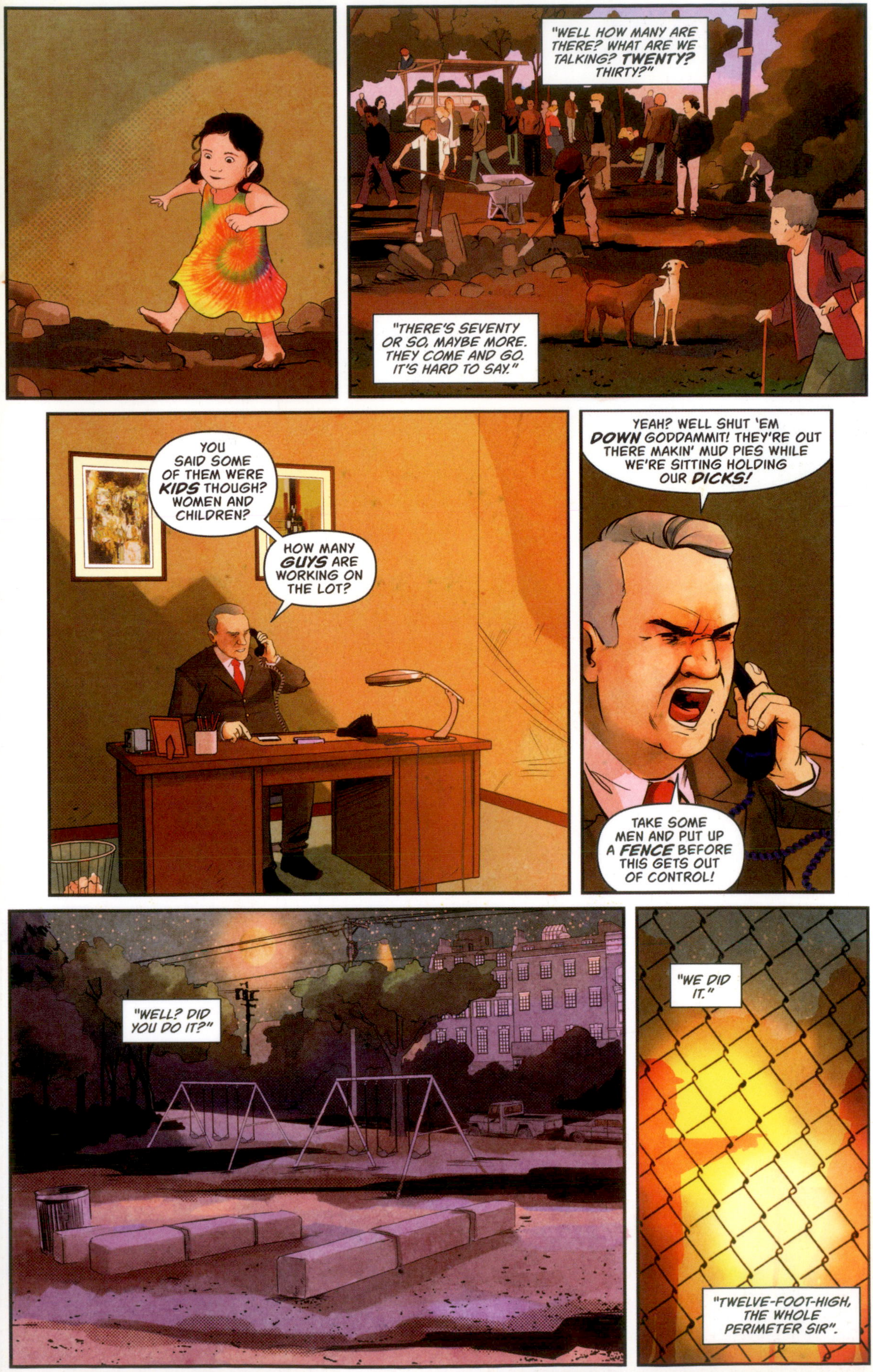
"WELL HOW MANY ARE THERE? WHAT ARE WE TALKING? TWENTY? THIRTY?"
"THERE'S SEVENTY OR SO, MAYBE MORE. THEY COME AND GO. IT'S HARD TO SAY."
YOU SAID SOME OF THEM WERE KIDS THOUGH? WOMEN AND CHILDREN?
HOW MANY GUYS ARE WORKING ON THE LOT?
YEAH? WELL SHUT 'EM DOWN GODDAMMIT! THEY'RE OUT THERE MAKIN' MUD PIES WHILE WE'RE SITTING HOLDING OUR DICKS!
TAKE SOME MEN AND PUT UP A FENCE BEFORE THIS GETS OUT OF CONTROL!
"WELL? DID YOU DO IT?"
"WE DID IT."
"TWELVE-FOOT-HIGH, THE WHOLE PERIMETER SIR".

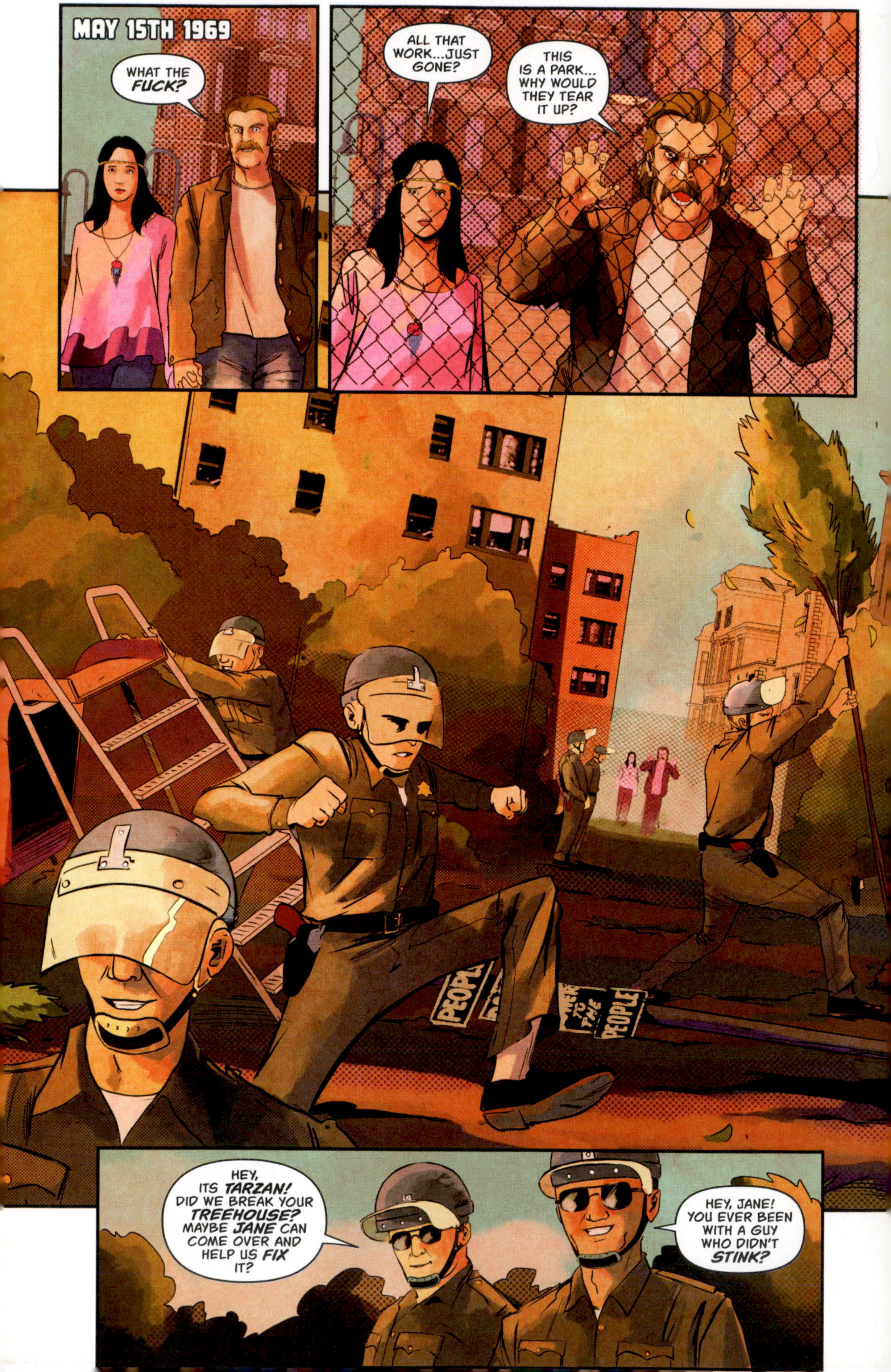
MAY 15TH 1969
WHAT THE FUCK?
ALL THAT WORK...JUST GONE?
THIS IS A PARK... WHY WOULD THEY TEAR IT UP?
HEY, ITS TARZAN! DID WE BREAK YOUR TREEHOUSE? MAYBE JANE CAN COME OVER AND HELP US FIX IT?
HEY, JANE! YOU EVER BEEN WITH A GUY WHO DIDN'T STINK?

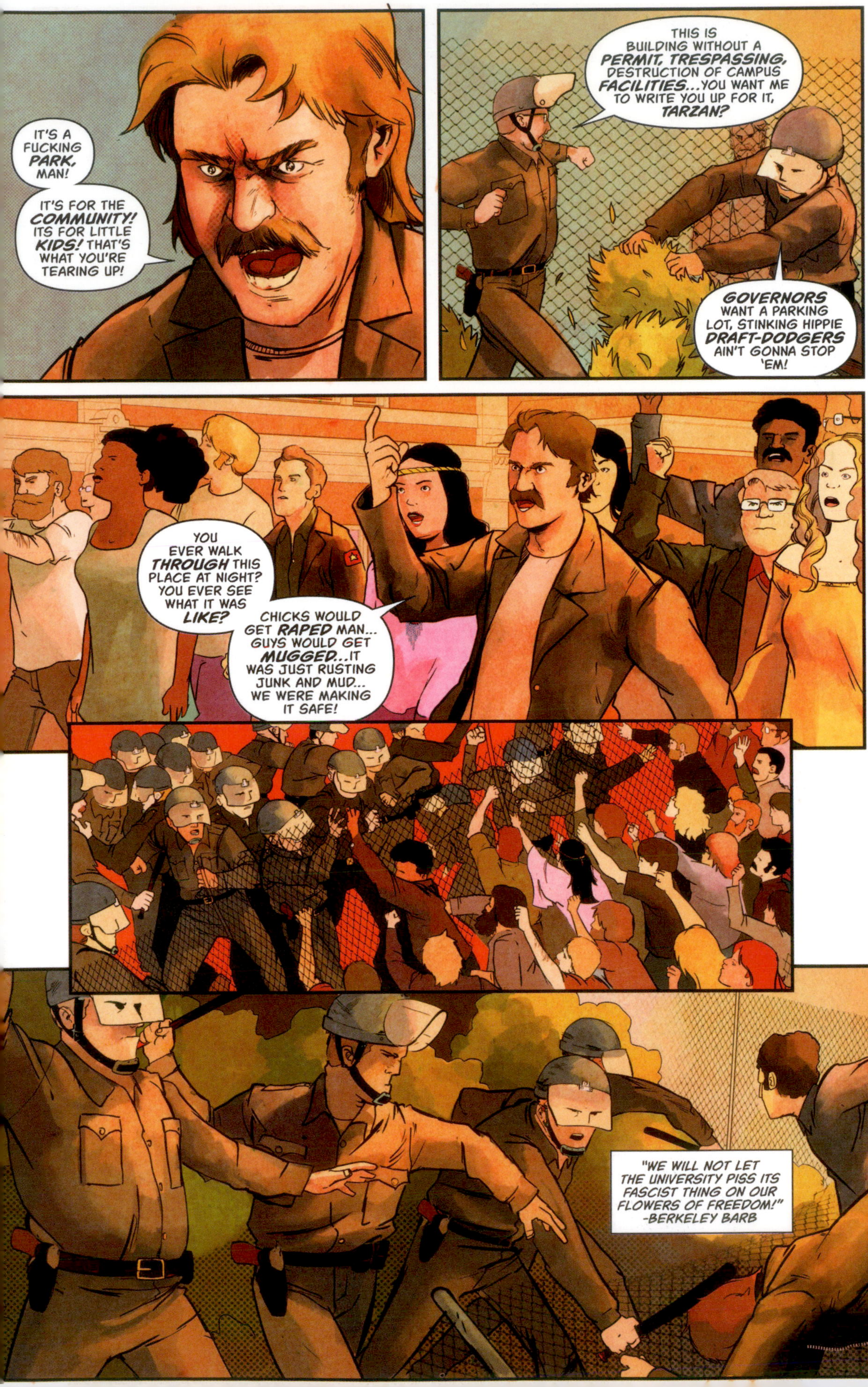
IT'S A FUCKING PARK, MAN!
IT'S FOR THE COMMUNITY! ITS FOR LITTLE KIDS! THAT'S WHAT YOU'RE TEARING UP!
THIS IS BUILDING WITHOUT A PERMIT, TRESPASSING, DESTRUCTION OF CAMPUS FACILITIES...YOU WANT ME TO WRITE YOU UP FOR IT, TARZAN?
GOVERNORS WANT A PARKING LOT, STINKING HIPPIE DRAFT-DODGERS AIN'T GONNA STOP 'EM!
YOU EVER WALK THROUGH THIS PLACE AT NIGHT? YOU EVER SEE WHAT IT WAS LIKE?
CHICKS WOULD GET RAPED MAN... GUYS WOULD GET MUGGED...IT WAS JUST RUSTING JUNK AND MUD... WE WERE MAKING IT SAFE!
"WE WILL NOT LET THE UNIVERSITY PISS ITS FASCIST THING ON OUR FLOWERS OF FREEDOM!" -BERKELEY BARB

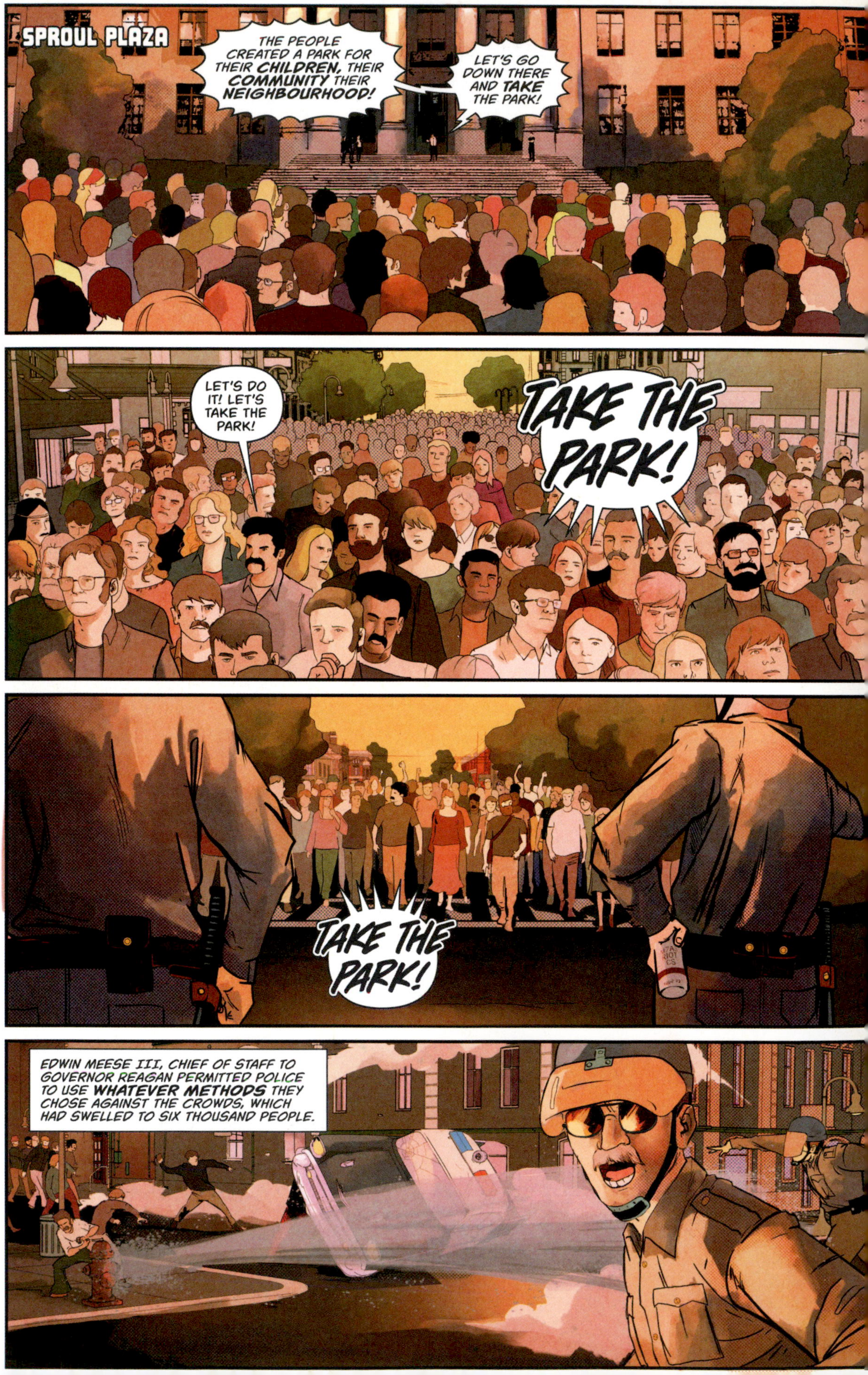
SPROUL PLAZA
THE PEOPLE CREATED A PARK FOR THEIR CHILDREN, THEIR COMMUNITY THEIR NEIGHBOURHOOD!
LET'S GO DOWN THERE AND TAKE THE PARK!
LET'S DO IT! LET'S TAKE THE PARK!
TAKE THE PARK!
TAKE THE PARK!
EDWIN MEESE III, CHIEF OF STAFF TO GOVERNOR REAGAN PERMITTED POLICE TO USE WHATEVER METHODS THEY CHOSE AGAINST THE CROWDS, WHICH HAD SWELLED TO SIX THOUSAND PEOPLE.

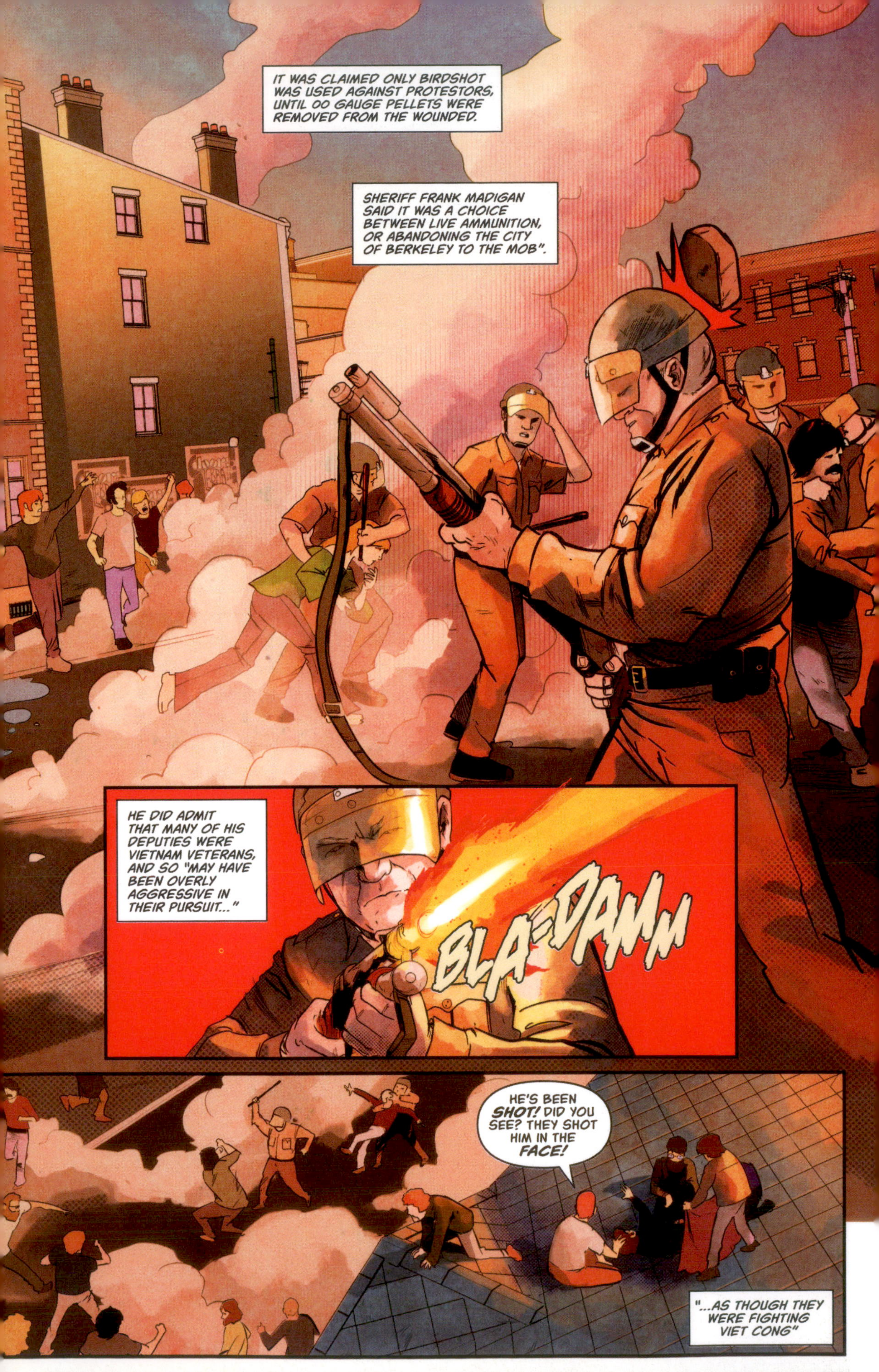
IT WAS CLAIMED ONLY BIRDSHOT WAS USED AGAINST PROTESTORS, UNTIL 00 GAUGE PELLETS WERE REMOVED FROM THE WOUNDED.
SHERIFF FRANK MADIGAN SAID IT WAS A CHOICE BETWEEN LIVE AMMUNITION, OR ABANDONING THE CITY OF BERKELEY TO THE MOB".
HE DID ADMIT THAT MANY OF HIS DEPUTIES WERE VIETNAM VETERANS, AND SO "MAY HAVE BEEN OVERLY AGGRESSIVE IN THEIR PURSUIT..."
BLA-DAMM
HE'S BEEN SHOT! DID YOU SEE? THEY SHOT HIM IN THE FACE!
"...AS THOUGH THEY WERE FIGHTING VIET CONG"

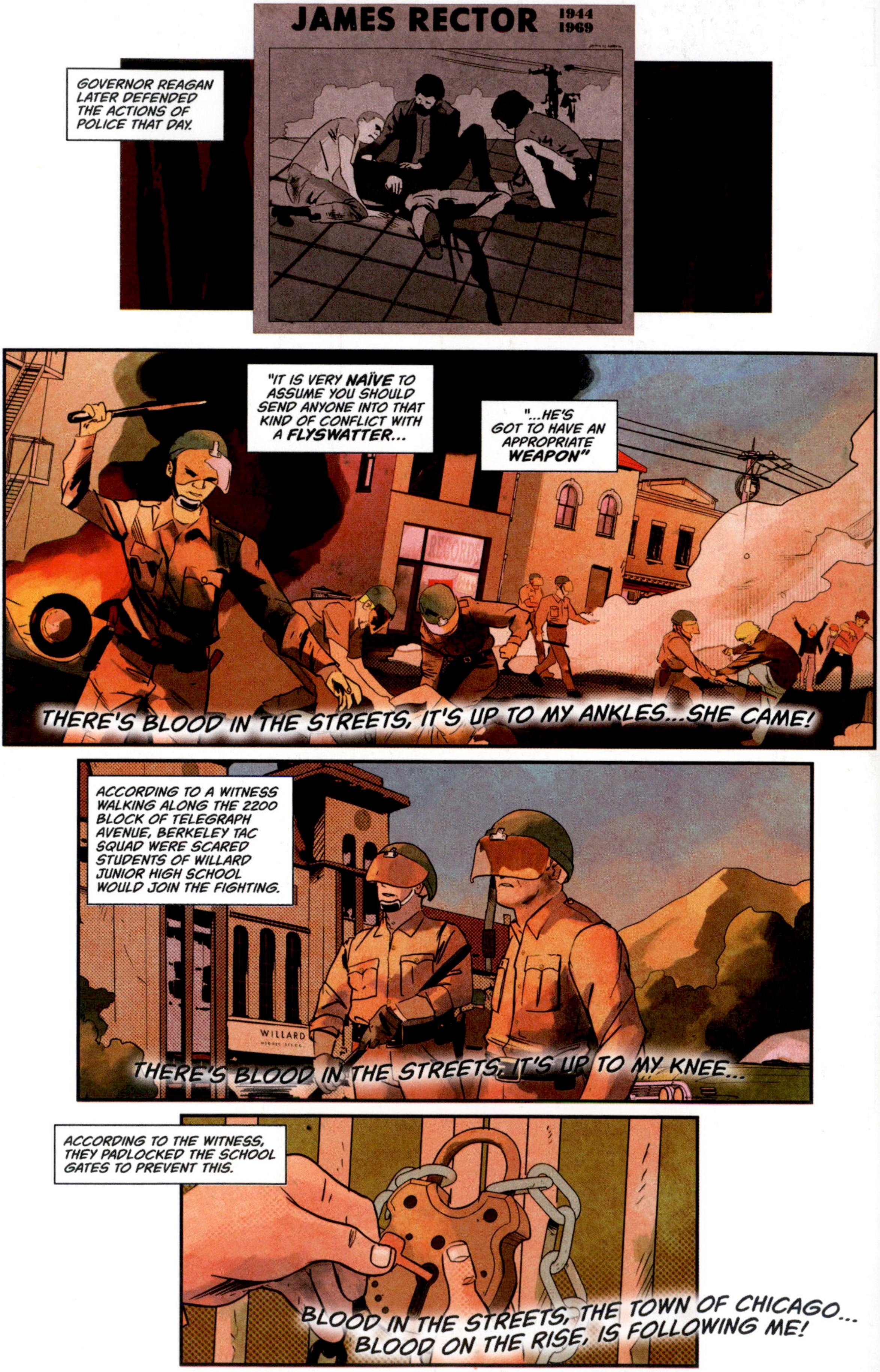

JAMES RECTOR 1944 1969
GOVERNOR REAGAN LATER DEFENDED THE ACTIONS OF POLICE THAT DAY.
"IT IS VERY NAÏVE TO ASSUME YOU SHOULD SEND ANYONE INTO THAT KIND OF CONFLICT WITH A FLYSWATTER...
"...HE'S GOT TO HAVE AN APPROPRIATE WEAPON"
RECORDS
THERE'S BLOOD IN THE STREETS, IT'S UP TO MY ANKLES...SHE CAME!
ACCORDING TO A WITNESS WALKING ALONG THE 2200 BLOCK OF TELEGRAPH AVENUE, BERKELEY TAC SQUAD WERE SCARED STUDENTS OF WILLARD JUNIOR HIGH SCHOOL WOULD JOIN THE FIGHTING.
WILLARD
THERE'S BLOOD IN THE STREETS, IT'S UP TO MY KNEE...
ACCORDING TO THE WITNESS, THEY PADLOCKED THE SCHOOL GATES TO PREVENT THIS.
BLOOD IN THE STREETS, THE TOWN OF CHICAGO...
BLOOD ON THE RISE, IS FOLLOWING ME!

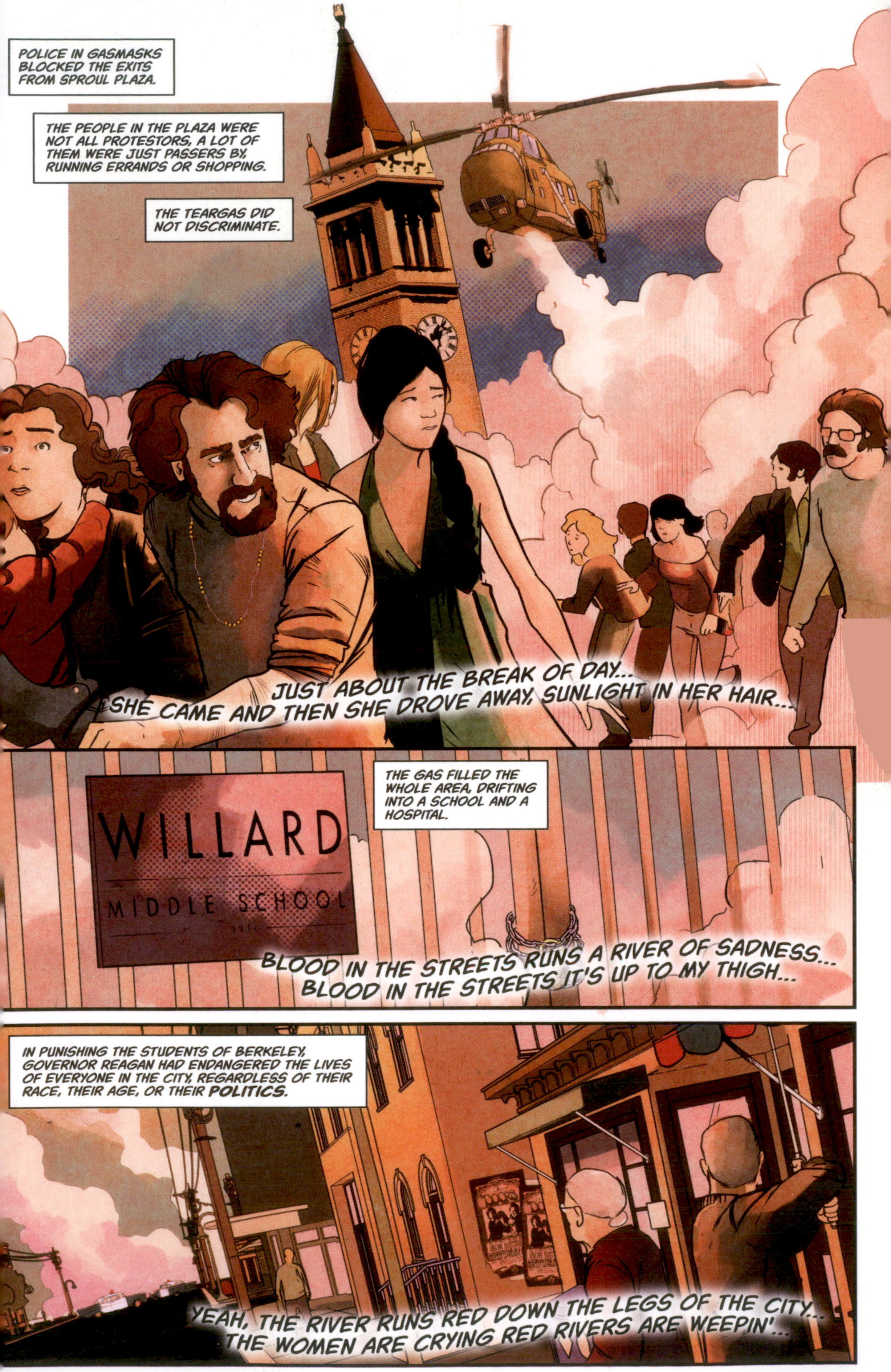
POLICE IN GASMASKS BLOCKED THE EXITS FROM SPROUL PLAZA.
THE PEOPLE IN THE PLAZA WERE NOT ALL PROTESTORS, A LOT OF THEM WERE JUST PASSERS BY, RUNNING ERRANDS OR SHOPPING.
THE TEARGAS DID NOT DISCRIMINATE.
JUST ABOUT THE BREAK OF DAY...
SHE CAME AND THEN SHE DROVE AWAY, SUNLIGHT IN HER HAIR...
WILLARD
MIDDLE SCHOOL
THE GAS FILLED THE WHOLE AREA, DRIFTING INTO A SCHOOL AND A HOSPITAL.
BLOOD IN THE STREETS RUNS A RIVER OF SADNESS...
BLOOD IN THE STREETS IT'S UP TO MY THIGH...
IN PUNISHING THE STUDENTS OF BERKELEY, GOVERNOR REAGAN HAD ENDANGERED THE LIVES OF EVERYONE IN THE CITY, REGARDLESS OF THEIR RACE, THEIR AGE, OR THEIR POLITICS.
YEAH, THE RIVER RUNS RED DOWN THE LEGS OF THE CITY...
THE WOMEN ARE CRYING RED RIVERS ARE WEEPIN'...

REAGAN DECLARED MARTIAL LAW IN BERKELEY.

800 NATIONAL GUARDSMEN WERE SENT TO SECURE THE CITY, AS IF IT WERE A BALKAN STATE.

SHE CAME IN TOWN AND THEN SHE DROVE AWAY...

MANY HAD ONLY JOINED THE NATIONAL GUARD TO AVOID BEING SENT TO VIETNAM.

FOR SOME OF THEM, IT WASN'T A CHORE.

...SUNLIGHT IN HER HAIR...

STORIES WERE RIFE OF LOCAL KIDS SELLING GUARDSMEN WEED.

PRETTY GIRLS GIVING THEM HASH BROWNIES.

INDIANS SCATTERED ON DAWN'S HIGHWAY BLEEDING... GHOSTS CROWD THE YOUNG CHILD'S FRAGILE EGGSHELL MIND...

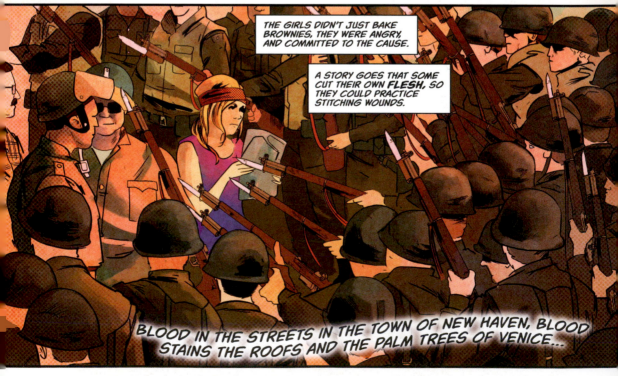

THE GIRLS DIDN'T JUST BAKE BROWNIES, THEY WERE ANGRY, AND COMMITTED TO THE CAUSE.

A STORY GOES THAT SOME CUT THEIR OWN FLESH, SO THEY COULD PRACTICE STITCHING WOUNDS.

BLOOD IN THE STREETS IN THE TOWN OF NEW HAVEN, BLOOD STAINS THE ROOFS AND THE PALM TREES OF VENICE...

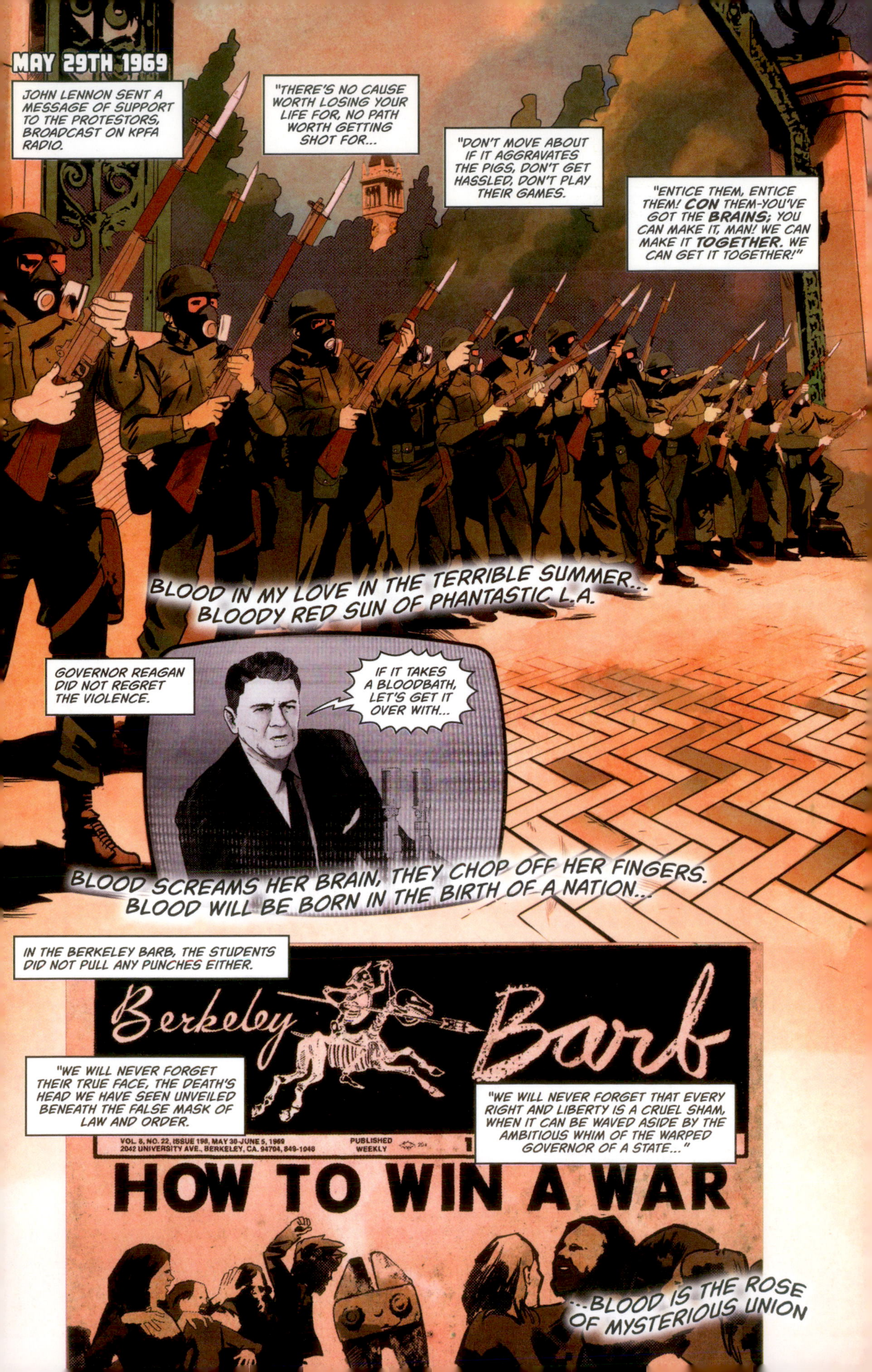

MAY 29TH 1969
JOHN LENNON SENT A MESSAGE OF SUPPORT TO THE PROTESTORS, BROADCAST ON KPFA RADIO.
"THERE'S NO CAUSE WORTH LOSING YOUR LIFE FOR, NO PATH WORTH GETTING SHOT FOR...
"DON'T MOVE ABOUT IF IT AGGRAVATES THE PIGS, DON'T GET HASSLED, DON'T PLAY THEIR GAMES.
"ENTICE THEM, ENTICE THEM! CON THEM-YOU'VE GOT THE BRAINS; YOU CAN MAKE IT, MAN! WE CAN MAKE IT TOGETHER. WE CAN GET IT TOGETHER!"
BLOOD IN MY LOVE IN THE TERRIBLE SUMMER... BLOODY RED SUN OF PHANTASTIC L.A.
GOVERNOR REAGAN DID NOT REGRET THE VIOLENCE.
IF IT TAKES A BLOODBATH, LET'S GET IT OVER WITH...
BLOOD SCREAMS HER BRAIN, THEY CHOP OFF HER FINGERS. BLOOD WILL BE BORN IN THE BIRTH OF A NATION...
IN THE BERKELEY BARB, THE STUDENTS DID NOT PULL ANY PUNCHES EITHER.
Berkeley Barb
"WE WILL NEVER FORGET THEIR TRUE FACE, THE DEATH'S HEAD WE HAVE SEEN UNVEILED BENEATH THE FALSE MASK OF LAW AND ORDER.
"WE WILL NEVER FORGET THAT EVERY RIGHT AND LIBERTY IS A CRUEL SHAM, WHEN IT CAN BE WAVED ASIDE BY THE AMBITIOUS WHIM OF THE WARPED GOVERNOR OF A STATE..."
VOL. 8, NO. 22, ISSUE 198, MAY 30-JUNE 5, 1969
2042 UNIVERSITY AVE., BERKELEY, CA. 94704, 849-1048
PUBLISHED WEEKLY
HOW TO WIN A WAR
...BLOOD IS THE ROSE OF MYSTERIOUS UNION

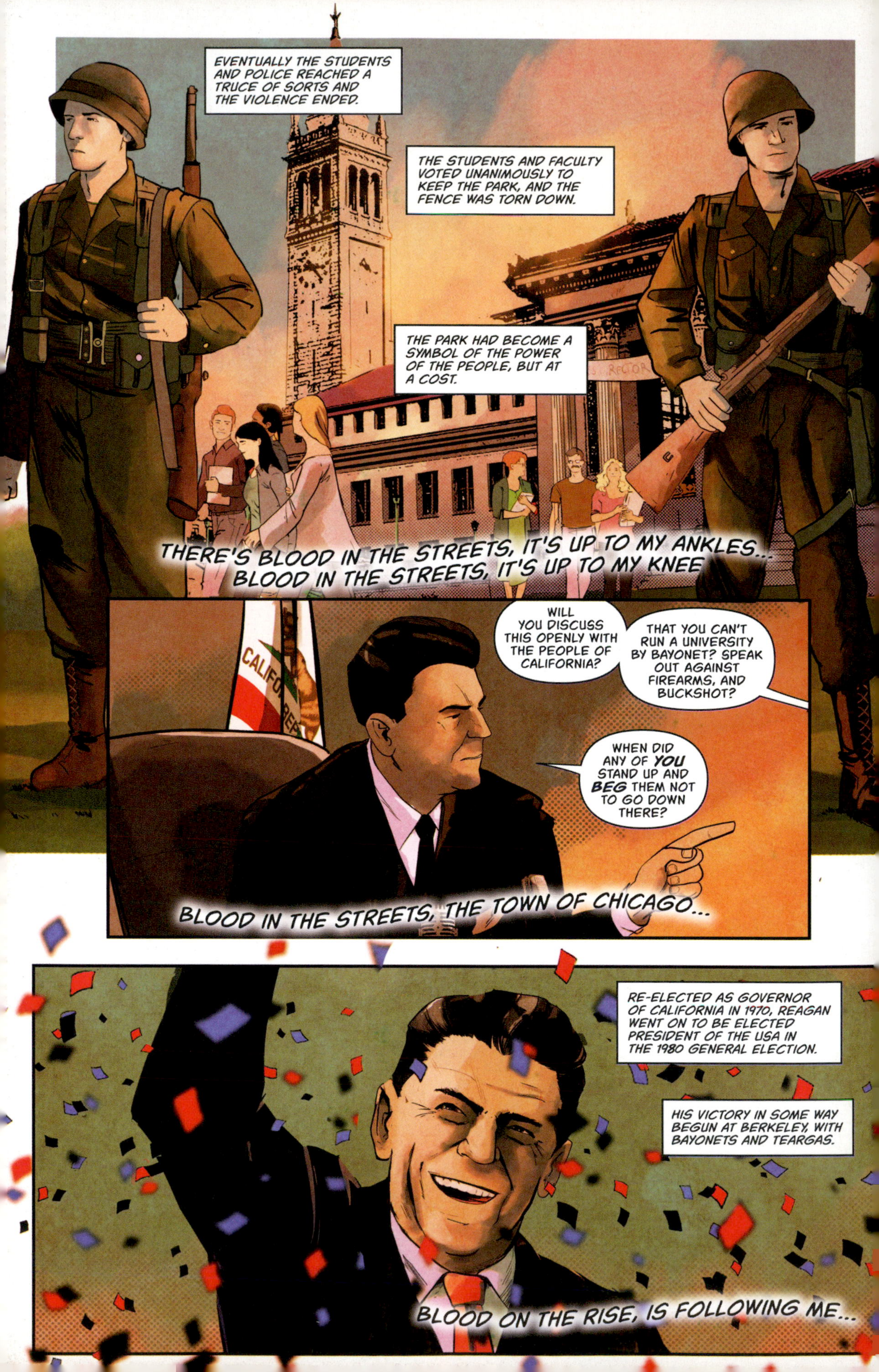
EVENTUALLY THE STUDENTS AND POLICE REACHED A TRUCE OF SORTS AND THE VIOLENCE ENDED.
THE STUDENTS AND FACULTY VOTED UNANIMOUSLY TO KEEP THE PARK, AND THE FENCE WAS TORN DOWN.
THE PARK HAD BECOME A SYMBOL OF THE POWER OF THE PEOPLE, BUT AT A COST.
THERE'S BLOOD IN THE STREETS, IT'S UP TO MY ANKLES... BLOOD IN THE STREETS, IT'S UP TO MY KNEE
WILL YOU DISCUSS THIS OPENLY WITH THE PEOPLE OF CALIFORNIA?
THAT YOU CAN'T RUN A UNIVERSITY BY BAYONET? SPEAK OUT AGAINST FIREARMS, AND BUCKSHOT?
WHEN DID ANY OF *YOU* STAND UP AND *BEG* THEM NOT TO GO DOWN THERE?
BLOOD IN THE STREETS, THE TOWN OF CHICAGO...
RE-ELECTED AS GOVERNOR OF CALIFORNIA IN 1970, REAGAN WENT ON TO BE ELECTED PRESIDENT OF THE USA IN THE 1980 GENERAL ELECTION.
HIS VICTORY IN SOME WAY BEGUN AT BERKELEY, WITH BAYONETS AND TEARGAS.
BLOOD ON THE RISE, IS FOLLOWING ME...

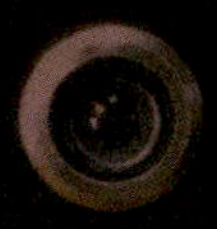

Blue Sunday

Artist . . . Guillermo Sanna
Colorist . . . Aladdin Collar

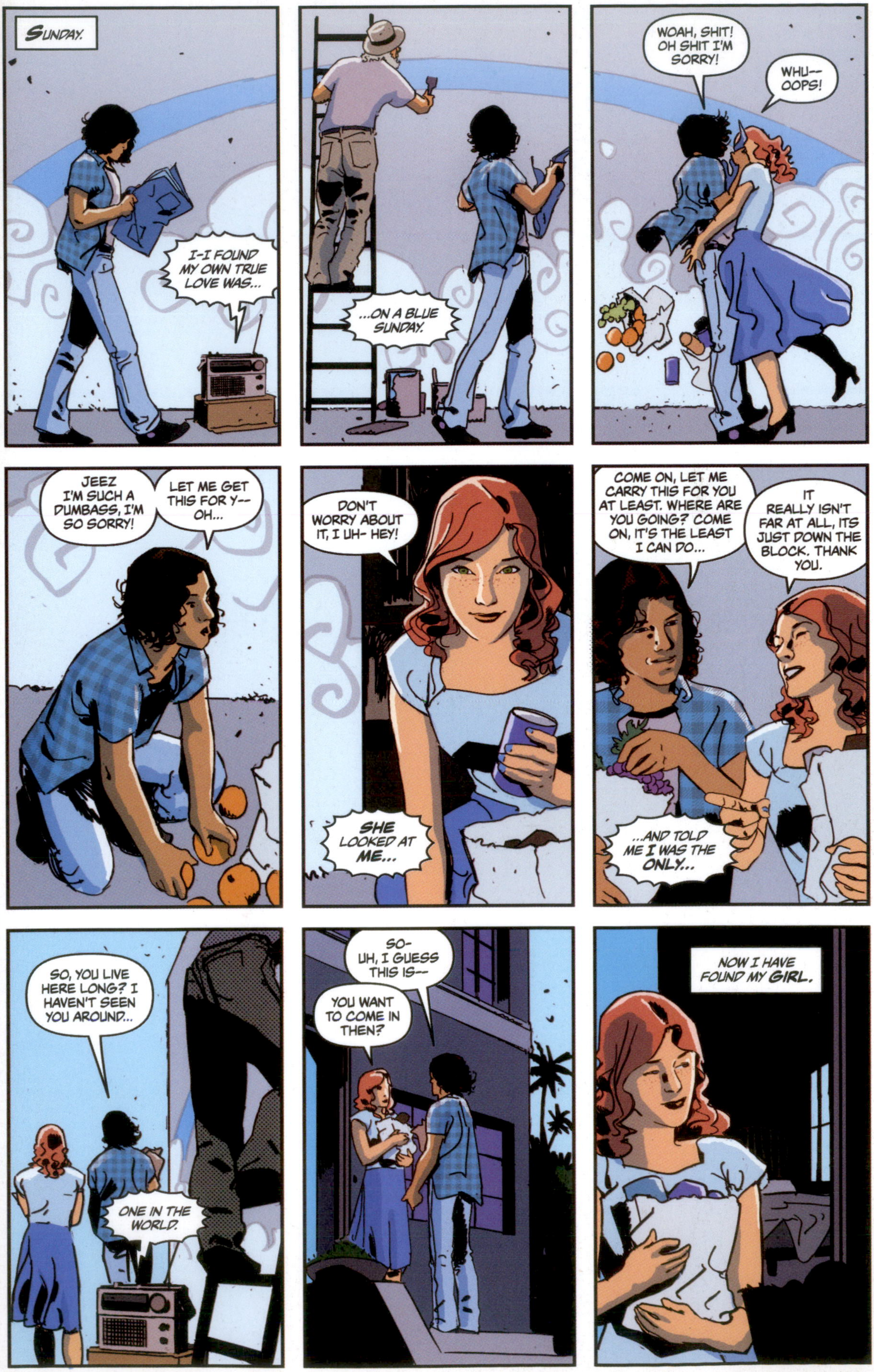
SUNDAY.
I-I FOUND MY OWN TRUE LOVE WAS...
...ON A BLUE SUNDAY.
WOAH, SHIT! OH SHIT I'M SORRY!
WHU-- OOPS!
JEEZ I'M SUCH A DUMBASS, I'M SO SORRY!
LET ME GET THIS FOR Y-- OH...
DON'T WORRY ABOUT IT, I UH- HEY!
SHE LOOKED AT ME...
COME ON, LET ME CARRY THIS FOR YOU AT LEAST. WHERE ARE YOU GOING? COME ON, IT'S THE LEAST I CAN DO...
IT REALLY ISN'T FAR AT ALL, ITS JUST DOWN THE BLOCK. THANK YOU.
...AND TOLD ME I WAS THE ONLY...
SO, YOU LIVE HERE LONG? I HAVEN'T SEEN YOU AROUND...
ONE IN THE WORLD.
SO- UH, I GUESS THIS IS--
YOU WANT TO COME IN THEN?
NOW I HAVE FOUND MY GIRL.

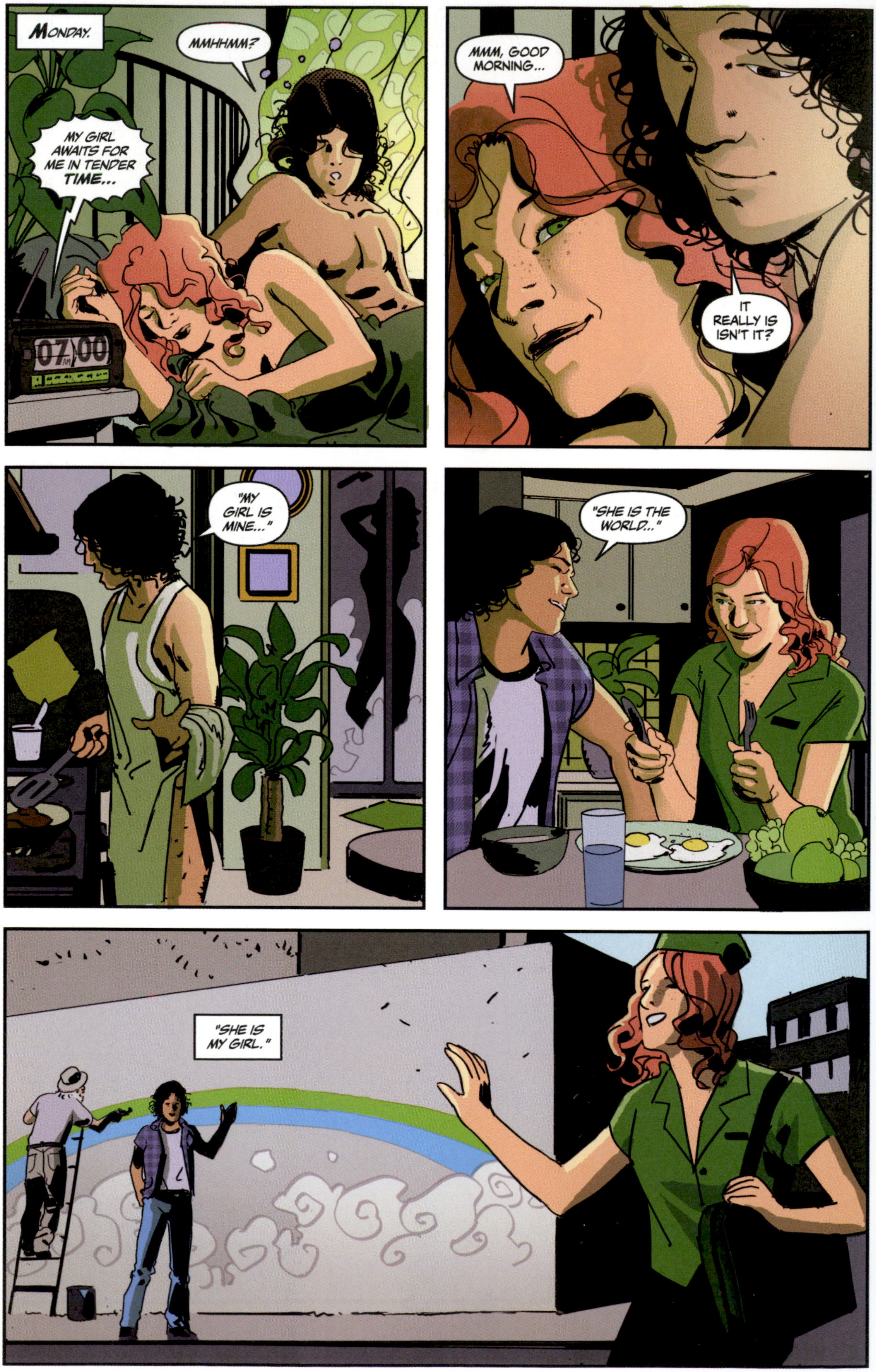
MONDAY.
MMHHMM?
MY GIRL AWAITS FOR ME IN TENDER TIME...
07:00
MMM, GOOD MORNING...
IT REALLY IS ISN'T IT?
"MY GIRL IS MINE..."
"SHE IS THE WORLD..."
"SHE IS MY GIRL."

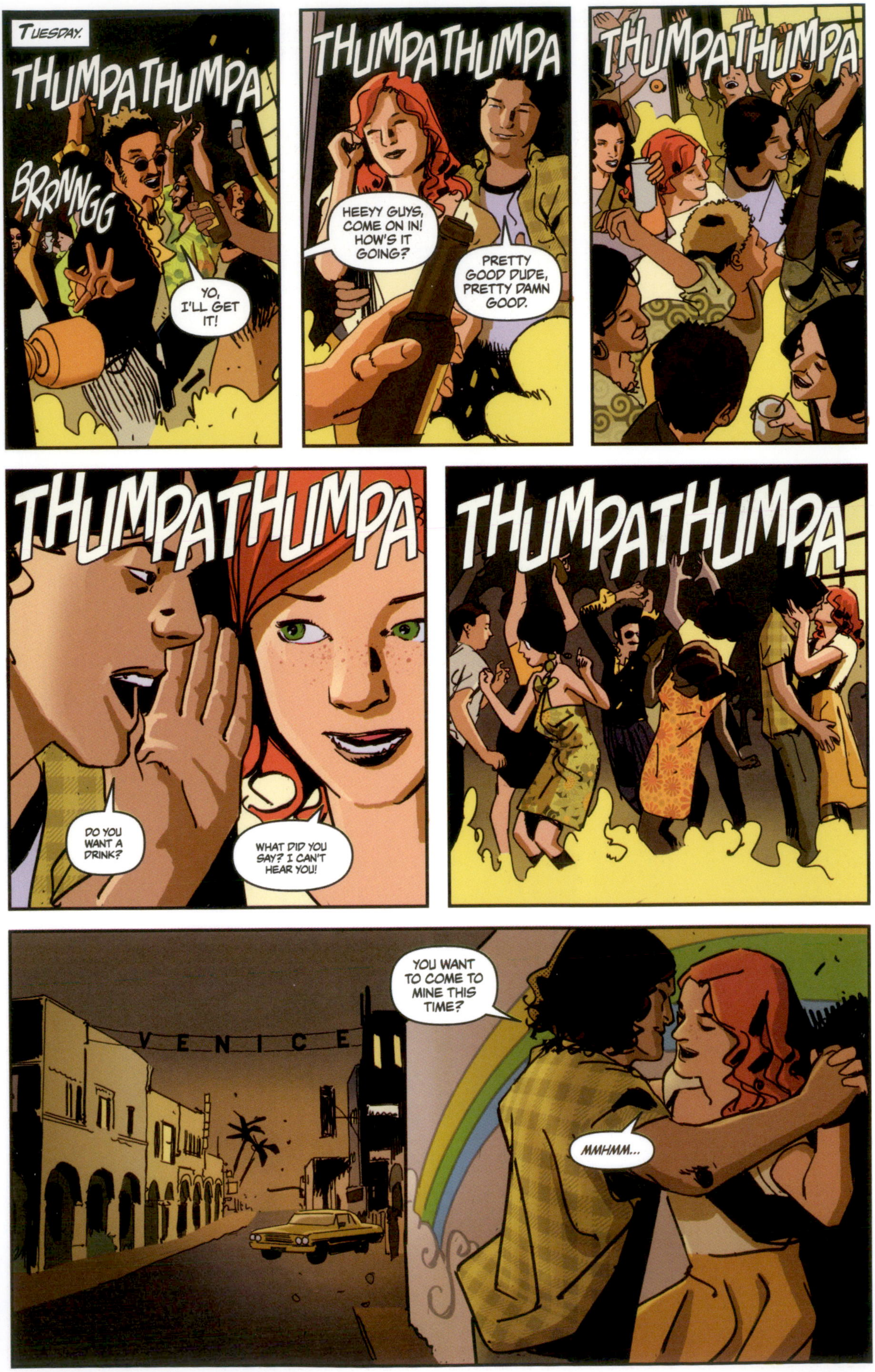

TUESDAY.
THUMPATHUMPA
BRRNNGG
YO, I'LL GET IT!
THUMPATHUMPA
HEEYY GUYS, COME ON IN! HOW'S IT GOING?
PRETTY GOOD DUDE, PRETTY DAMN GOOD.
THUMPATHUMPA
THUMPATHUMPA
DO YOU WANT A DRINK?
WHAT DID YOU SAY? I CAN'T HEAR YOU!
THUMPATHUMPA
VENICE
YOU WANT TO COME TO MINE THIS TIME?
MMHMM...

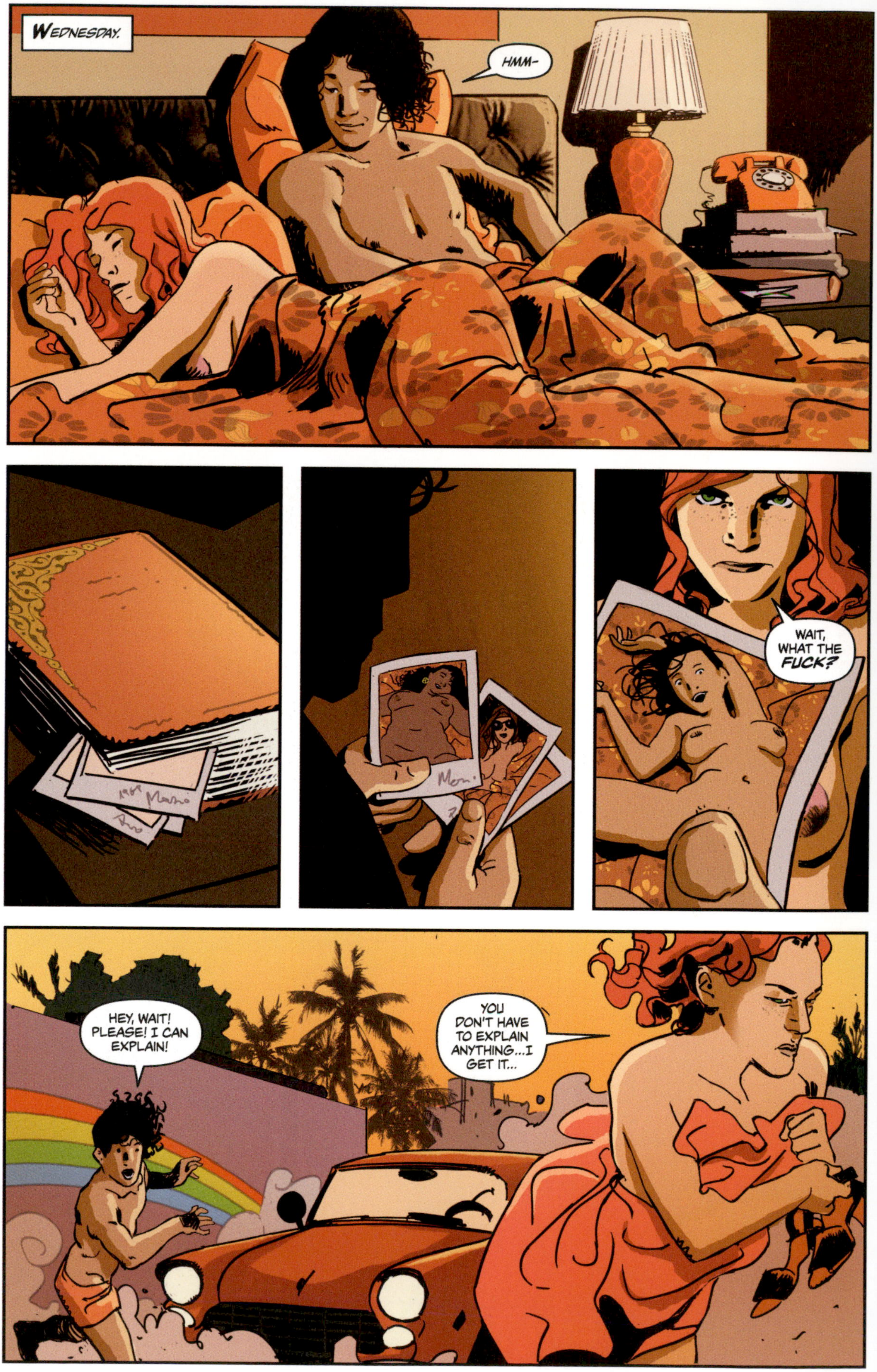
WEDNESDAY.
HMM-
WAIT, WHAT THE FUCK?
HEY, WAIT! PLEASE! I CAN EXPLAIN!
YOU DON'T HAVE TO EXPLAIN ANYTHING...I GET IT...

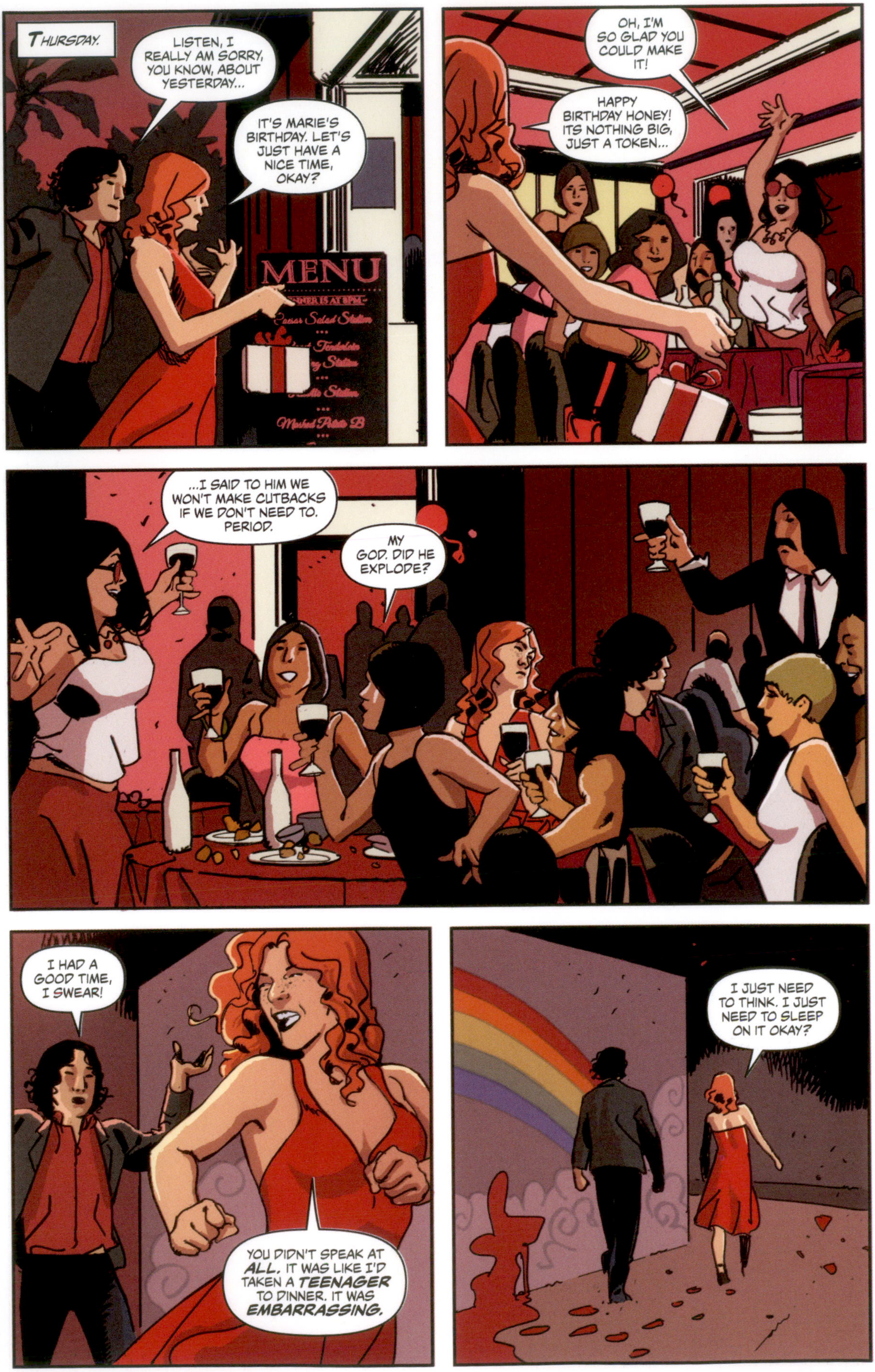
THURSDAY.
LISTEN, I REALLY AM SORRY, YOU KNOW, ABOUT YESTERDAY...
IT'S MARIE'S BIRTHDAY. LET'S JUST HAVE A NICE TIME, OKAY?
MENU
Caesar Salad Station
OH, I'M SO GLAD YOU COULD MAKE IT!
HAPPY BIRTHDAY HONEY! ITS NOTHING BIG, JUST A TOKEN...
...I SAID TO HIM WE WON'T MAKE CUTBACKS IF WE DON'T NEED TO. PERIOD.
MY GOD. DID HE EXPLODE?
I HAD A GOOD TIME, I SWEAR!
YOU DIDN'T SPEAK AT ALL. IT WAS LIKE I'D TAKEN A TEENAGER TO DINNER. IT WAS EMBARRASSING.
I JUST NEED TO THINK. I JUST NEED TO SLEEP ON IT OKAY?

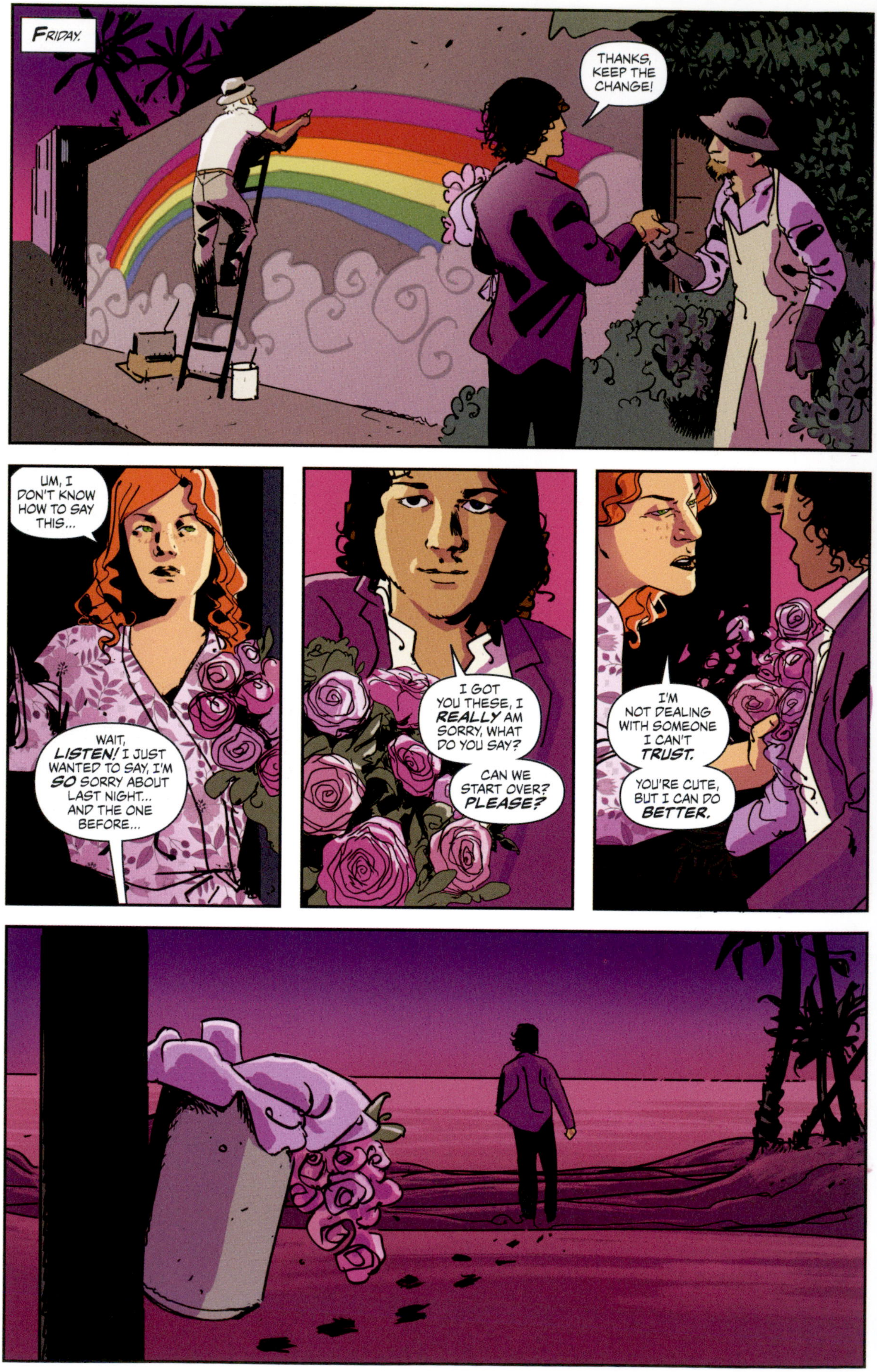
FRIDAY.
THANKS, KEEP THE CHANGE!
UM, I DON'T KNOW HOW TO SAY THIS...
WAIT, LISTEN! I JUST WANTED TO SAY, I'M SO SORRY ABOUT LAST NIGHT... AND THE ONE BEFORE...
I GOT YOU THESE, I REALLY AM SORRY, WHAT DO YOU SAY?
CAN WE START OVER? PLEASE?
I'M NOT DEALING WITH SOMEONE I CAN'T TRUST.
YOU'RE CUTE, BUT I CAN DO BETTER.

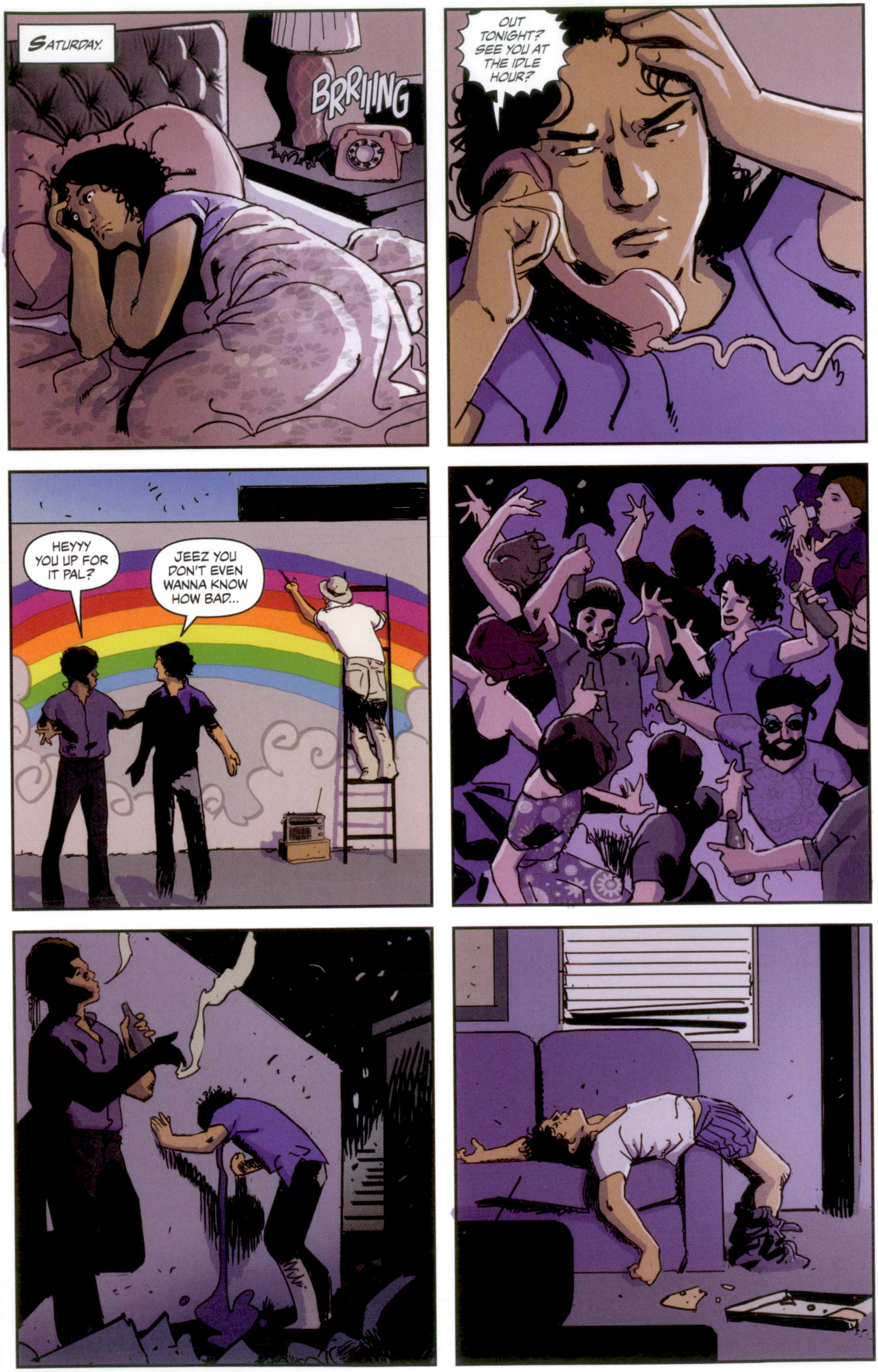
SATURDAY.
BRRIIING
OUT TONIGHT? SEE YOU AT THE IDLE HOUR?
HEYYY YOU UP FOR IT PAL?
JEEZ YOU DON'T EVEN WANNA KNOW HOW BAD...

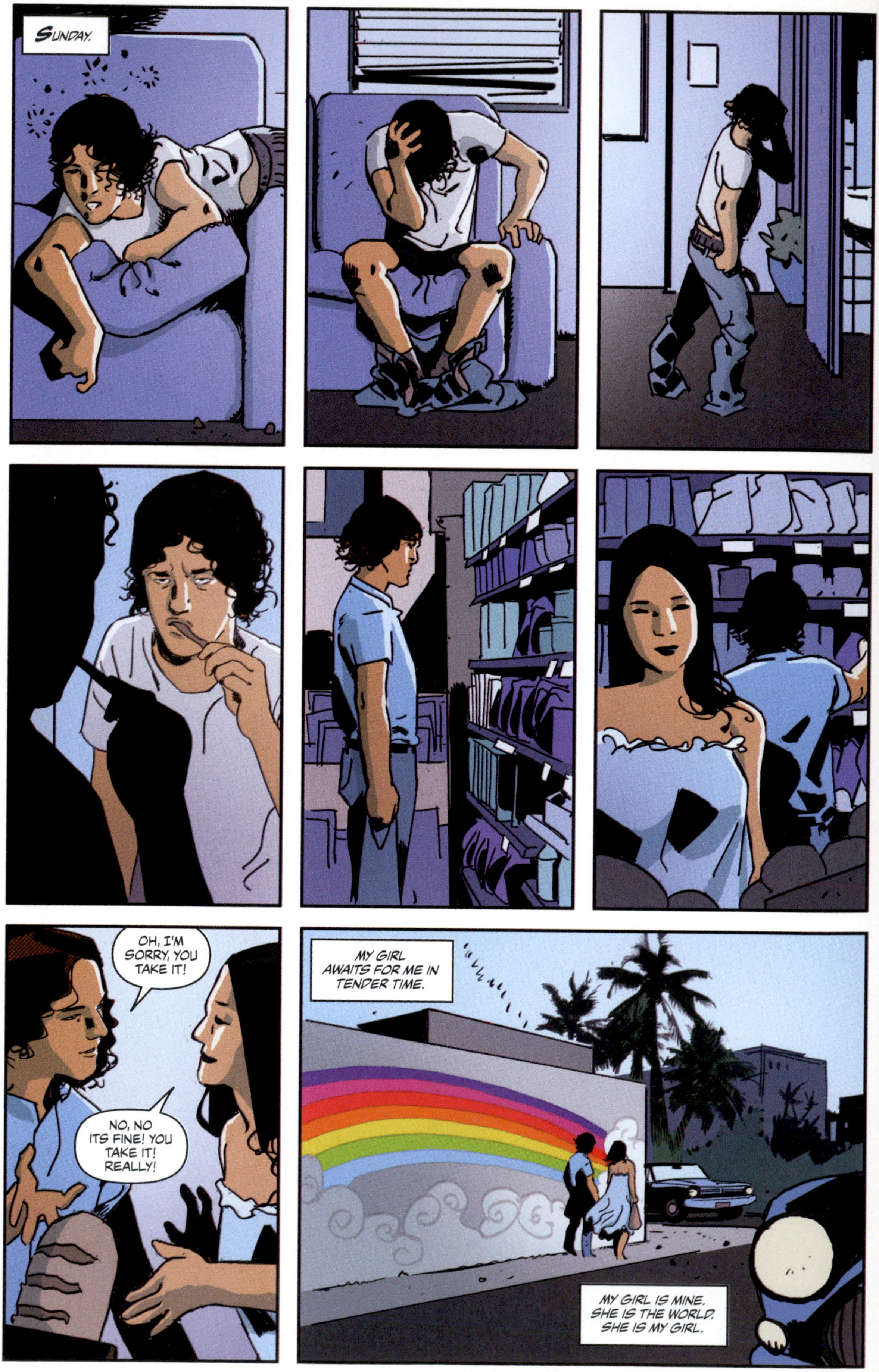
SUNDAY.
OH, I'M SORRY, YOU TAKE IT!
NO, NO ITS FINE! YOU TAKE IT! REALLY!
MY GIRL AWAITS FOR ME IN TENDER TIME.
MY GIRL IS MINE. SHE IS THE WORLD. SHE IS MY GIRL.

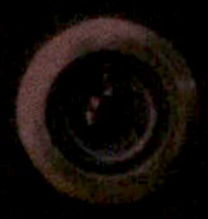

Ship of Fools

Artist . . . Colleen Doran

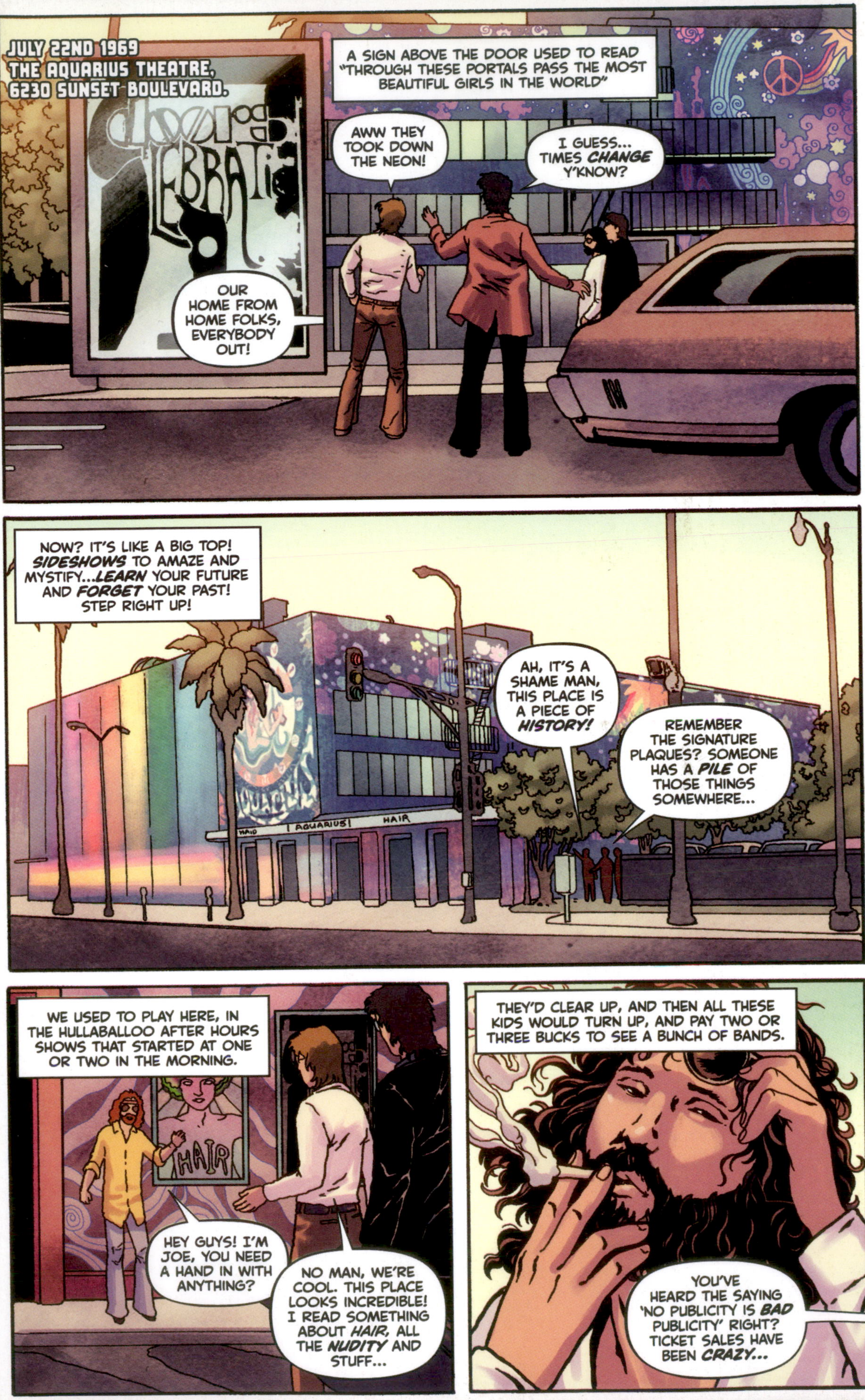
JULY 22ND 1969
THE AQUARIUS THEATRE, 6230 SUNSET BOULEVARD.
A SIGN ABOVE THE DOOR USED TO READ "THROUGH THESE PORTALS PASS THE MOST BEAUTIFUL GIRLS IN THE WORLD"
AWW THEY TOOK DOWN THE NEON!
I GUESS... TIMES *CHANGE* Y'KNOW?
OUR HOME FROM HOME FOLKS, EVERYBODY OUT!
NOW? IT'S LIKE A BIG TOP! *SIDESHOWS* TO AMAZE AND MYSTIFY...*LEARN* YOUR FUTURE AND *FORGET* YOUR PAST! STEP RIGHT UP!
AH, IT'S A SHAME MAN, THIS PLACE IS A PIECE OF *HISTORY!*
REMEMBER THE SIGNATURE PLAQUES? SOMEONE HAS A *PILE* OF THOSE THINGS SOMEWHERE...
AQUARIUS
HAIR
WE USED TO PLAY HERE, IN THE HULLABALLOO AFTER HOURS SHOWS THAT STARTED AT ONE OR TWO IN THE MORNING.
HAIR
HEY GUYS! I'M JOE, YOU NEED A HAND IN WITH ANYTHING?
NO MAN, WE'RE COOL. THIS PLACE LOOKS INCREDIBLE! I READ SOMETHING ABOUT *HAIR*, ALL THE *NUDITY* AND STUFF...
THEY'D CLEAR UP, AND THEN ALL THESE KIDS WOULD TURN UP, AND PAY TWO OR THREE BUCKS TO SEE A BUNCH OF BANDS.
YOU'VE HEARD THE SAYING 'NO PUBLICITY IS *BAD* PUBLICITY' RIGHT? TICKET SALES HAVE BEEN *CRAZY*...

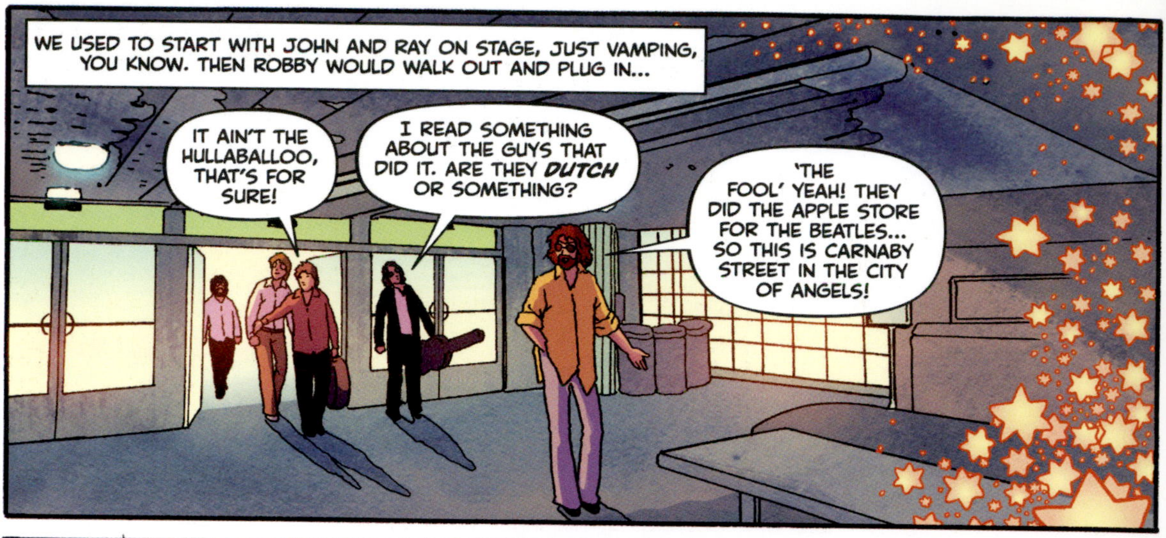

WE USED TO START WITH JOHN AND RAY ON STAGE, JUST VAMPING, YOU KNOW. THEN ROBBY WOULD WALK OUT AND PLUG IN...
IT AIN'T THE HULLABALLOO, THAT'S FOR SURE!
I READ SOMETHING ABOUT THE GUYS THAT DID IT. ARE THEY *DUTCH* OR SOMETHING?
'THE FOOL' YEAH! THEY DID THE APPLE STORE FOR THE BEATLES... SO THIS IS CARNABY STREET IN THE CITY OF ANGELS!

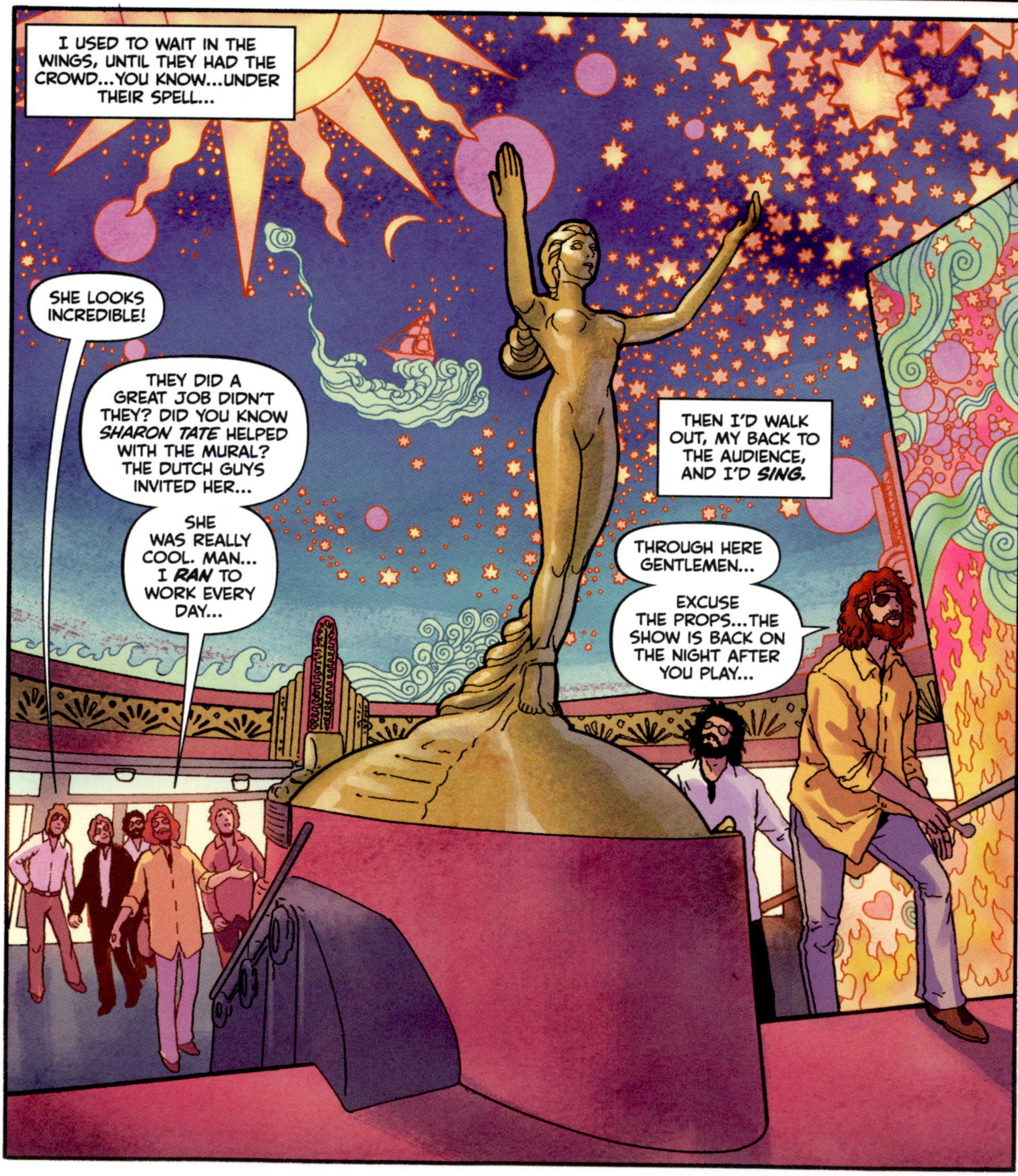

I USED TO WAIT IN THE WINGS, UNTIL THEY HAD THE CROWD...YOU KNOW...UNDER THEIR SPELL...
SHE LOOKS INCREDIBLE!
THEY DID A GREAT JOB DIDN'T THEY? DID YOU KNOW *SHARON TATE* HELPED WITH THE MURAL? THE DUTCH GUYS INVITED HER...
SHE WAS REALLY COOL. MAN... I *RAN* TO WORK EVERY DAY...
THEN I'D WALK OUT, MY BACK TO THE AUDIENCE, AND I'D *SING.*
THROUGH HERE GENTLEMEN...
EXCUSE THE PROPS...THE SHOW IS BACK ON THE NIGHT AFTER YOU PLAY...

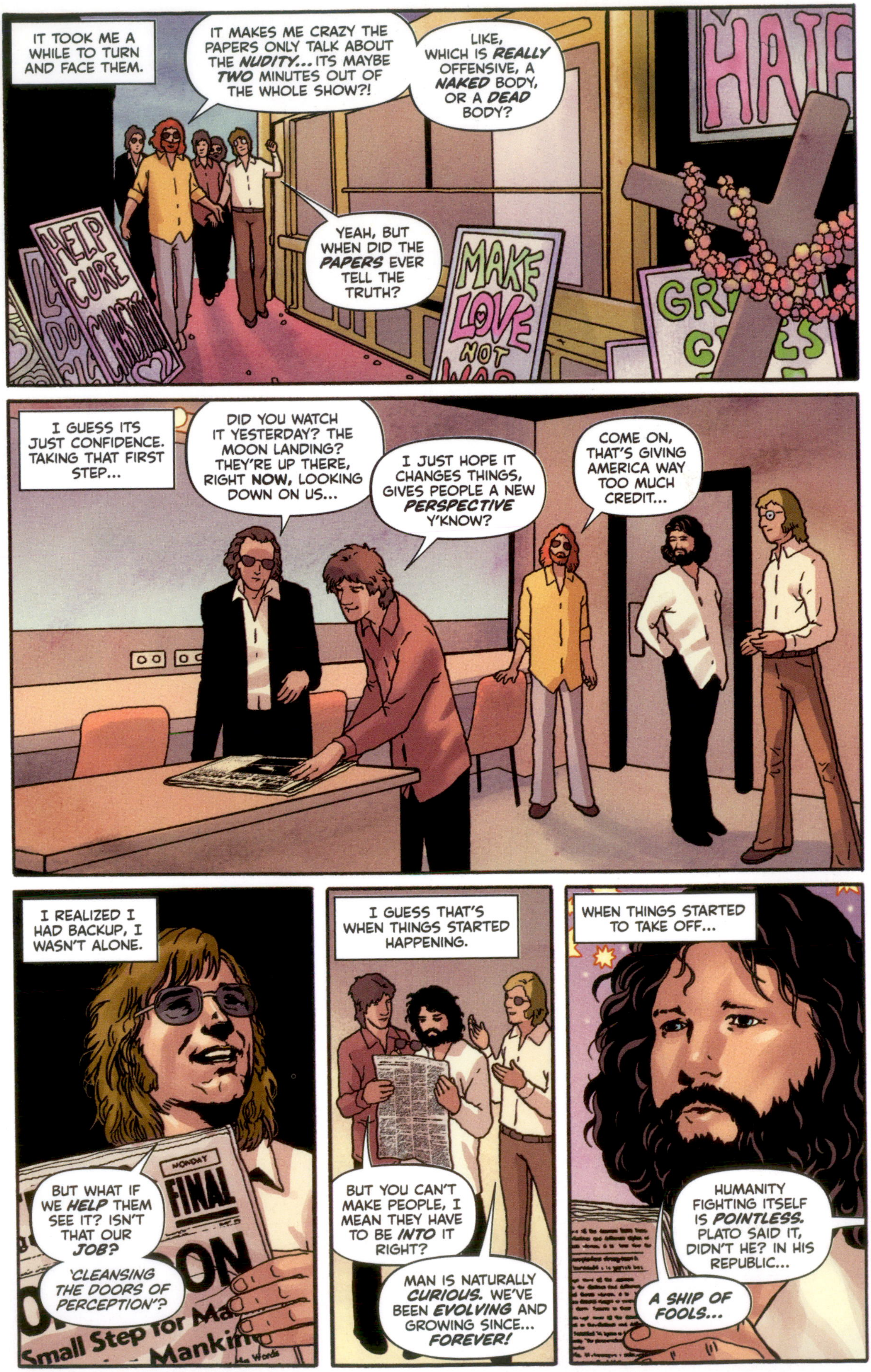
IT TOOK ME A WHILE TO TURN AND FACE THEM.
IT MAKES ME CRAZY THE PAPERS ONLY TALK ABOUT THE *NUDITY...* ITS MAYBE *TWO* MINUTES OUT OF THE WHOLE SHOW?!
LIKE, WHICH IS *REALLY* OFFENSIVE, A *NAKED* BODY, OR A *DEAD* BODY?
YEAH, BUT WHEN DID THE *PAPERS* EVER TELL THE TRUTH?
HATE
HELP CURE
MAKE LOVE NOT
I GUESS ITS JUST CONFIDENCE. TAKING THAT FIRST STEP...
DID YOU WATCH IT YESTERDAY? THE MOON LANDING? THEY'RE UP THERE, RIGHT **NOW**, LOOKING DOWN ON US...
I JUST HOPE IT CHANGES THINGS, GIVES PEOPLE A NEW *PERSPECTIVE* Y'KNOW?
COME ON, THAT'S GIVING AMERICA WAY TOO MUCH CREDIT...
I REALIZED I HAD BACKUP, I WASN'T ALONE.
MONDAY
FINAL
BUT WHAT IF WE *HELP* THEM SEE IT? ISN'T THAT OUR *JOB?*
'CLEANSING THE DOORS OF PERCEPTION'?
I GUESS THAT'S WHEN THINGS STARTED HAPPENING.
BUT YOU CAN'T MAKE PEOPLE, I MEAN THEY HAVE TO BE *INTO* IT RIGHT?
MAN IS NATURALLY *CURIOUS.* WE'VE BEEN *EVOLVING* AND GROWING SINCE... *FOREVER!*
WHEN THINGS STARTED TO TAKE OFF...
HUMANITY FIGHTING ITSELF IS *POINTLESS.* PLATO SAID IT, DIDN'T HE? IN HIS REPUBLIC...
A SHIP OF FOOLS...

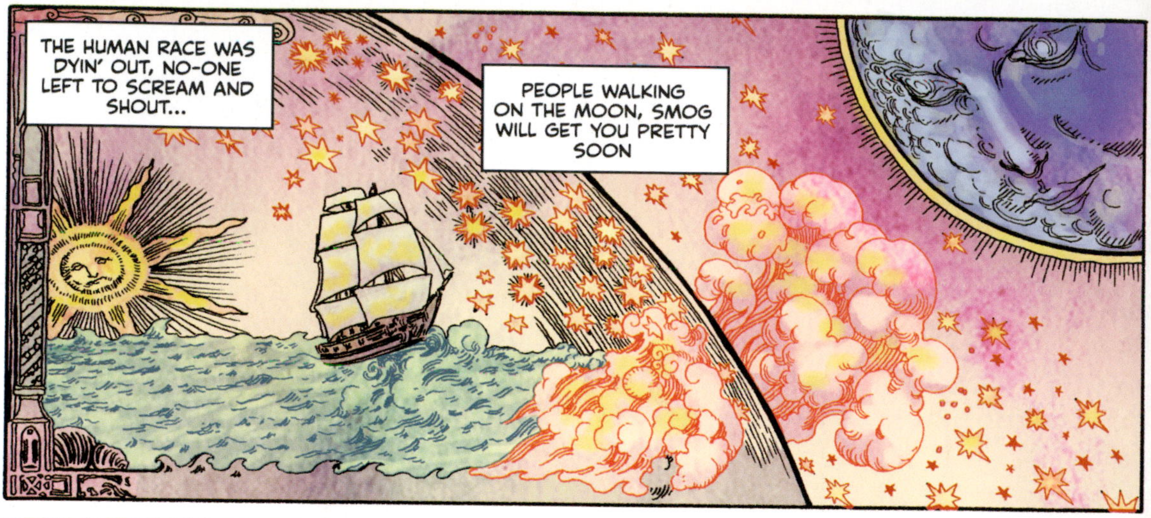
THE HUMAN RACE WAS DYIN' OUT, NO-ONE LEFT TO SCREAM AND SHOUT...
PEOPLE WALKING ON THE MOON, SMOG WILL GET YOU PRETTY SOON

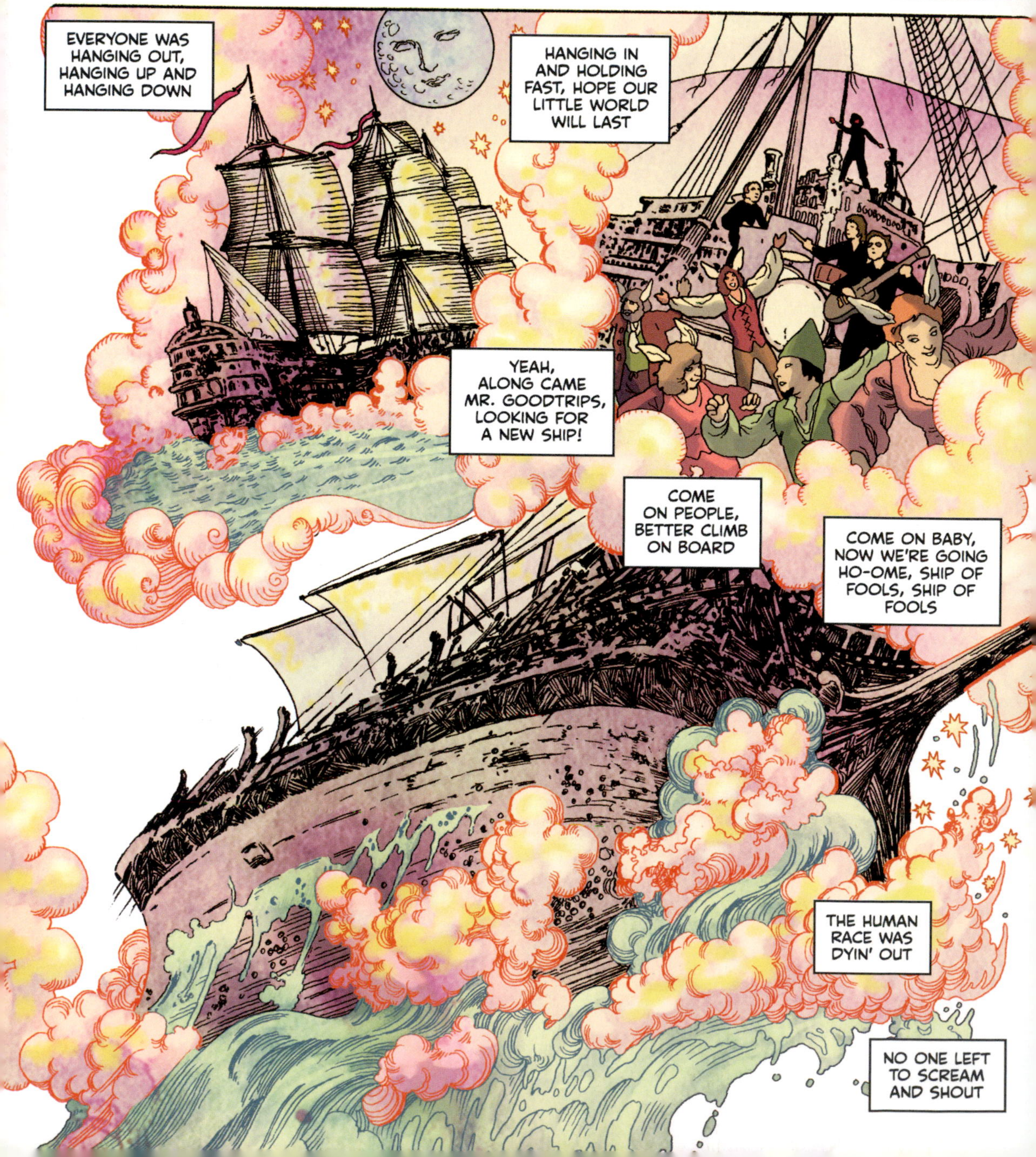
EVERYONE WAS HANGING OUT, HANGING UP AND HANGING DOWN
HANGING IN AND HOLDING FAST, HOPE OUR LITTLE WORLD WILL LAST
YEAH, ALONG CAME MR. GOODTRIPS, LOOKING FOR A NEW SHIP!
COME ON PEOPLE, BETTER CLIMB ON BOARD
COME ON BABY, NOW WE'RE GOING HO-OME, SHIP OF FOOLS, SHIP OF FOOLS
THE HUMAN RACE WAS DYIN' OUT
NO ONE LEFT TO SCREAM AND SHOUT

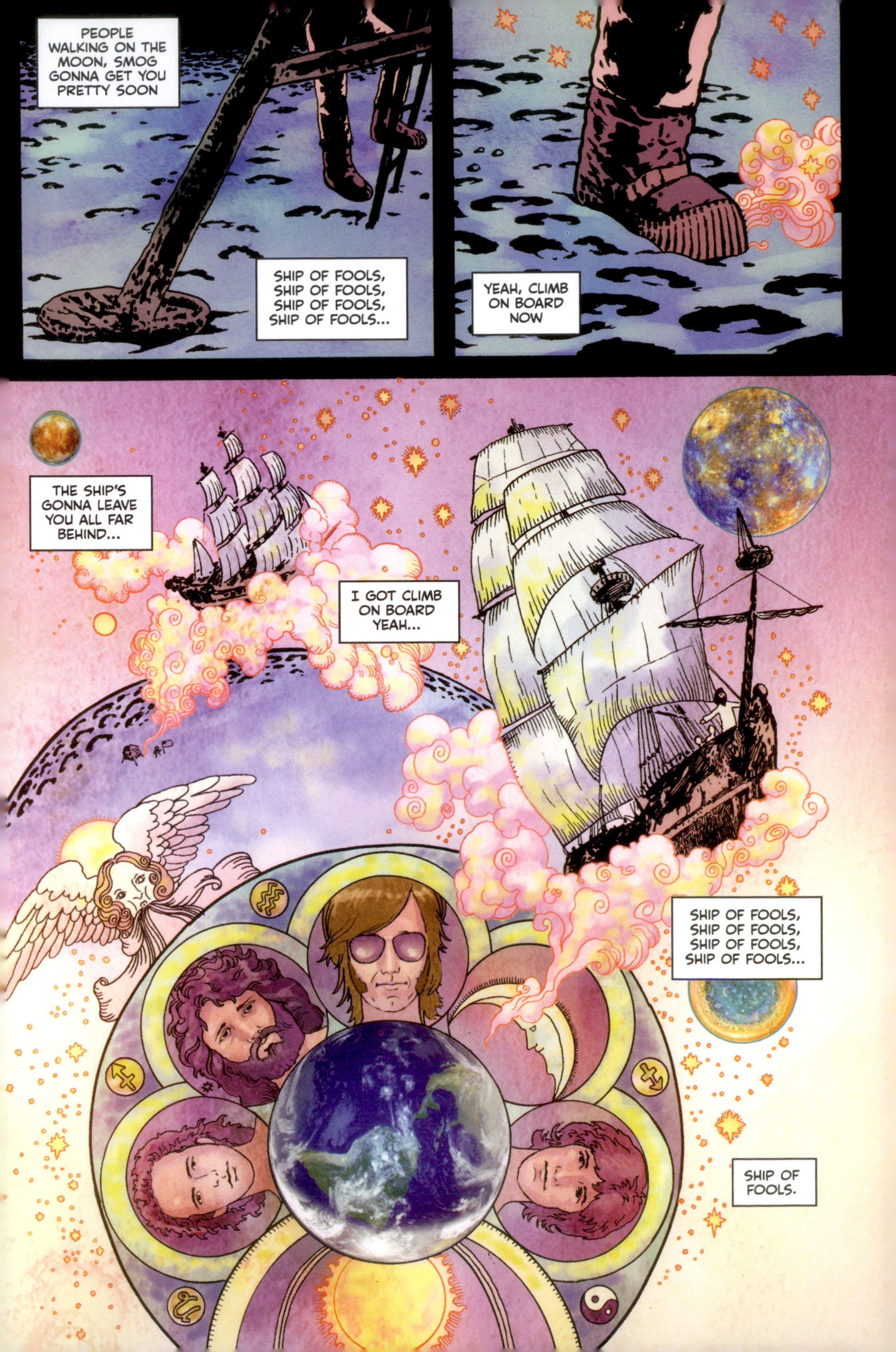
PEOPLE WALKING ON THE MOON, SMOG GONNA GET YOU PRETTY SOON
SHIP OF FOOLS, SHIP OF FOOLS, SHIP OF FOOLS, SHIP OF FOOLS...
YEAH, CLIMB ON BOARD NOW
THE SHIP'S GONNA LEAVE YOU ALL FAR BEHIND...
I GOT CLIMB ON BOARD YEAH...
SHIP OF FOOLS, SHIP OF FOOLS, SHIP OF FOOLS, SHIP OF FOOLS...
SHIP OF FOOLS.

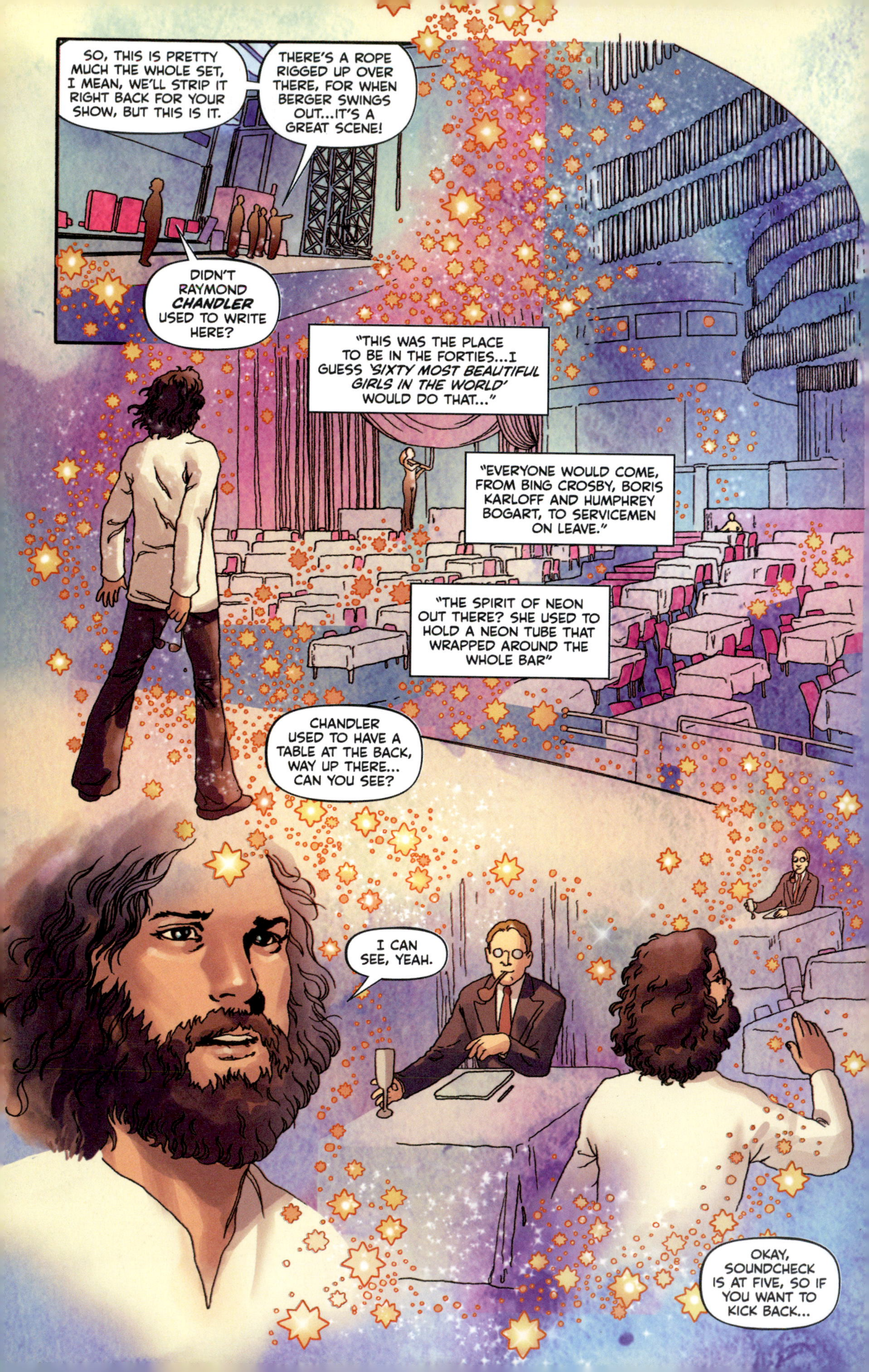
SO, THIS IS PRETTY MUCH THE WHOLE SET, I MEAN, WE'LL STRIP IT RIGHT BACK FOR YOUR SHOW, BUT THIS IS IT.
THERE'S A ROPE RIGGED UP OVER THERE, FOR WHEN BERGER SWINGS OUT...IT'S A GREAT SCENE!
DIDN'T RAYMOND *CHANDLER* USED TO WRITE HERE?
"THIS WAS THE PLACE TO BE IN THE FORTIES...I GUESS *'SIXTY MOST BEAUTIFUL GIRLS IN THE WORLD'* WOULD DO THAT..."
"EVERYONE WOULD COME, FROM BING CROSBY, BORIS KARLOFF AND HUMPHREY BOGART, TO SERVICEMEN ON LEAVE."
"THE SPIRIT OF NEON OUT THERE? SHE USED TO HOLD A NEON TUBE THAT WRAPPED AROUND THE WHOLE BAR"
CHANDLER USED TO HAVE A TABLE AT THE BACK, WAY UP THERE... CAN YOU SEE?
I CAN SEE, YEAH.
OKAY, SOUNDCHECK IS AT FIVE, SO IF YOU WANT TO KICK BACK...

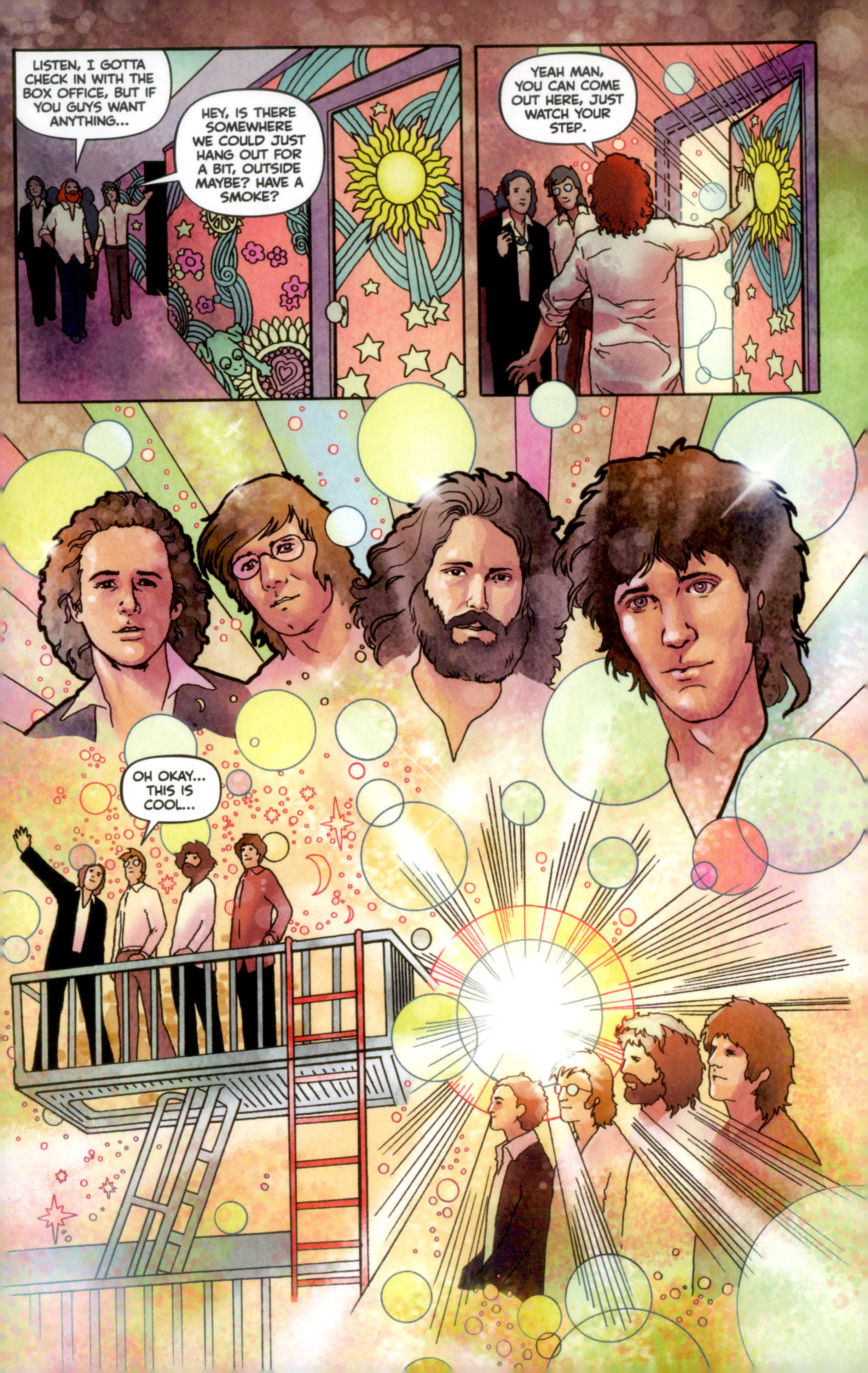
LISTEN, I GOTTA CHECK IN WITH THE BOX OFFICE, BUT IF YOU GUYS WANT ANYTHING...
HEY, IS THERE SOMEWHERE WE COULD JUST HANG OUT FOR A BIT, OUTSIDE MAYBE? HAVE A SMOKE?
YEAH MAN, YOU CAN COME OUT HERE, JUST WATCH YOUR STEP.
OH OKAY... THIS IS COOL...

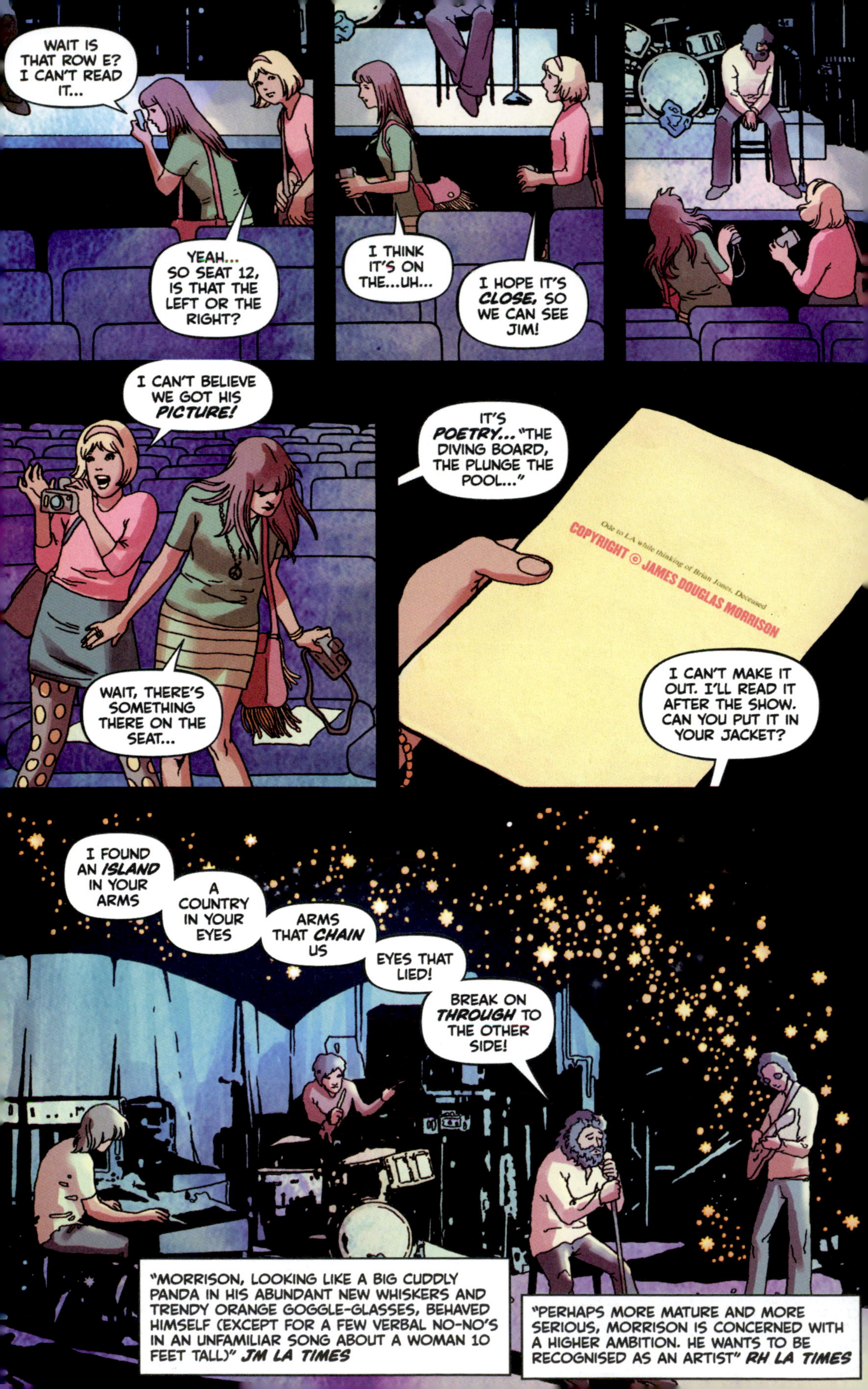
WAIT IS THAT ROW E? I CAN'T READ IT...
YEAH... SO SEAT 12, IS THAT THE LEFT OR THE RIGHT?
I THINK IT'S ON THE...UH...
I HOPE IT'S CLOSE, SO WE CAN SEE JIM!
I CAN'T BELIEVE WE GOT HIS PICTURE!
WAIT, THERE'S SOMETHING THERE ON THE SEAT...
IT'S POETRY... "THE DIVING BOARD, THE PLUNGE THE POOL..."
Ode to LA while thinking of Brian Jones, Deceased
COPYRIGHT © JAMES DOUGLAS MORRISON
I CAN'T MAKE IT OUT. I'LL READ IT AFTER THE SHOW. CAN YOU PUT IT IN YOUR JACKET?
I FOUND AN ISLAND IN YOUR ARMS
A COUNTRY IN YOUR EYES
ARMS THAT CHAIN US
EYES THAT LIED!
BREAK ON THROUGH TO THE OTHER SIDE!
"MORRISON, LOOKING LIKE A BIG CUDDLY PANDA IN HIS ABUNDANT NEW WHISKERS AND TRENDY ORANGE GOGGLE-GLASSES, BEHAVED HIMSELF (EXCEPT FOR A FEW VERBAL NO-NO'S IN AN UNFAMILIAR SONG ABOUT A WOMAN 10 FEET TALL)" JM LA TIMES
"PERHAPS MORE MATURE AND MORE SERIOUS, MORRISON IS CONCERNED WITH A HIGHER AMBITION. HE WANTS TO BE RECOGNISED AS AN ARTIST" RH LA TIMES

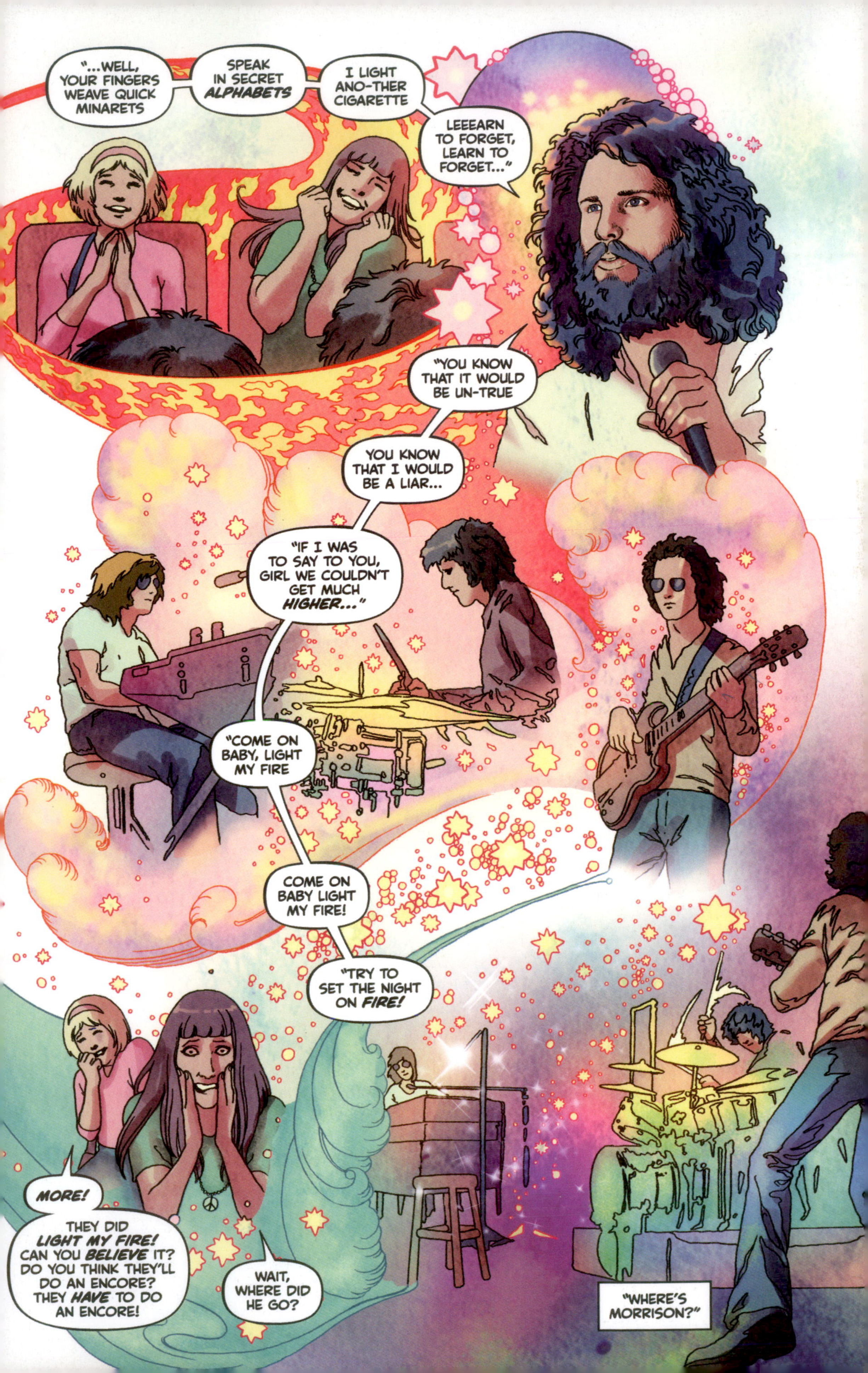
"...WELL, YOUR FINGERS WEAVE QUICK MINARETS
SPEAK IN SECRET *ALPHABETS*
I LIGHT ANO-THER CIGARETTE
LEEEARN TO FORGET, LEARN TO FORGET..."
"YOU KNOW THAT IT WOULD BE UN-TRUE
YOU KNOW THAT I WOULD BE A LIAR...
"IF I WAS TO SAY TO YOU, GIRL WE COULDN'T GET MUCH *HIGHER...*"
"COME ON BABY, LIGHT MY FIRE
COME ON BABY LIGHT MY FIRE!
"TRY TO SET THE NIGHT ON *FIRE!*
MORE!
THEY DID *LIGHT MY FIRE!* CAN YOU *BELIEVE* IT? DO YOU THINK THEY'LL DO AN ENCORE? THEY *HAVE* TO DO AN ENCORE!
WAIT, WHERE DID HE GO?
"WHERE'S MORRISON?"

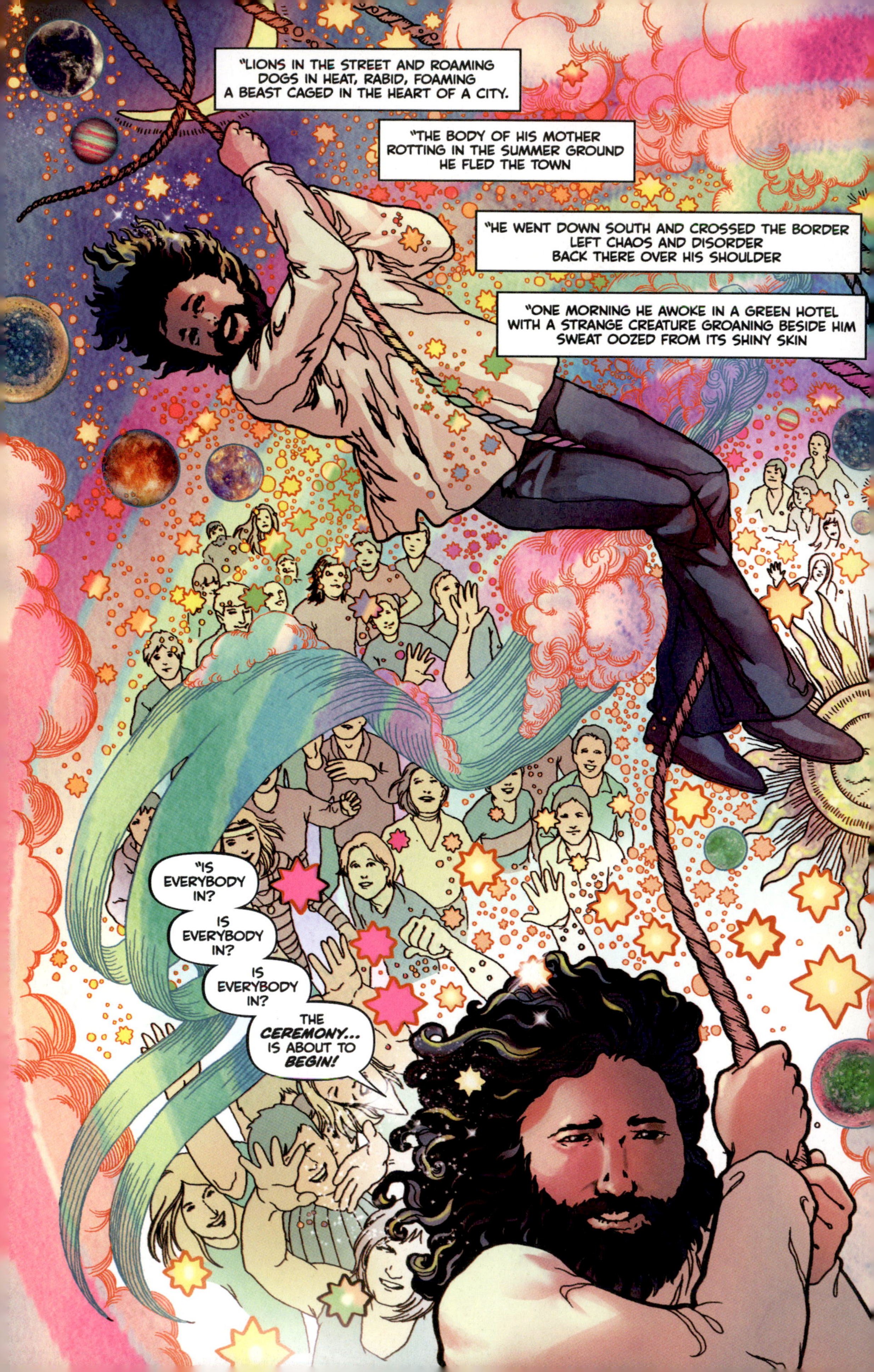
"LIONS IN THE STREET AND ROAMING DOGS IN HEAT, RABID, FOAMING A BEAST CAGED IN THE HEART OF A CITY.
"THE BODY OF HIS MOTHER ROTTING IN THE SUMMER GROUND HE FLED THE TOWN
"HE WENT DOWN SOUTH AND CROSSED THE BORDER LEFT CHAOS AND DISORDER BACK THERE OVER HIS SHOULDER
"ONE MORNING HE AWOKE IN A GREEN HOTEL WITH A STRANGE CREATURE GROANING BESIDE HIM SWEAT OOZED FROM ITS SHINY SKIN
"IS EVERYBODY IN?
IS EVERYBODY IN?
IS EVERYBODY IN?
THE *CEREMONY...* IS ABOUT TO *BEGIN!*

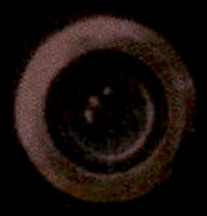

Land Ho!

Artist . . . . Ryan Kelly
Colorist . . . Aladdin Collar

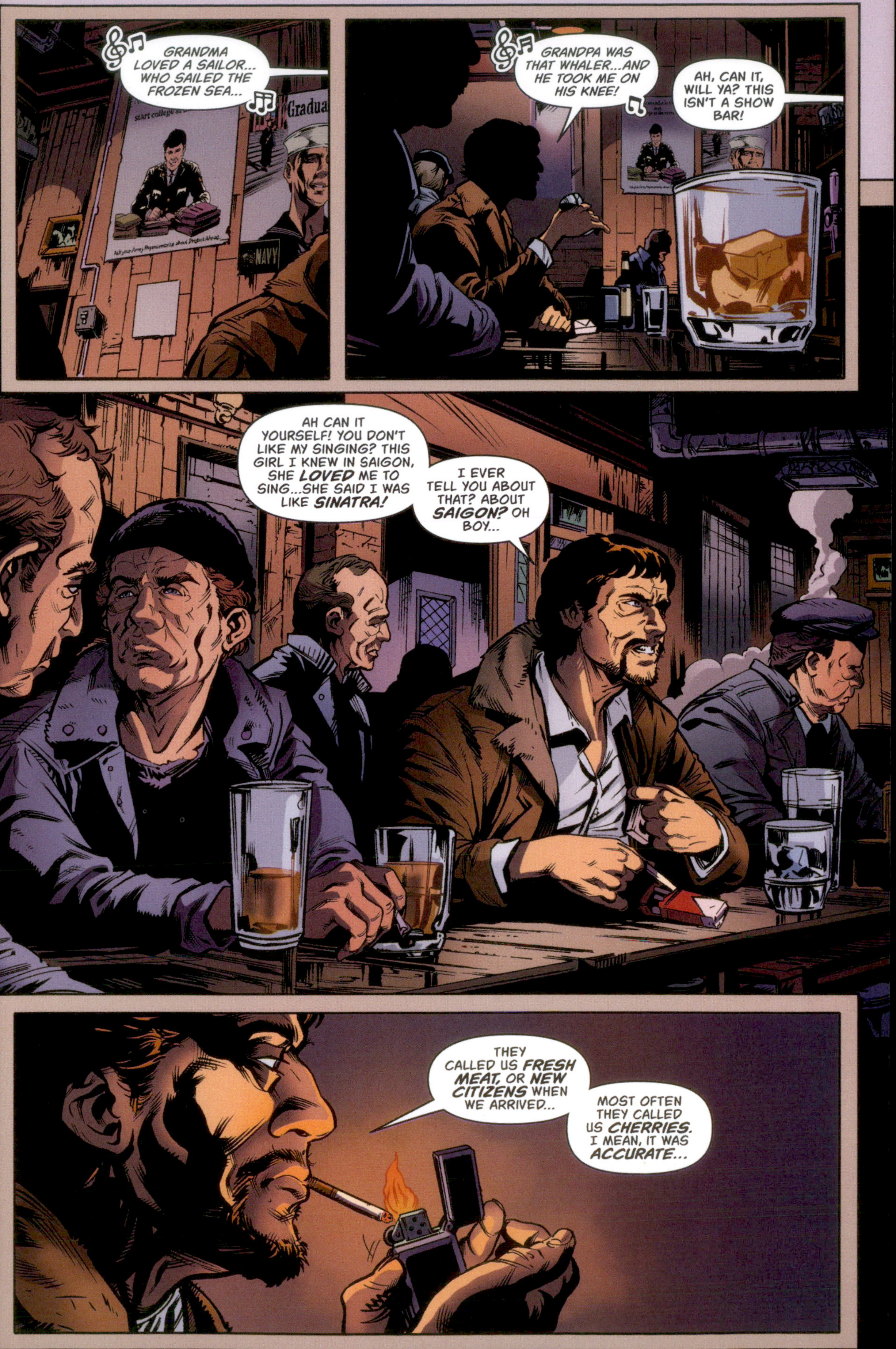
GRANDMA LOVED A SAILOR... WHO SAILED THE FROZEN SEA...
Gradua
NAVY
GRANDPA WAS THAT WHALER...AND HE TOOK ME ON HIS KNEE!
AH, CAN IT, WILL YA? THIS ISN'T A SHOW BAR!
AH CAN IT YOURSELF! YOU DON'T LIKE MY SINGING? THIS GIRL I KNEW IN SAIGON, SHE **LOVED** ME TO SING...SHE SAID I WAS LIKE **SINATRA!**
I EVER TELL YOU ABOUT THAT? ABOUT **SAIGON?** OH BOY...
THEY CALLED US **FRESH MEAT,** OR **NEW CITIZENS** WHEN WE ARRIVED...
MOST OFTEN THEY CALLED US **CHERRIES.** I MEAN, IT WAS **ACCURATE...**

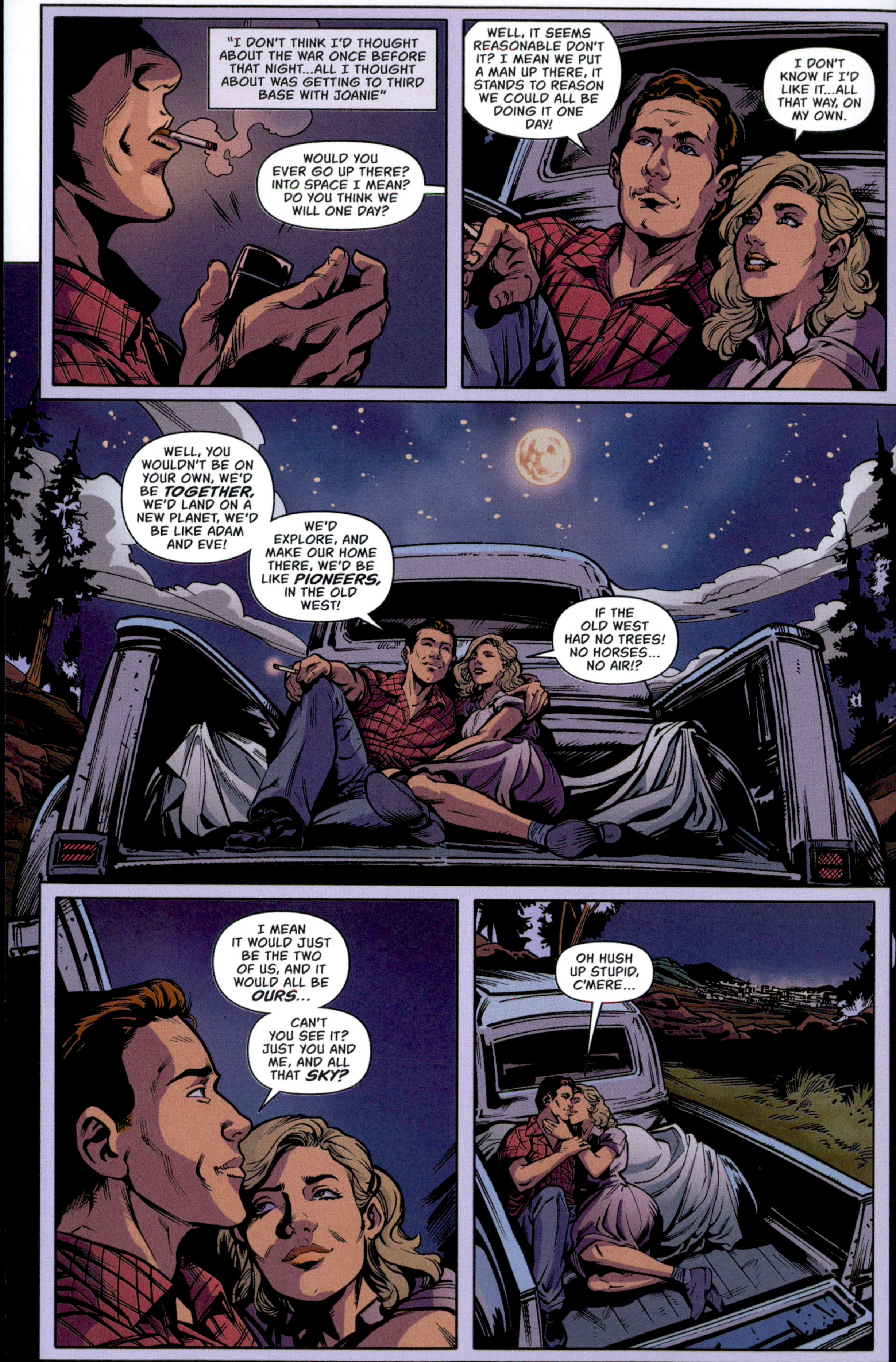
"I DON'T THINK I'D THOUGHT ABOUT THE WAR ONCE BEFORE THAT NIGHT...ALL I THOUGHT ABOUT WAS GETTING TO THIRD BASE WITH JOANIE"
WOULD YOU EVER GO UP THERE? INTO SPACE I MEAN? DO YOU THINK WE WILL ONE DAY?
WELL, IT SEEMS REASONABLE DON'T IT? I MEAN WE PUT A MAN UP THERE, IT STANDS TO REASON WE COULD ALL BE DOING IT ONE DAY!
I DON'T KNOW IF I'D LIKE IT...ALL THAT WAY, ON MY OWN.
WELL, YOU WOULDN'T BE ON YOUR OWN, WE'D BE TOGETHER, WE'D LAND ON A NEW PLANET, WE'D BE LIKE ADAM AND EVE!
WE'D EXPLORE, AND MAKE OUR HOME THERE, WE'D BE LIKE PIONEERS, IN THE OLD WEST!
IF THE OLD WEST HAD NO TREES! NO HORSES... NO AIR!?
I MEAN IT WOULD JUST BE THE TWO OF US, AND IT WOULD ALL BE OURS...
CAN'T YOU SEE IT? JUST YOU AND ME, AND ALL THAT SKY?
OH HUSH UP STUPID, C'MERE...

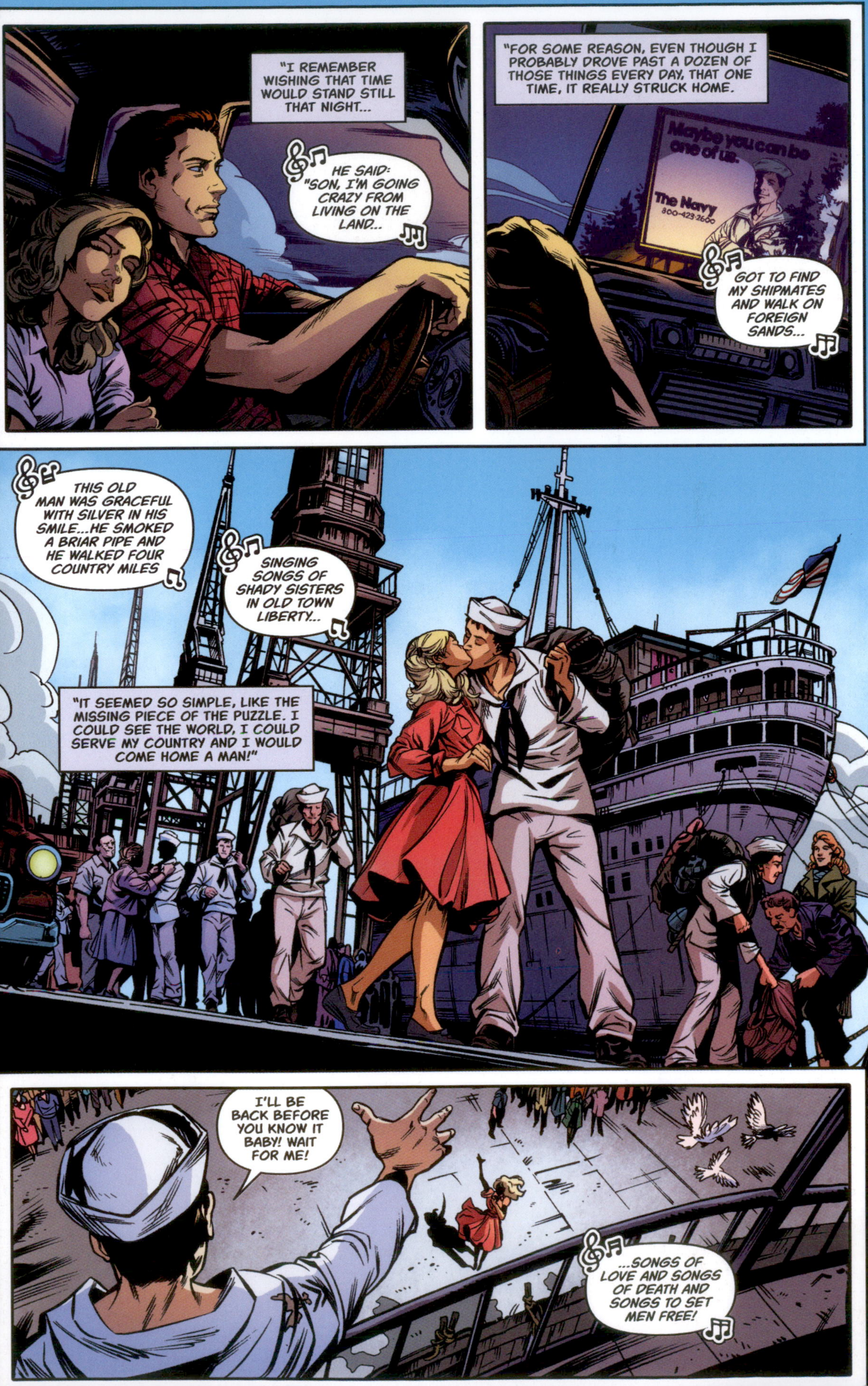
"I REMEMBER WISHING THAT TIME WOULD STAND STILL THAT NIGHT...
HE SAID: "SON, I'M GOING CRAZY FROM LIVING ON THE LAND...
"FOR SOME REASON, EVEN THOUGH I PROBABLY DROVE PAST A DOZEN OF THOSE THINGS EVERY DAY, THAT ONE TIME, IT REALLY STRUCK HOME.
Maybe you can be one of us.
The Navy
800-423-2600
GOT TO FIND MY SHIPMATES AND WALK ON FOREIGN SANDS...
THIS OLD MAN WAS GRACEFUL WITH SILVER IN HIS SMILE...HE SMOKED A BRIAR PIPE AND HE WALKED FOUR COUNTRY MILES
SINGING SONGS OF SHADY SISTERS IN OLD TOWN LIBERTY...
"IT SEEMED SO SIMPLE, LIKE THE MISSING PIECE OF THE PUZZLE. I COULD SEE THE WORLD, I COULD SERVE MY COUNTRY AND I WOULD COME HOME A MAN!"
The Navy
I'LL BE BACK BEFORE YOU KNOW IT BABY! WAIT FOR ME!
...SONGS OF LOVE AND SONGS OF DEATH AND SONGS TO SET MEN FREE!

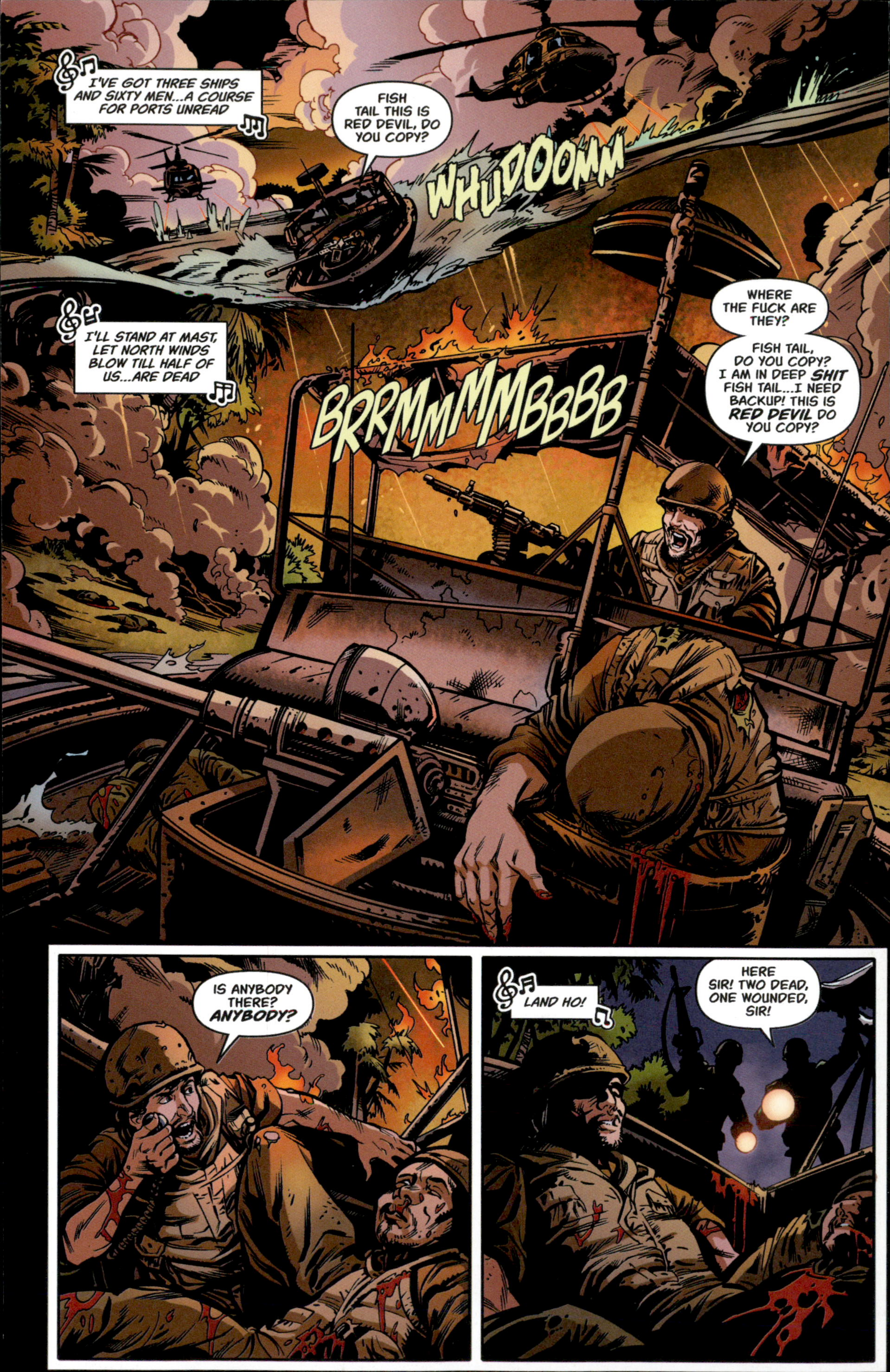

I'VE GOT THREE SHIPS AND SIXTY MEN...A COURSE FOR PORTS UNREAD
FISH TAIL THIS IS RED DEVIL, DO YOU COPY?
WHUDOOMM
I'LL STAND AT MAST, LET NORTH WINDS BLOW TILL HALF OF US...ARE DEAD
BRRMMMMMBBBB
WHERE THE FUCK ARE THEY?
FISH TAIL, DO YOU COPY? I AM IN DEEP SHIT FISH TAIL...I NEED BACKUP! THIS IS RED DEVIL DO YOU COPY?
IS ANYBODY THERE? ANYBODY?
LAND HO!
HERE SIR! TWO DEAD, ONE WOUNDED, SIR!

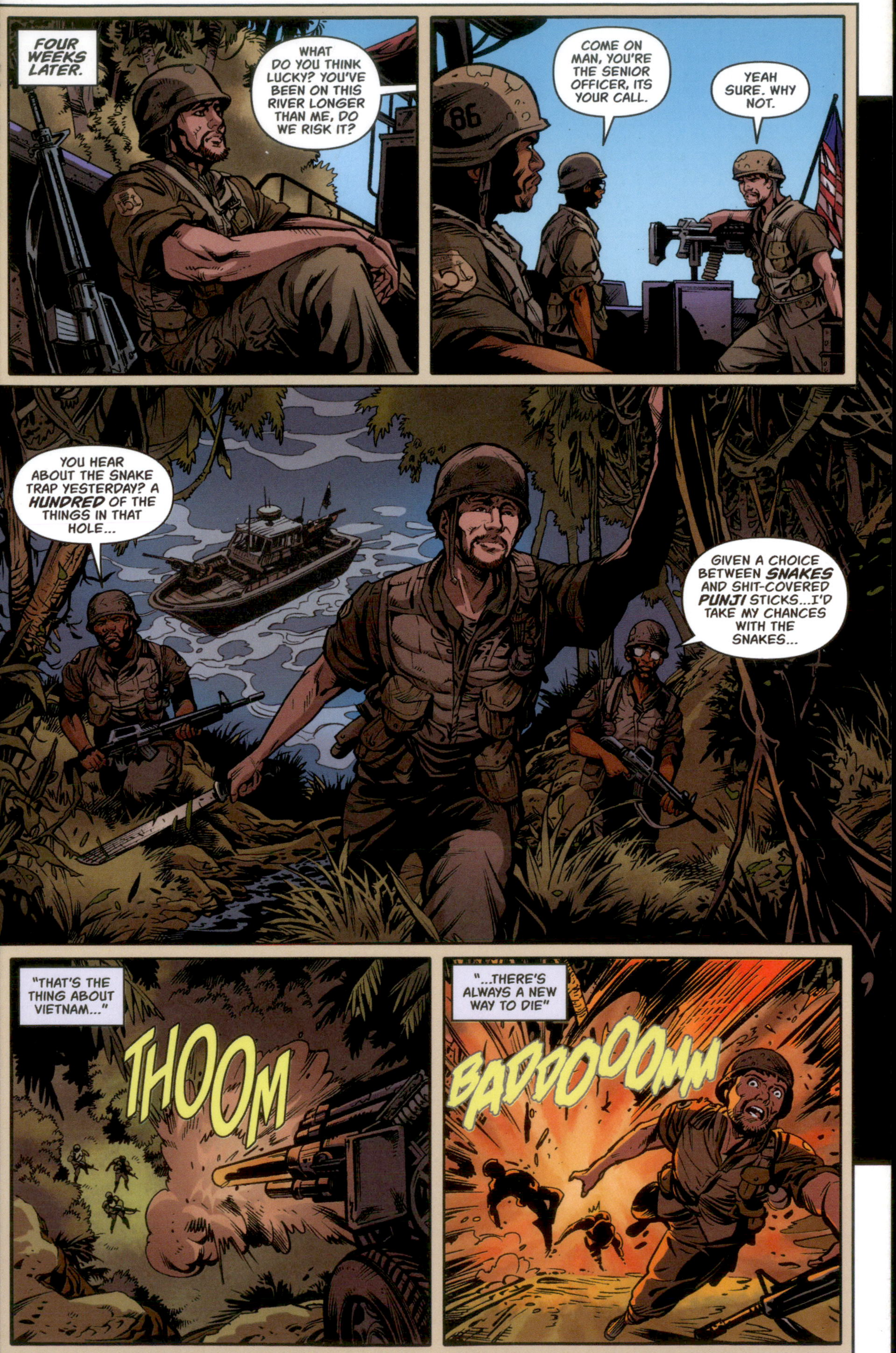
FOUR WEEKS LATER.
WHAT DO YOU THINK LUCKY? YOU'VE BEEN ON THIS RIVER LONGER THAN ME, DO WE RISK IT?
COME ON MAN, YOU'RE THE SENIOR OFFICER, ITS YOUR CALL.
YEAH SURE. WHY NOT.
YOU HEAR ABOUT THE SNAKE TRAP YESTERDAY? A HUNDRED OF THE THINGS IN THAT HOLE...
GIVEN A CHOICE BETWEEN SNAKES AND SHIT-COVERED PUNJI STICKS...I'D TAKE MY CHANCES WITH THE SNAKES...
"THAT'S THE THING ABOUT VIETNAM..."
THOOM
"...THERE'S ALWAYS A NEW WAY TO DIE"
BADDOOOMM

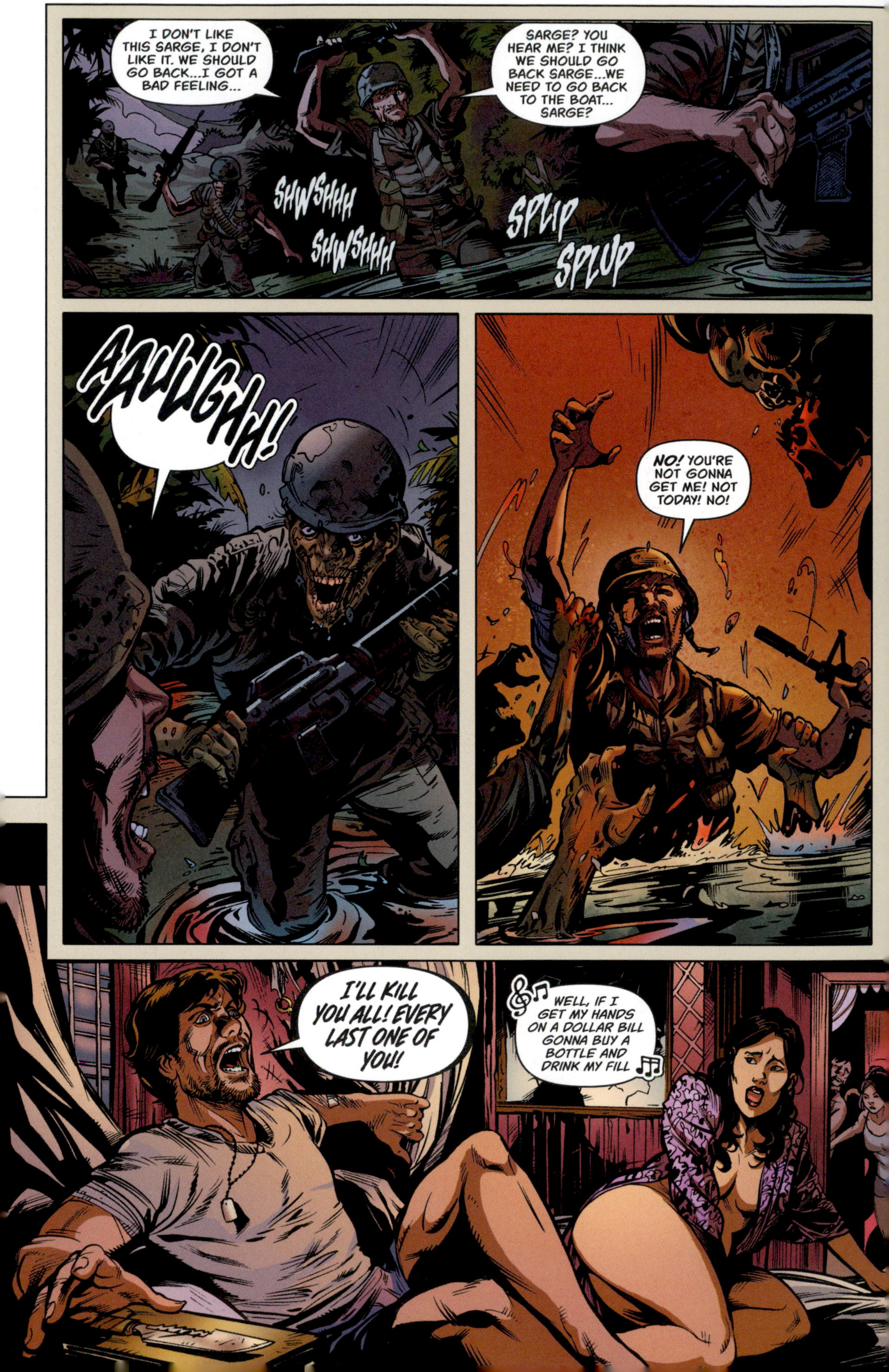
I DON'T LIKE THIS SARGE, I DON'T LIKE IT. WE SHOULD GO BACK...I GOT A BAD FEELING...
SARGE? YOU HEAR ME? I THINK WE SHOULD GO BACK SARGE...WE NEED TO GO BACK TO THE BOAT... SARGE?
SHWSHHH
SHWSHHH
SPLIP
SPLUP
AAUUGHH!
NO! YOU'RE NOT GONNA GET ME! NOT TODAY! NO!
I'LL KILL YOU ALL! EVERY LAST ONE OF YOU!
WELL, IF I GET MY HANDS ON A DOLLAR BILL GONNA BUY A BOTTLE AND DRINK MY FILL

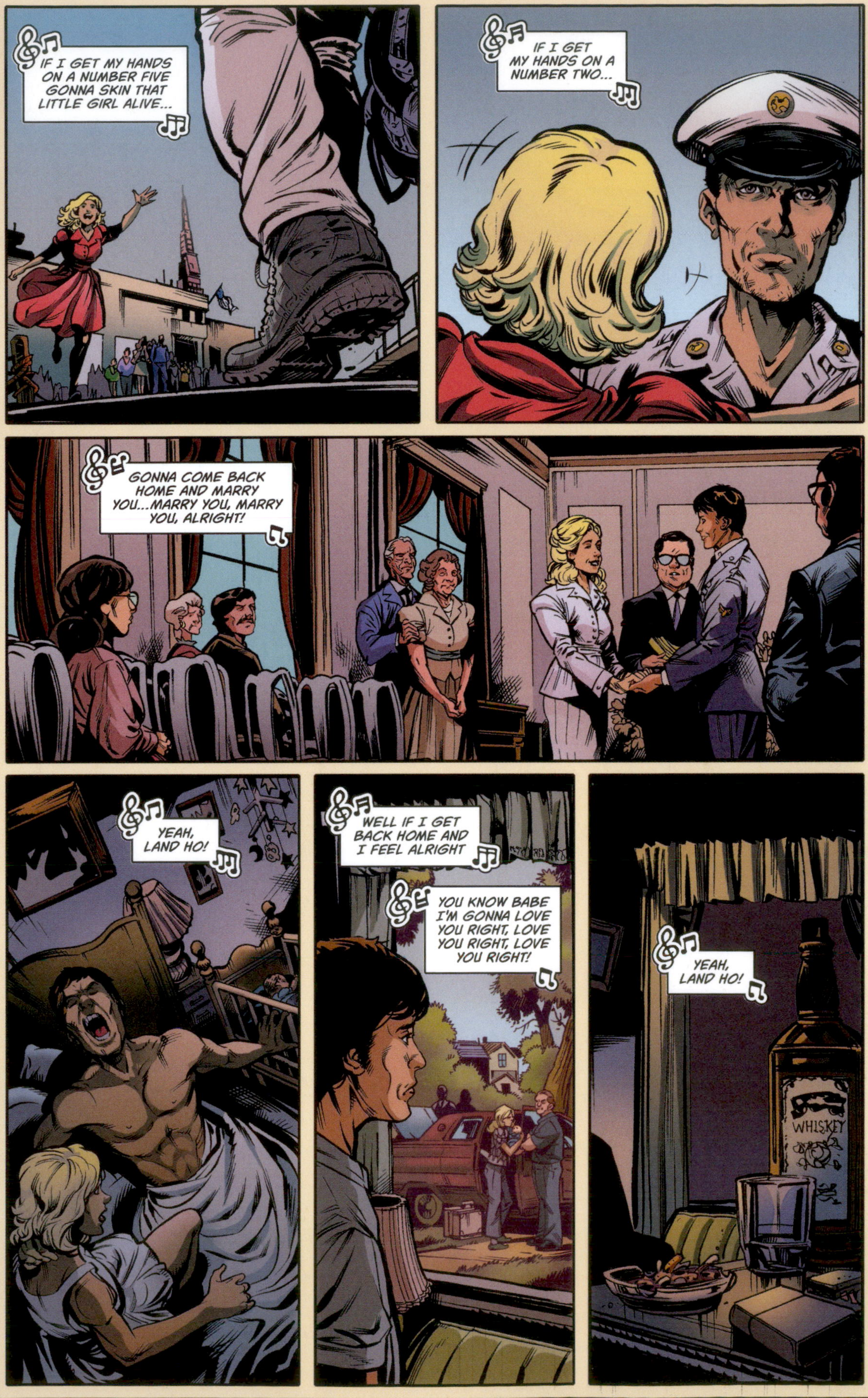
IF I GET MY HANDS ON A NUMBER FIVE GONNA SKIN THAT LITTLE GIRL ALIVE...
IF I GET MY HANDS ON A NUMBER TWO...
GONNA COME BACK HOME AND MARRY YOU...MARRY YOU, MARRY YOU, ALRIGHT!
YEAH, LAND HO!
WELL IF I GET BACK HOME AND I FEEL ALRIGHT
YOU KNOW BABE I'M GONNA LOVE YOU RIGHT, LOVE YOU RIGHT, LOVE YOU RIGHT!
YEAH, LAND HO!
WHISKEY

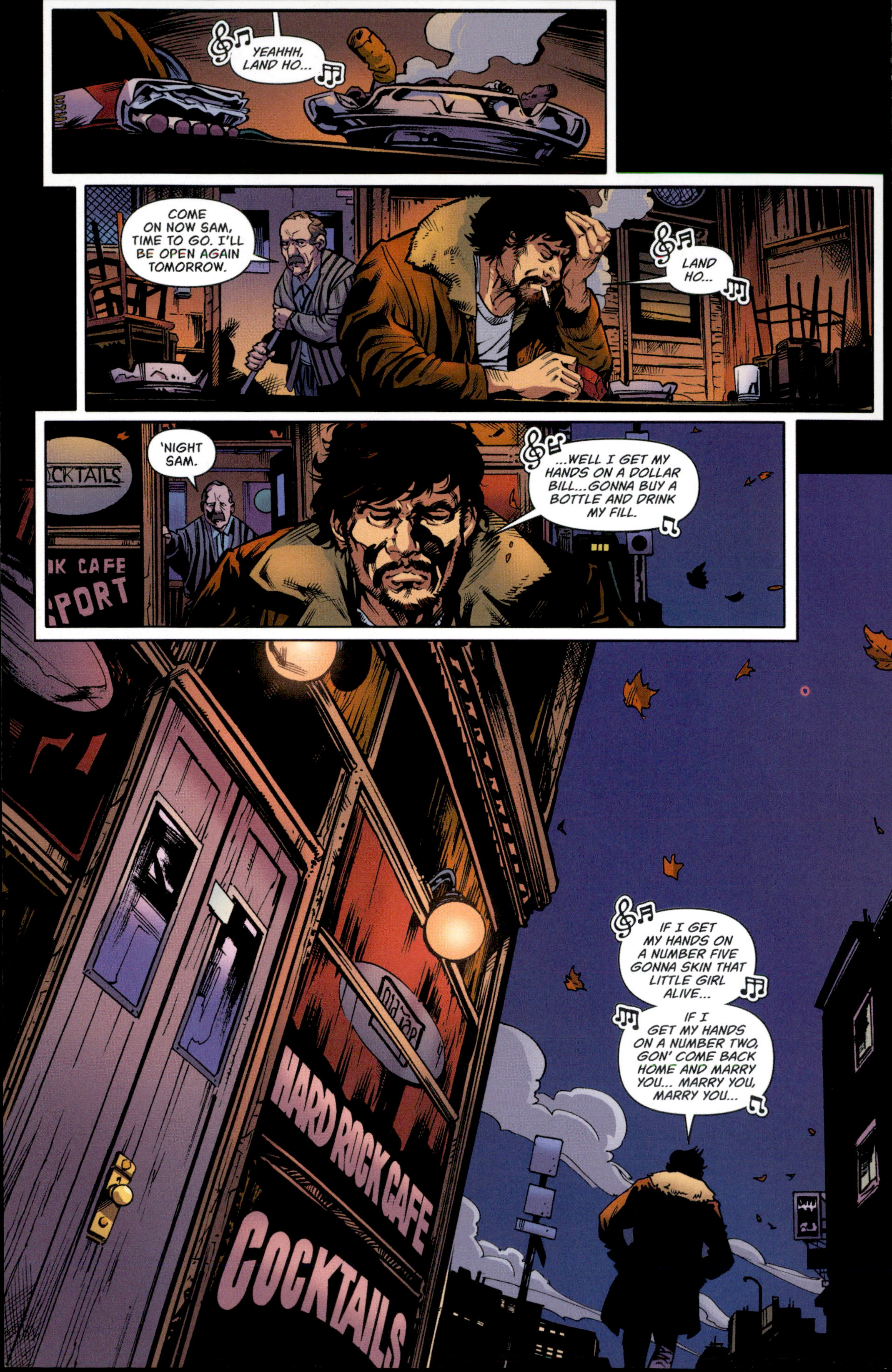
YEAHHH, LAND HO...
COME ON NOW SAM, TIME TO GO. I'LL BE OPEN AGAIN TOMORROW.
LAND HO...
'NIGHT SAM.
...WELL I GET MY HANDS ON A DOLLAR BILL...GONNA BUY A BOTTLE AND DRINK MY FILL.
IF I GET MY HANDS ON A NUMBER FIVE GONNA SKIN THAT LITTLE GIRL ALIVE...
IF I GET MY HANDS ON A NUMBER TWO, GON' COME BACK HOME AND MARRY YOU... MARRY YOU, MARRY YOU...
HARD ROCK CAFE
COCKTAILS

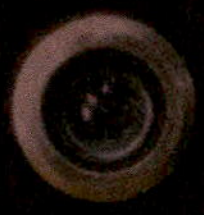

The Spy

Artist . . . . Armitano
Colorist . . . . . Ellie Wright

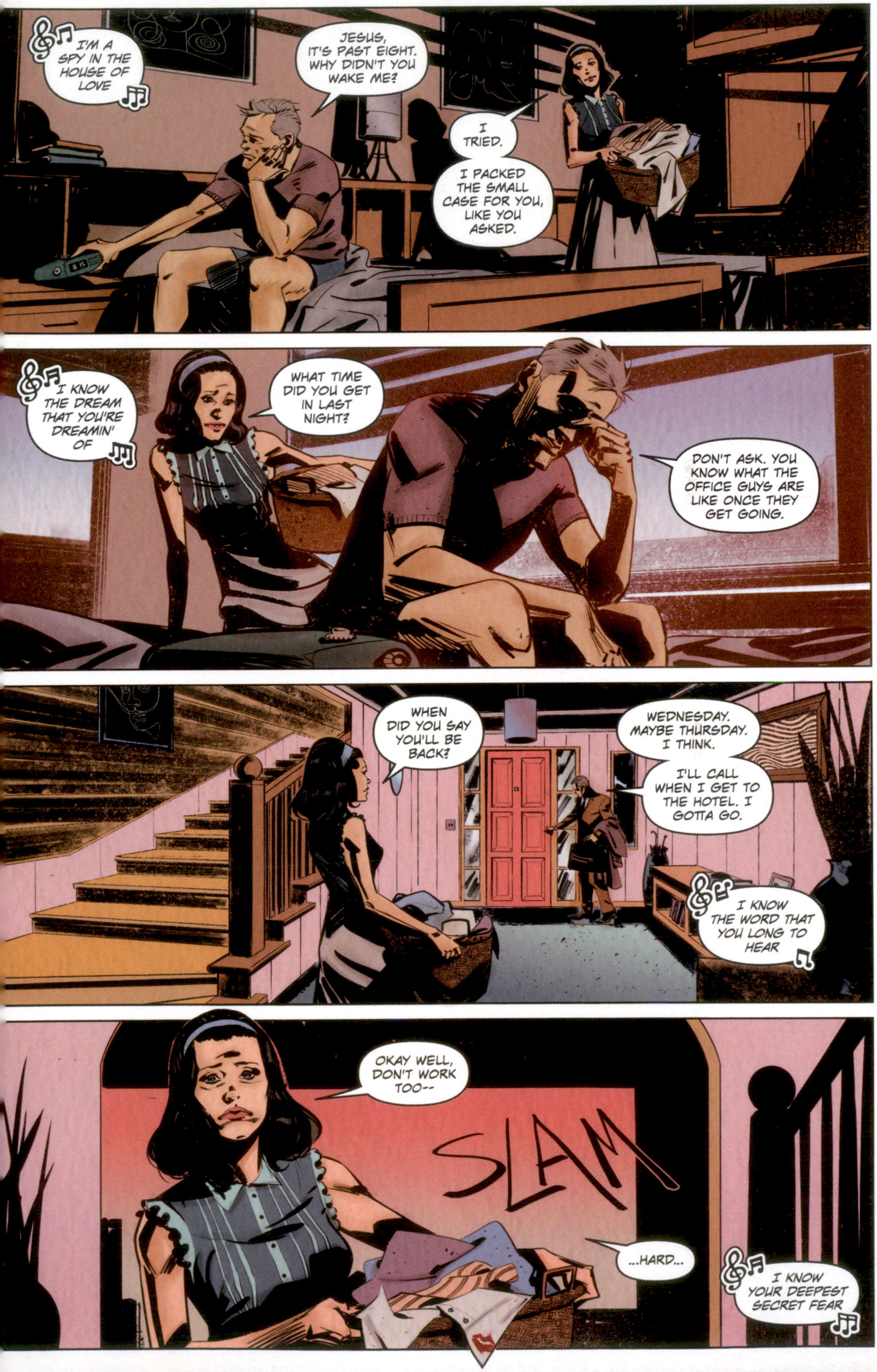

I'M A SPY IN THE HOUSE OF LOVE
JESUS, IT'S PAST EIGHT. WHY DIDN'T YOU WAKE ME?
I TRIED.
I PACKED THE SMALL CASE FOR YOU, LIKE YOU ASKED.
I KNOW THE DREAM THAT YOU'RE DREAMIN' OF
WHAT TIME DID YOU GET IN LAST NIGHT?
DON'T ASK. YOU KNOW WHAT THE OFFICE GUYS ARE LIKE ONCE THEY GET GOING.
WHEN DID YOU SAY YOU'LL BE BACK?
WEDNESDAY. MAYBE THURSDAY. I THINK.
I'LL CALL WHEN I GET TO THE HOTEL. I GOTTA GO.
I KNOW THE WORD THAT YOU LONG TO HEAR
OKAY WELL, DON'T WORK TOO--
SLAM
...HARD...
I KNOW YOUR DEEPEST SECRET FEAR

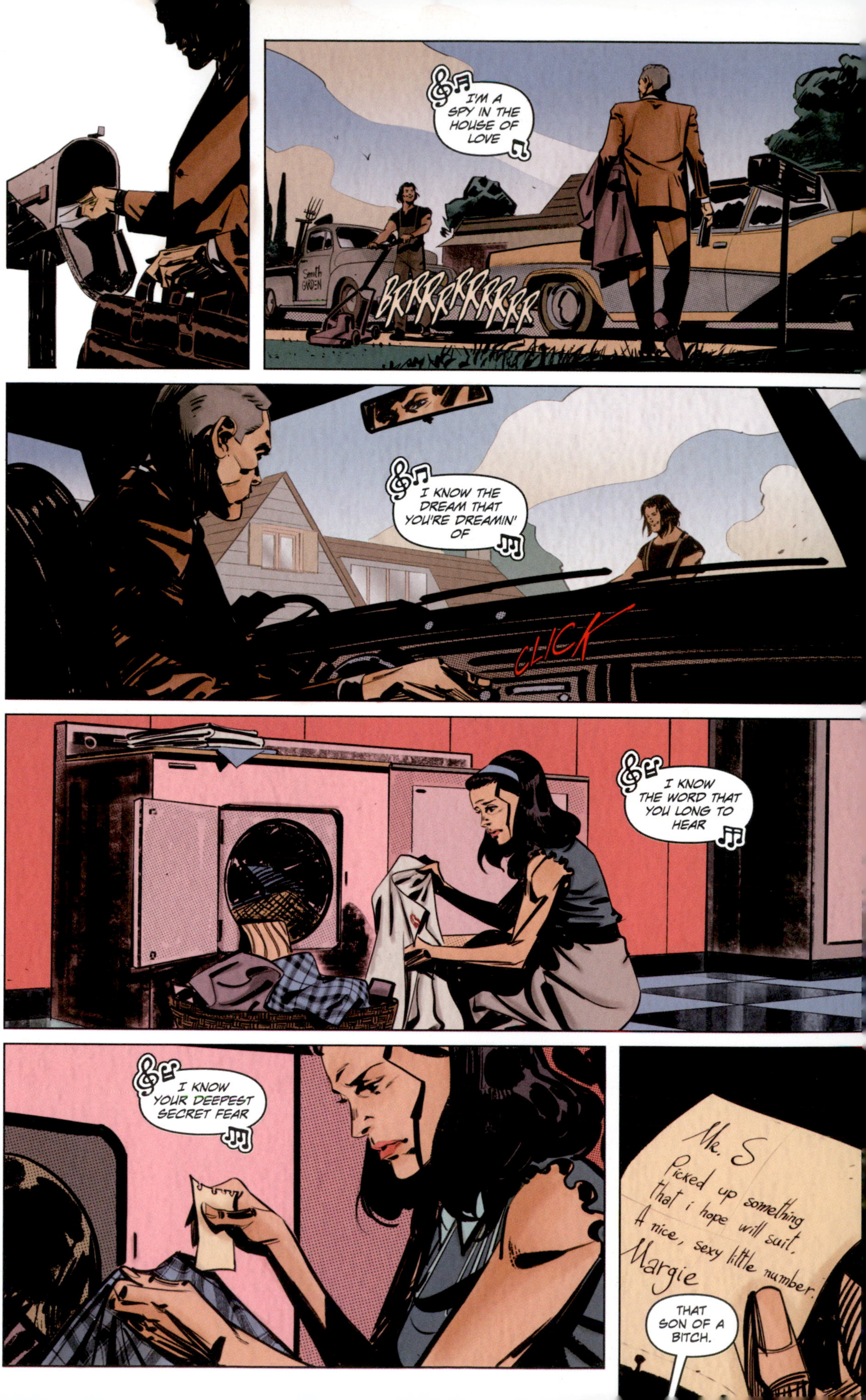
I'M A SPY IN THE HOUSE OF LOVE
Smith GARDEN
BRRRRRRRRRRRR
I KNOW THE DREAM THAT YOU'RE DREAMIN' OF
CLICK
I KNOW THE WORD THAT YOU LONG TO HEAR
I KNOW YOUR DEEPEST SECRET FEAR
Mr. S
Picked up something that i hope will suit. A nice, sexy little number.
Margie
THAT SON OF A BITCH.

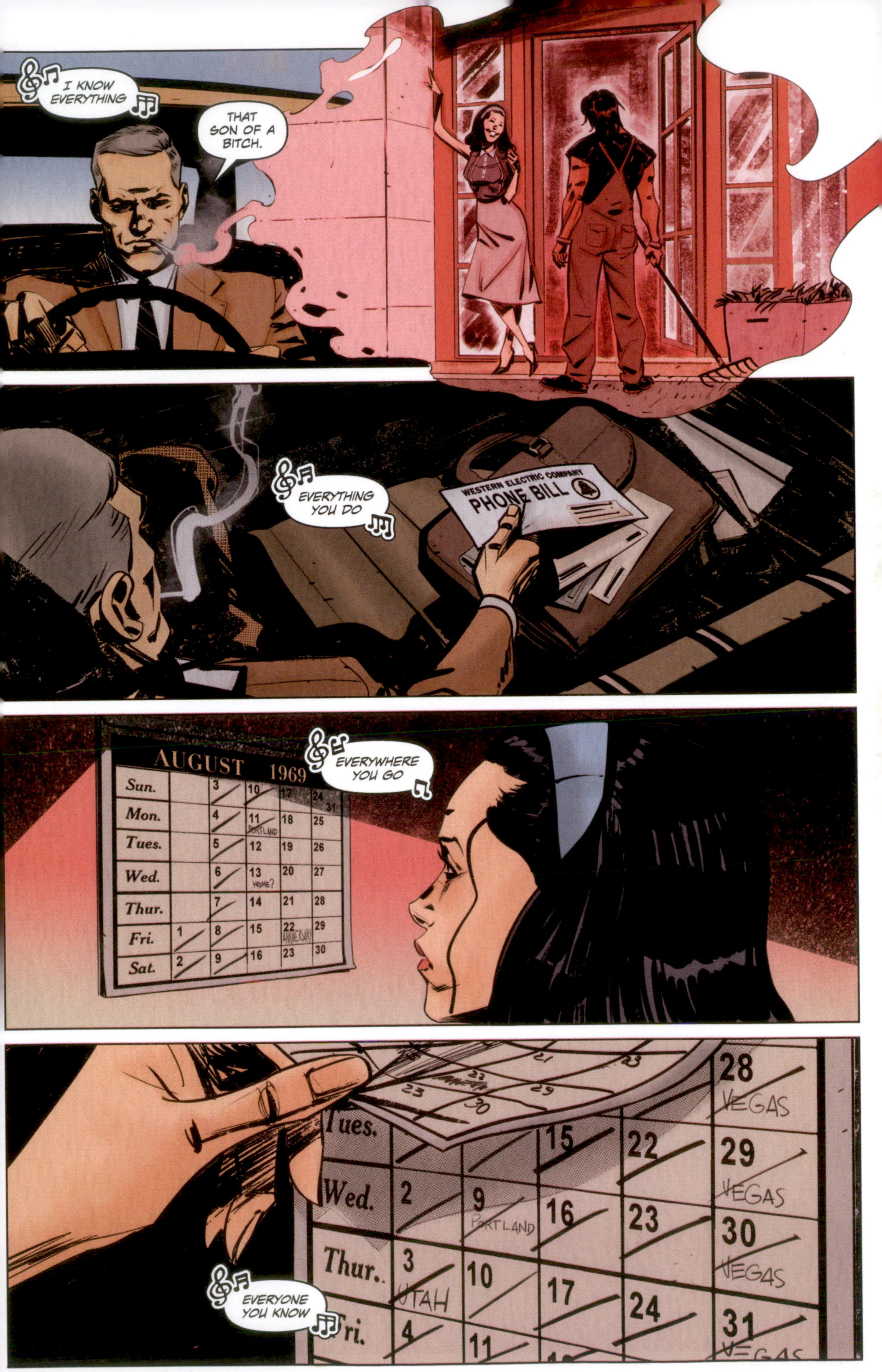
I KNOW EVERYTHING
THAT SON OF A BITCH.
WESTERN ELECTRIC COMPANY
PHONE BILL
EVERYTHING YOU DO
AUGUST 1969
EVERYWHERE YOU GO
EVERYONE YOU KNOW

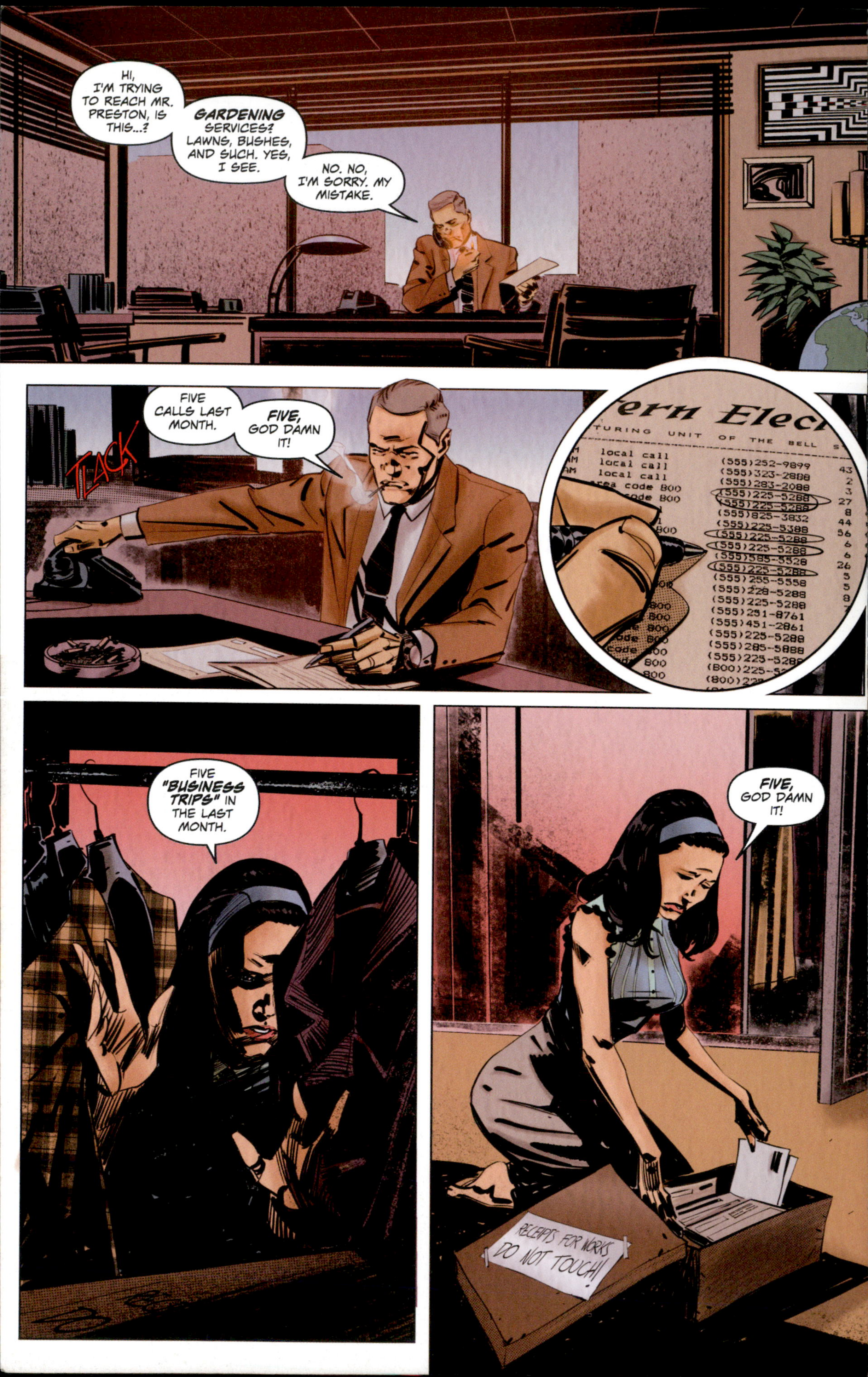

HI, I'M TRYING TO REACH MR. PRESTON, IS THIS...?
GARDENING SERVICES? LAWNS, BUSHES, AND SUCH. YES, I SEE.
NO. NO, I'M SORRY. MY MISTAKE.
TLACK
FIVE CALLS LAST MONTH.
FIVE, GOD DAMN IT!
local call (555)252-9899
local call (555)323-2888
local call (555)283-2088
(555)225-5288
(555)225-5288
(555)825-3832
(555)225-5388
(555)225-5288
(555)225-5288
(555)585-5528
(555)225-5288
(555)255-5558
(555)228-5288
(555)225-5288
(555)251-8761
(555)451-2861
(555)225-5288
(555)285-5888
FIVE "BUSINESS TRIPS" IN THE LAST MONTH.
FIVE, GOD DAMN IT!
RECEIPTS FOR WORKS DO NOT TOUCH!

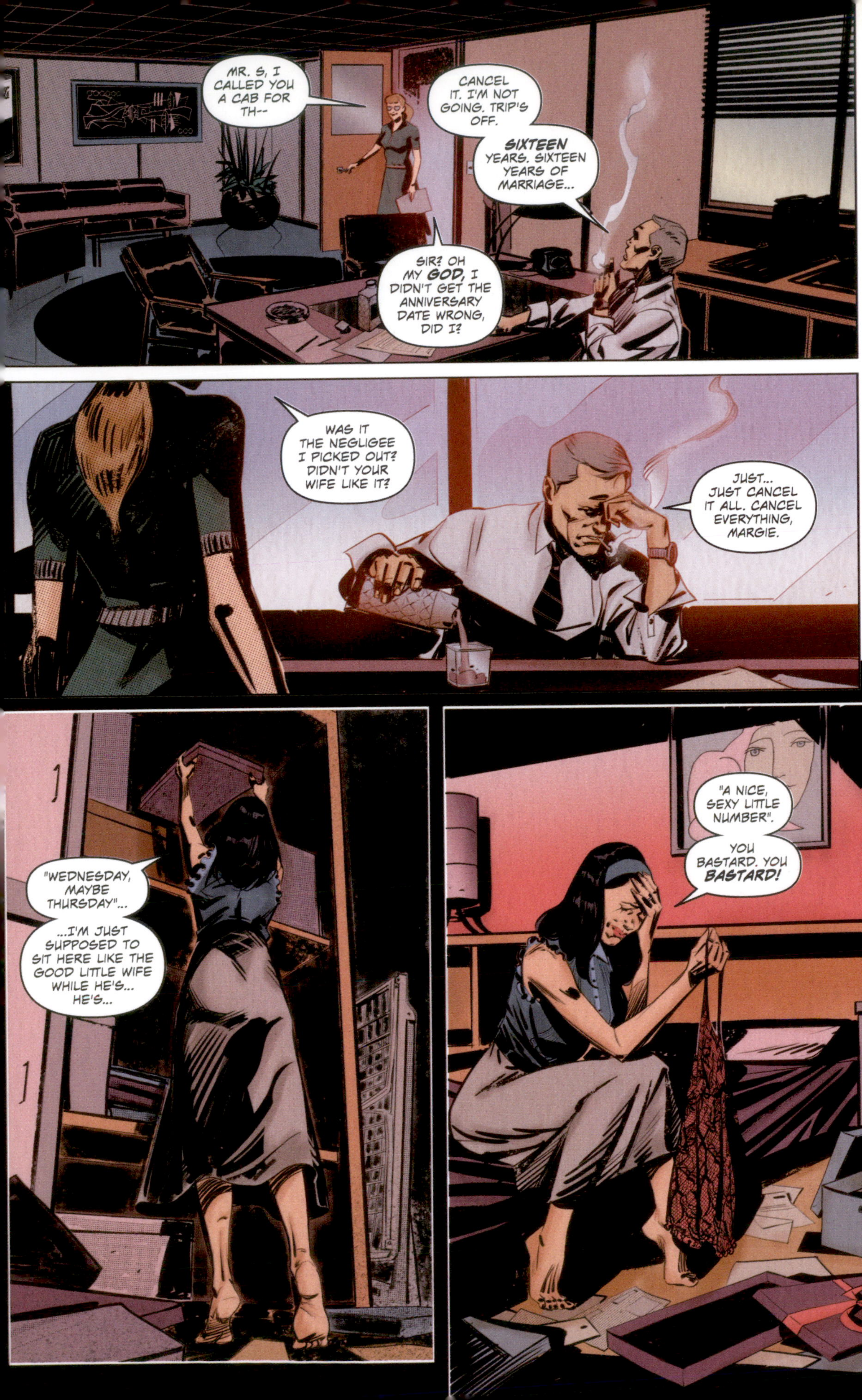
MR. S, I CALLED YOU A CAB FOR TH--
CANCEL IT. I'M NOT GOING. TRIP'S OFF.
SIXTEEN YEARS. SIXTEEN YEARS OF MARRIAGE...
SIR? OH MY GOD, I DIDN'T GET THE ANNIVERSARY DATE WRONG, DID I?
WAS IT THE NEGLIGEE I PICKED OUT? DIDN'T YOUR WIFE LIKE IT?
JUST... JUST CANCEL IT ALL. CANCEL EVERYTHING, MARGIE.
"WEDNESDAY, MAYBE THURSDAY"...
...I'M JUST SUPPOSED TO SIT HERE LIKE THE GOOD LITTLE WIFE WHILE HE'S... HE'S...
"A NICE, SEXY LITTLE NUMBER".
YOU BASTARD. YOU BASTARD!

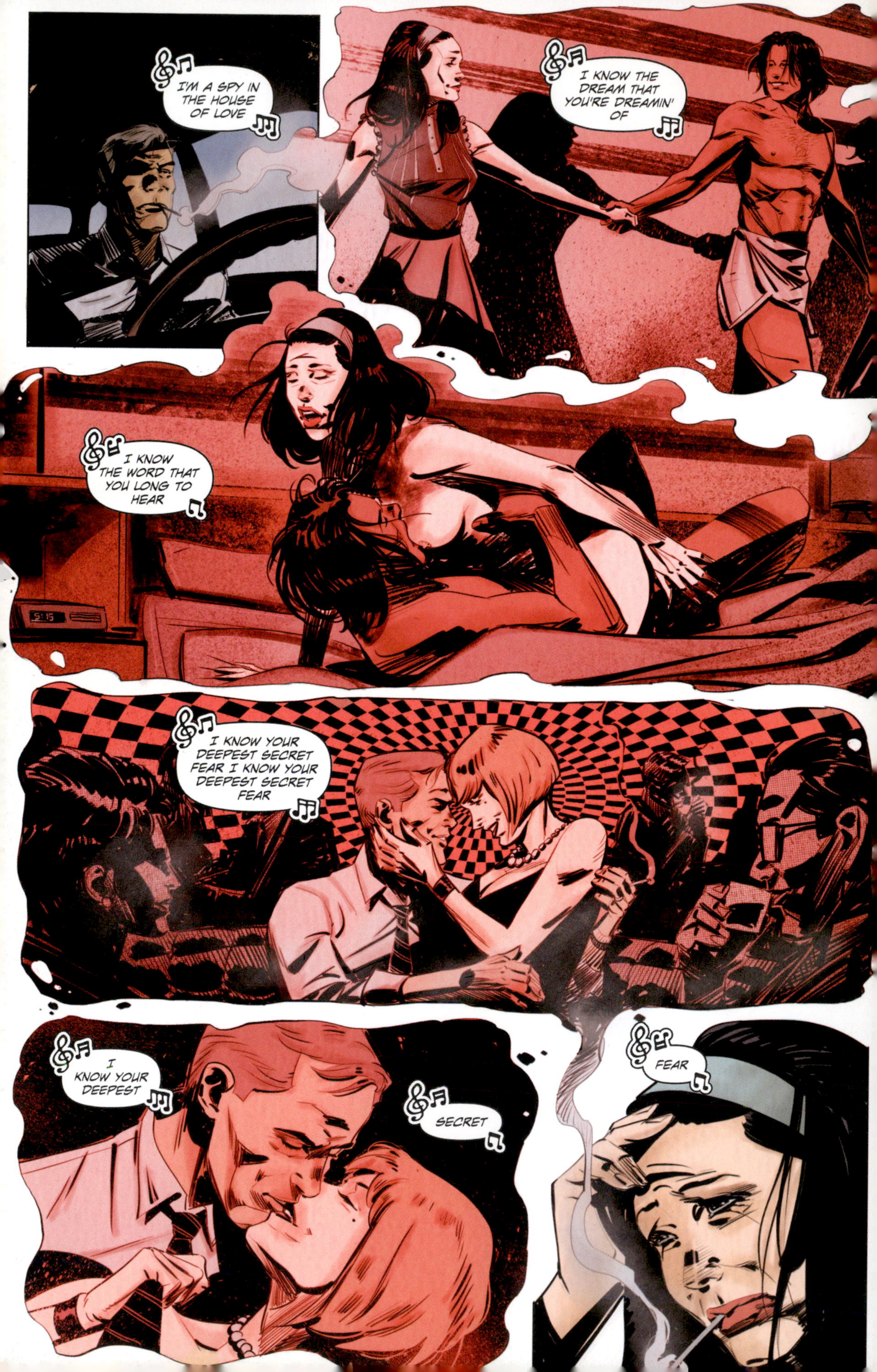
I'M A SPY IN THE HOUSE OF LOVE
I KNOW THE DREAM THAT YOU'RE DREAMIN' OF
I KNOW THE WORD THAT YOU LONG TO HEAR
I KNOW YOUR DEEPEST SECRET FEAR I KNOW YOUR DEEPEST SECRET FEAR
I KNOW YOUR DEEPEST
SECRET
FEAR

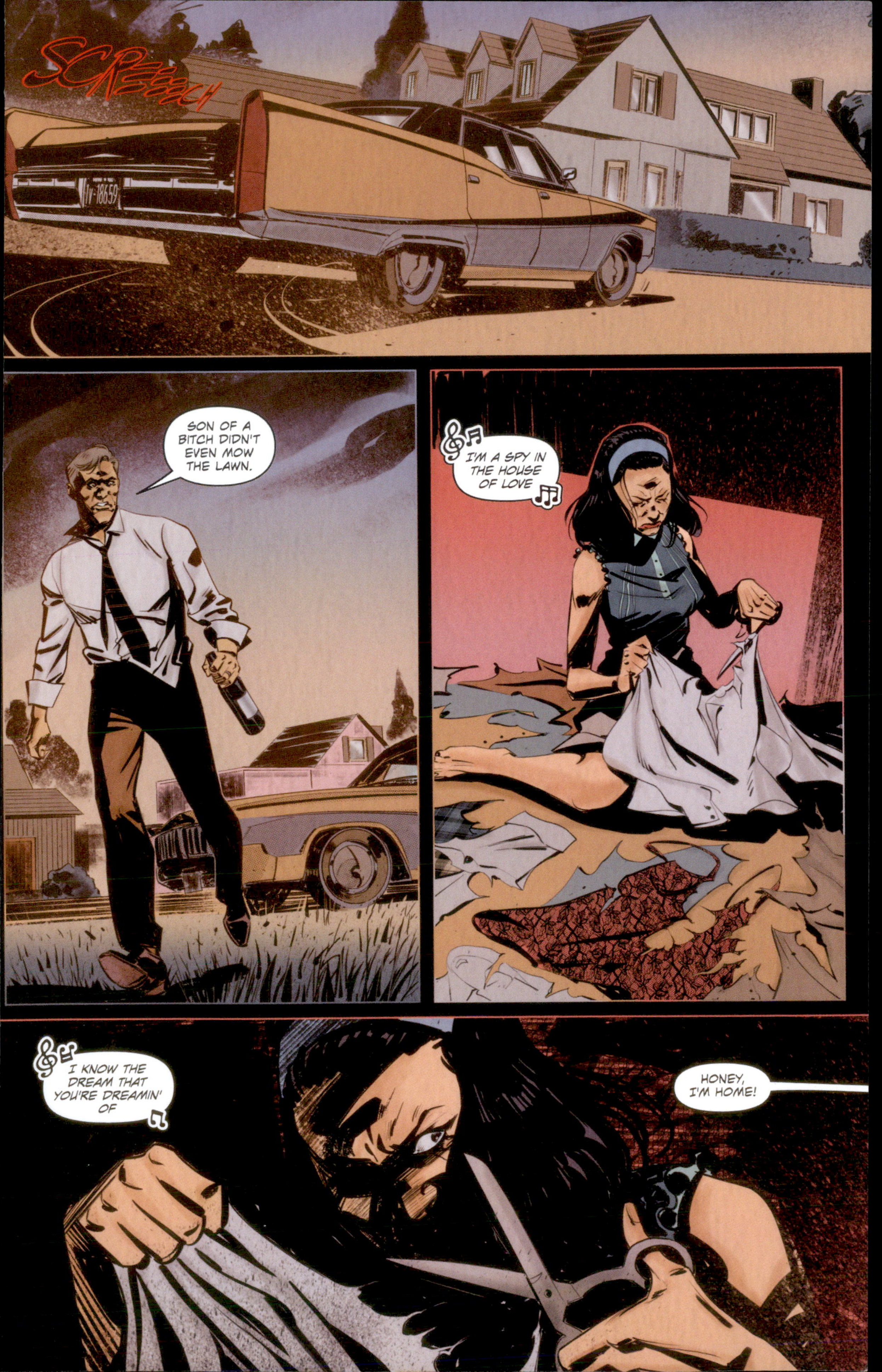
SCREEECH
SON OF A BITCH DIDN'T EVEN MOW THE LAWN.
I'M A SPY IN THE HOUSE OF LOVE
I KNOW THE DREAM THAT YOU'RE DREAMIN' OF
HONEY, I'M HOME!

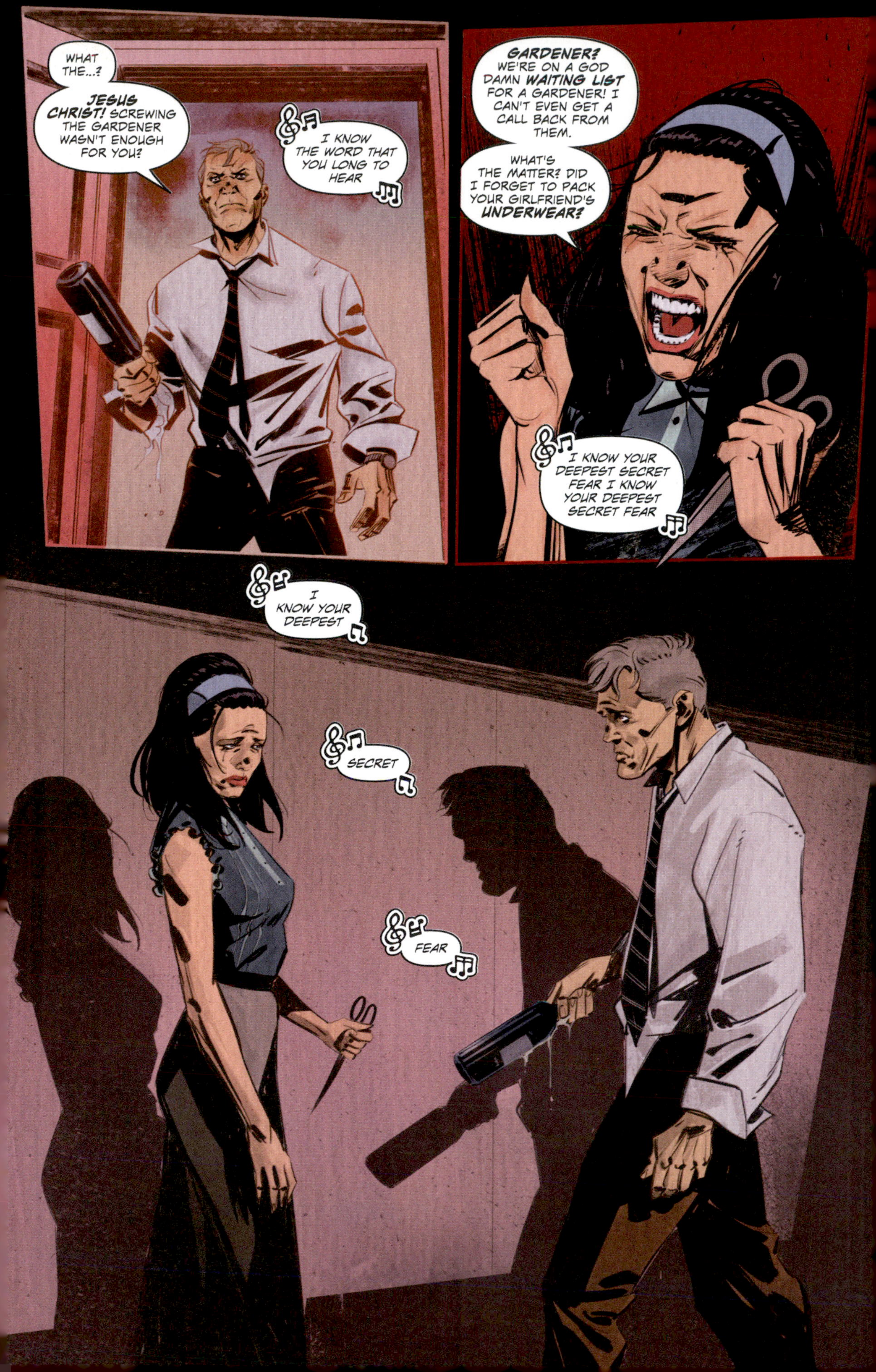
WHAT THE...?
JESUS CHRIST! SCREWING THE GARDENER WASN'T ENOUGH FOR YOU?
I KNOW THE WORD THAT YOU LONG TO HEAR
GARDENER? WE'RE ON A GOD DAMN WAITING LIST FOR A GARDENER! I CAN'T EVEN GET A CALL BACK FROM THEM.
WHAT'S THE MATTER? DID I FORGET TO PACK YOUR GIRLFRIEND'S UNDERWEAR?
I KNOW YOUR DEEPEST SECRET FEAR I KNOW YOUR DEEPEST SECRET FEAR
I KNOW YOUR DEEPEST
SECRET
FEAR

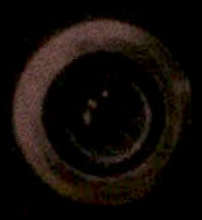

Queen of the Highway

Artist . . . Vasilis Lolos

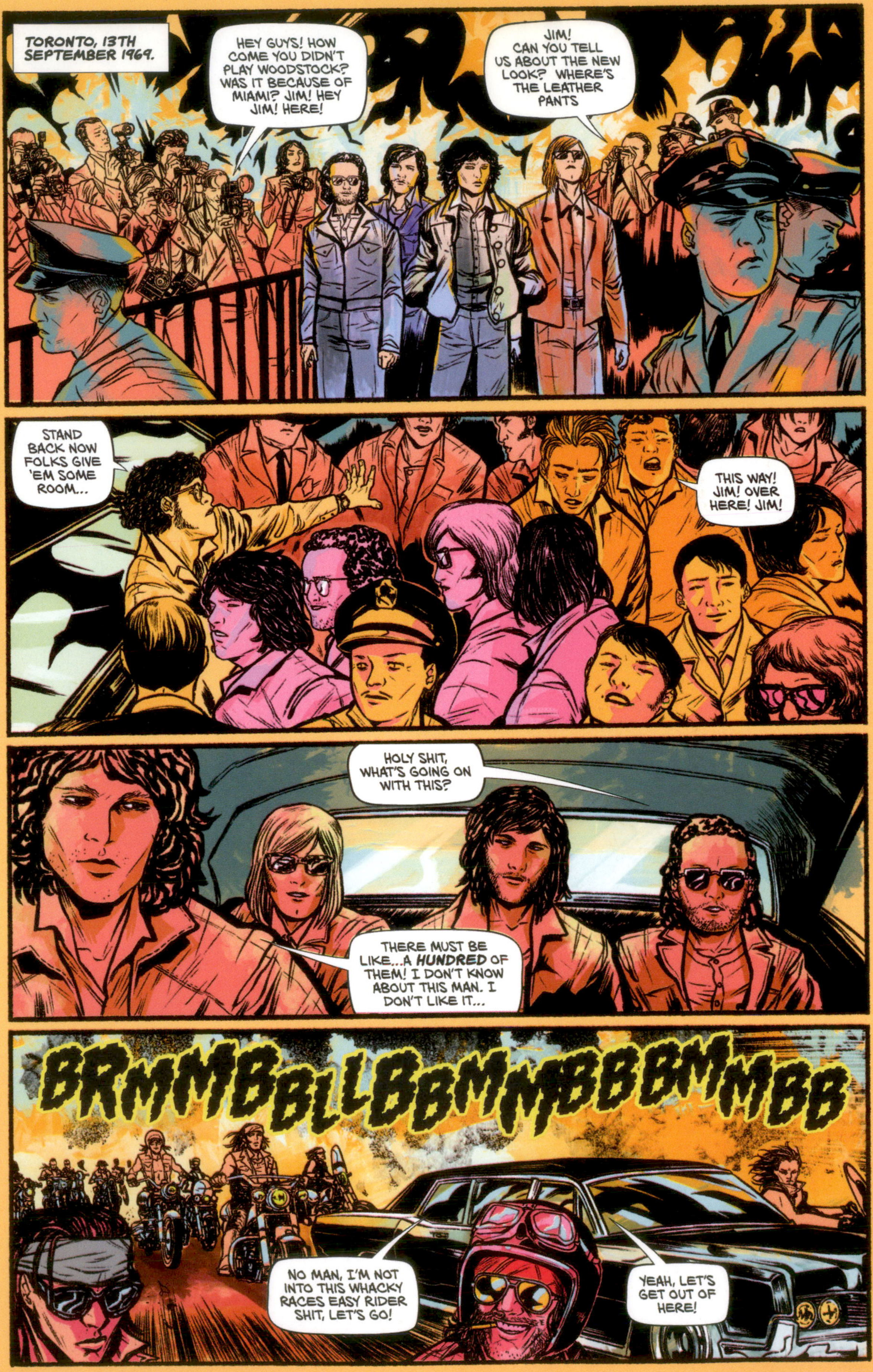
TORONTO, 13TH SEPTEMBER 1969.
HEY GUYS! HOW COME YOU DIDN'T PLAY WOODSTOCK? WAS IT BECAUSE OF MIAMI? JIM! HEY JIM! HERE!
JIM! CAN YOU TELL US ABOUT THE NEW LOOK? WHERE'S THE LEATHER PANTS
STAND BACK NOW FOLKS GIVE 'EM SOME ROOM...
THIS WAY! JIM! OVER HERE! JIM!
HOLY SHIT, WHAT'S GOING ON WITH THIS?
THERE MUST BE LIKE...A HUNDRED OF THEM! I DON'T KNOW ABOUT THIS MAN. I DON'T LIKE IT...
BRMMBBLLBBMMBBBMMBB
NO MAN, I'M NOT INTO THIS WHACKY RACES EASY RIDER SHIT, LET'S GO!
YEAH, LET'S GET OUT OF HERE!

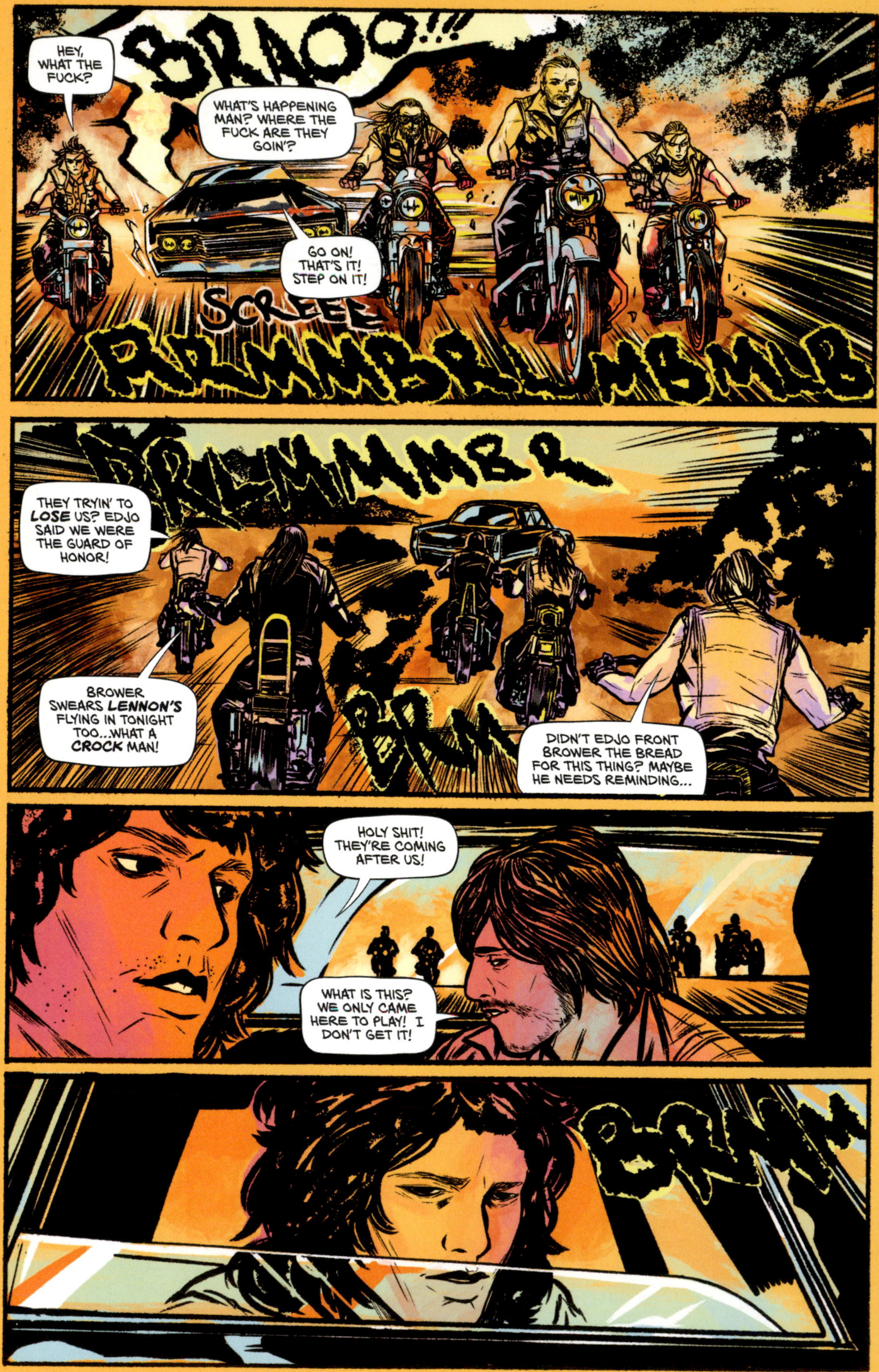
BRAOO!!!
HEY, WHAT THE FUCK?
WHAT'S HAPPENING MAN? WHERE THE FUCK ARE THEY GOIN'?
GO ON! THAT'S IT! STEP ON IT!
SCREEE
RRUMMBRUUMBMUB
BRUMMMBR
THEY TRYIN' TO LOSE US? EDJO SAID WE WERE THE GUARD OF HONOR!
BROWER SWEARS LENNON'S FLYING IN TONIGHT TOO...WHAT A CROCK MAN!
BRM
DIDN'T EDJO FRONT BROWER THE BREAD FOR THIS THING? MAYBE HE NEEDS REMINDING...
HOLY SHIT! THEY'RE COMING AFTER US!
WHAT IS THIS? WE ONLY CAME HERE TO PLAY! I DON'T GET IT!
BRMM

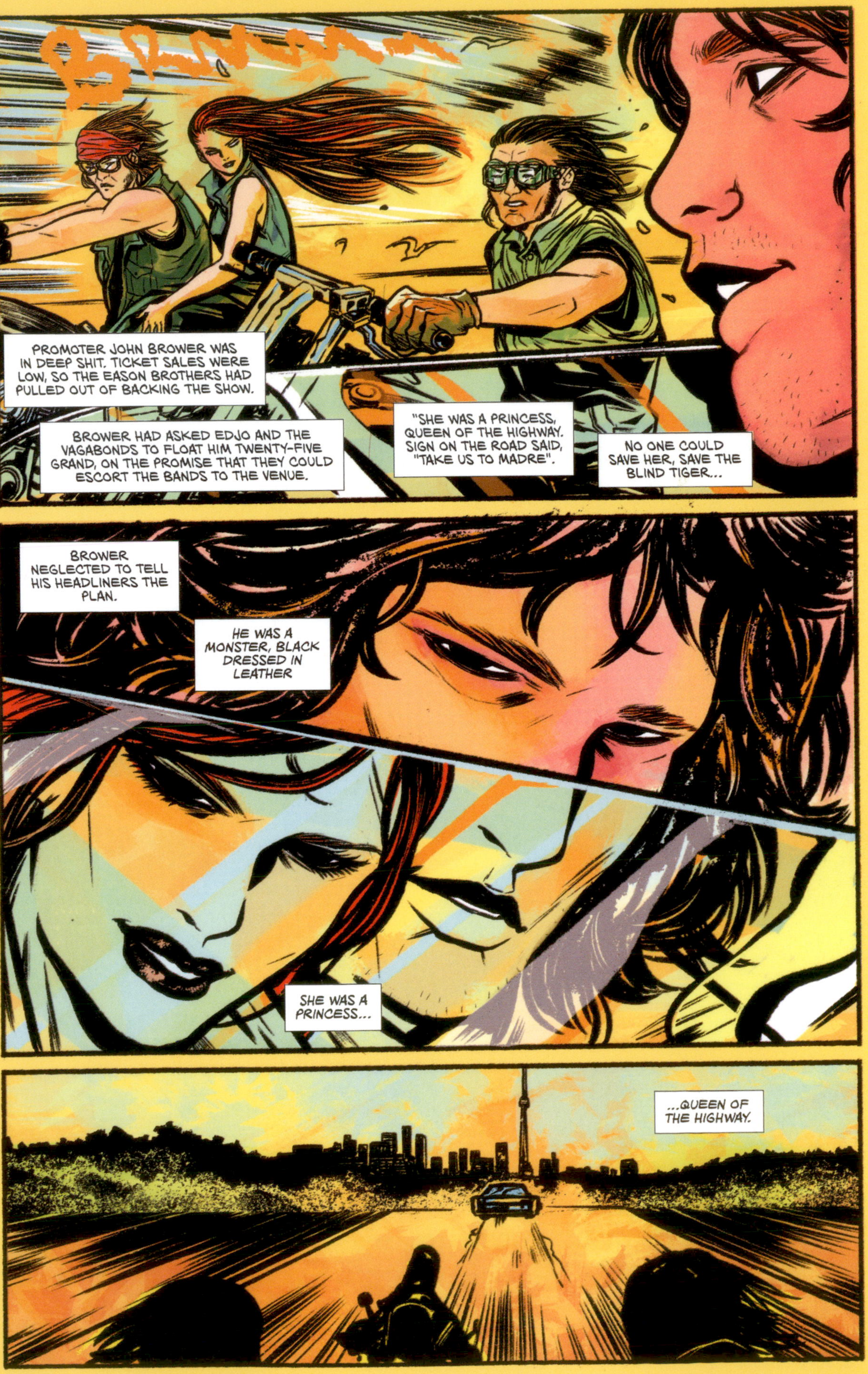
BRMMM
PROMOTER JOHN BROWER WAS IN DEEP SHIT. TICKET SALES WERE LOW, SO THE EASON BROTHERS HAD PULLED OUT OF BACKING THE SHOW.
BROWER HAD ASKED EDJO AND THE VAGABONDS TO FLOAT HIM TWENTY-FIVE GRAND, ON THE PROMISE THAT THEY COULD ESCORT THE BANDS TO THE VENUE.
"SHE WAS A PRINCESS, QUEEN OF THE HIGHWAY. SIGN ON THE ROAD SAID, "TAKE US TO MADRE".
NO ONE COULD SAVE HER, SAVE THE BLIND TIGER...
BROWER NEGLECTED TO TELL HIS HEADLINERS THE PLAN.
HE WAS A MONSTER, BLACK DRESSED IN LEATHER
SHE WAS A PRINCESS...
...QUEEN OF THE HIGHWAY.

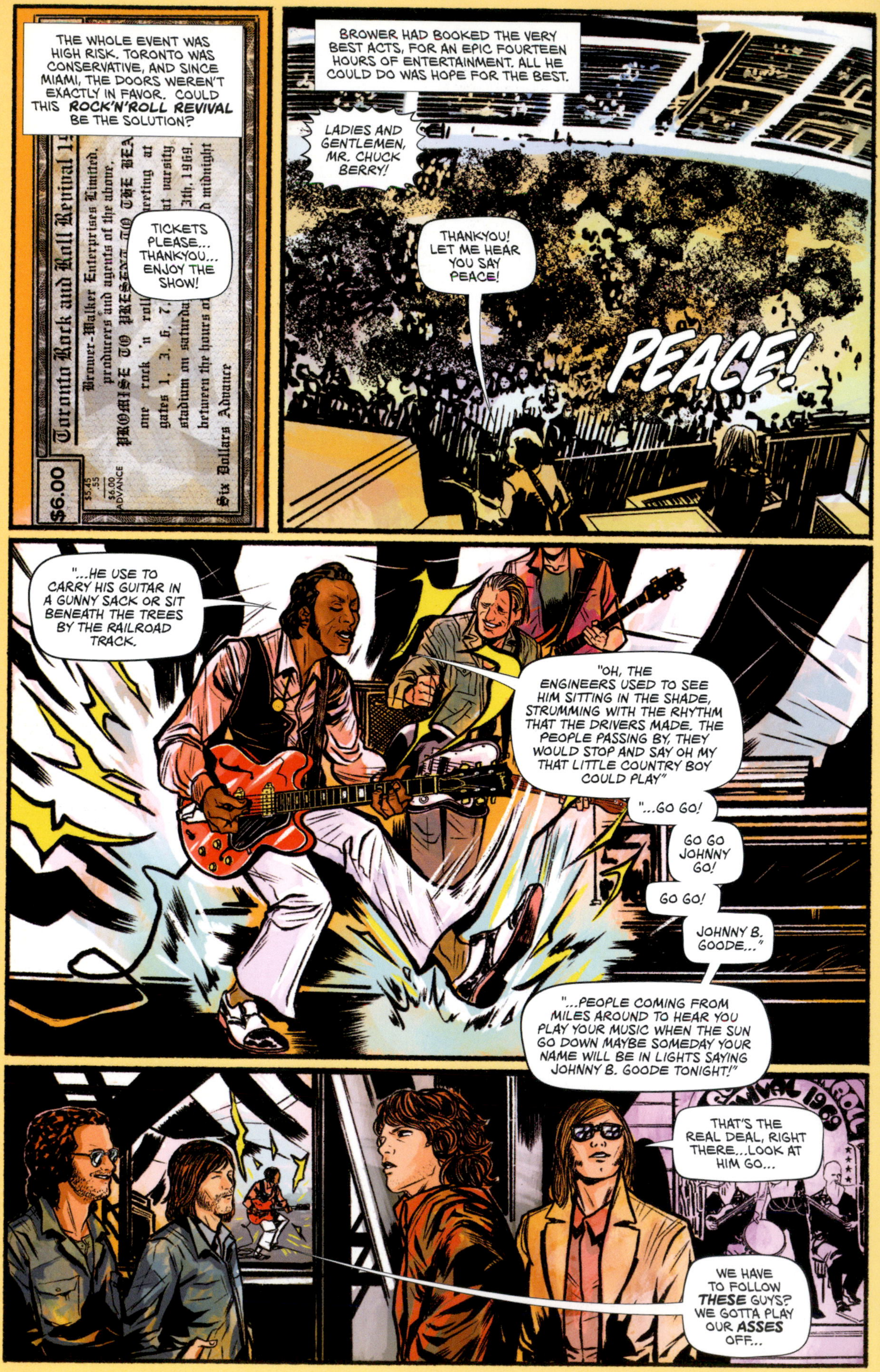
THE WHOLE EVENT WAS HIGH RISK. TORONTO WAS CONSERVATIVE, AND SINCE MIAMI, THE DOORS WEREN'T EXACTLY IN FAVOR. COULD THIS ROCK'N'ROLL REVIVAL BE THE SOLUTION?
Toronto Rock and Roll Revival
Brower-Walker Enterprises Limited,
producers and agents of the above,
Six Dollars Advance
$6.00
TICKETS PLEASE... THANKYOU... ENJOY THE SHOW!
BROWER HAD BOOKED THE VERY BEST ACTS, FOR AN EPIC FOURTEEN HOURS OF ENTERTAINMENT. ALL HE COULD DO WAS HOPE FOR THE BEST.
LADIES AND GENTLEMEN, MR. CHUCK BERRY!
THANKYOU! LET ME HEAR YOU SAY PEACE!
PEACE!
"...HE USE TO CARRY HIS GUITAR IN A GUNNY SACK OR SIT BENEATH THE TREES BY THE RAILROAD TRACK.
"OH, THE ENGINEERS USED TO SEE HIM SITTING IN THE SHADE, STRUMMING WITH THE RHYTHM THAT THE DRIVERS MADE. THE PEOPLE PASSING BY, THEY WOULD STOP AND SAY OH MY THAT LITTLE COUNTRY BOY COULD PLAY"
"...GO GO!
GO GO JOHNNY GO!
GO GO!
JOHNNY B. GOODE..."
"...PEOPLE COMING FROM MILES AROUND TO HEAR YOU PLAY YOUR MUSIC WHEN THE SUN GO DOWN MAYBE SOMEDAY YOUR NAME WILL BE IN LIGHTS SAYING JOHNNY B. GOODE TONIGHT!"
THAT'S THE REAL DEAL, RIGHT THERE...LOOK AT HIM GO...
WE HAVE TO FOLLOW THESE GUYS? WE GOTTA PLAY OUR ASSES OFF...

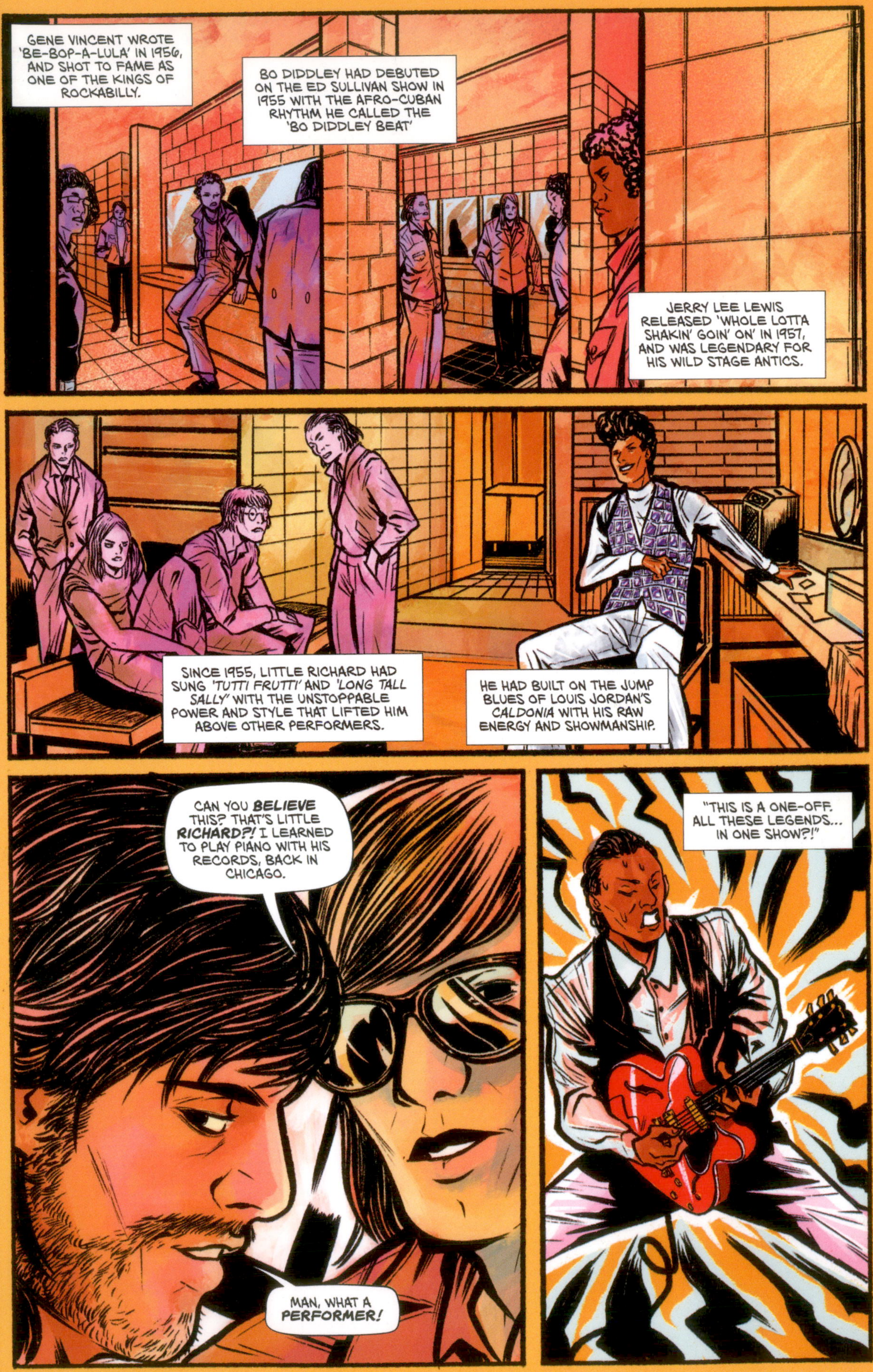
GENE VINCENT WROTE 'BE-BOP-A-LULA' IN 1956, AND SHOT TO FAME AS ONE OF THE KINGS OF ROCKABILLY.
BO DIDDLEY HAD DEBUTED ON THE ED SULLIVAN SHOW IN 1955 WITH THE AFRO-CUBAN RHYTHM HE CALLED THE 'BO DIDDLEY BEAT'
JERRY LEE LEWIS RELEASED 'WHOLE LOTTA SHAKIN' GOIN' ON' IN 1957, AND WAS LEGENDARY FOR HIS WILD STAGE ANTICS.
SINCE 1955, LITTLE RICHARD HAD SUNG *'TUTTI FRUTTI'* AND *'LONG TALL SALLY'* WITH THE UNSTOPPABLE POWER AND STYLE THAT LIFTED HIM ABOVE OTHER PERFORMERS.
HE HAD BUILT ON THE JUMP BLUES OF LOUIS JORDAN'S *CALDONIA* WITH HIS RAW ENERGY AND SHOWMANSHIP.
CAN YOU **BELIEVE** THIS? THAT'S LITTLE ***RICHARD?!*** I LEARNED TO PLAY PIANO WITH HIS RECORDS, BACK IN CHICAGO.
MAN, WHAT A ***PERFORMER!***
"THIS IS A ONE-OFF. ALL THESE LEGENDS... IN ONE SHOW?!"

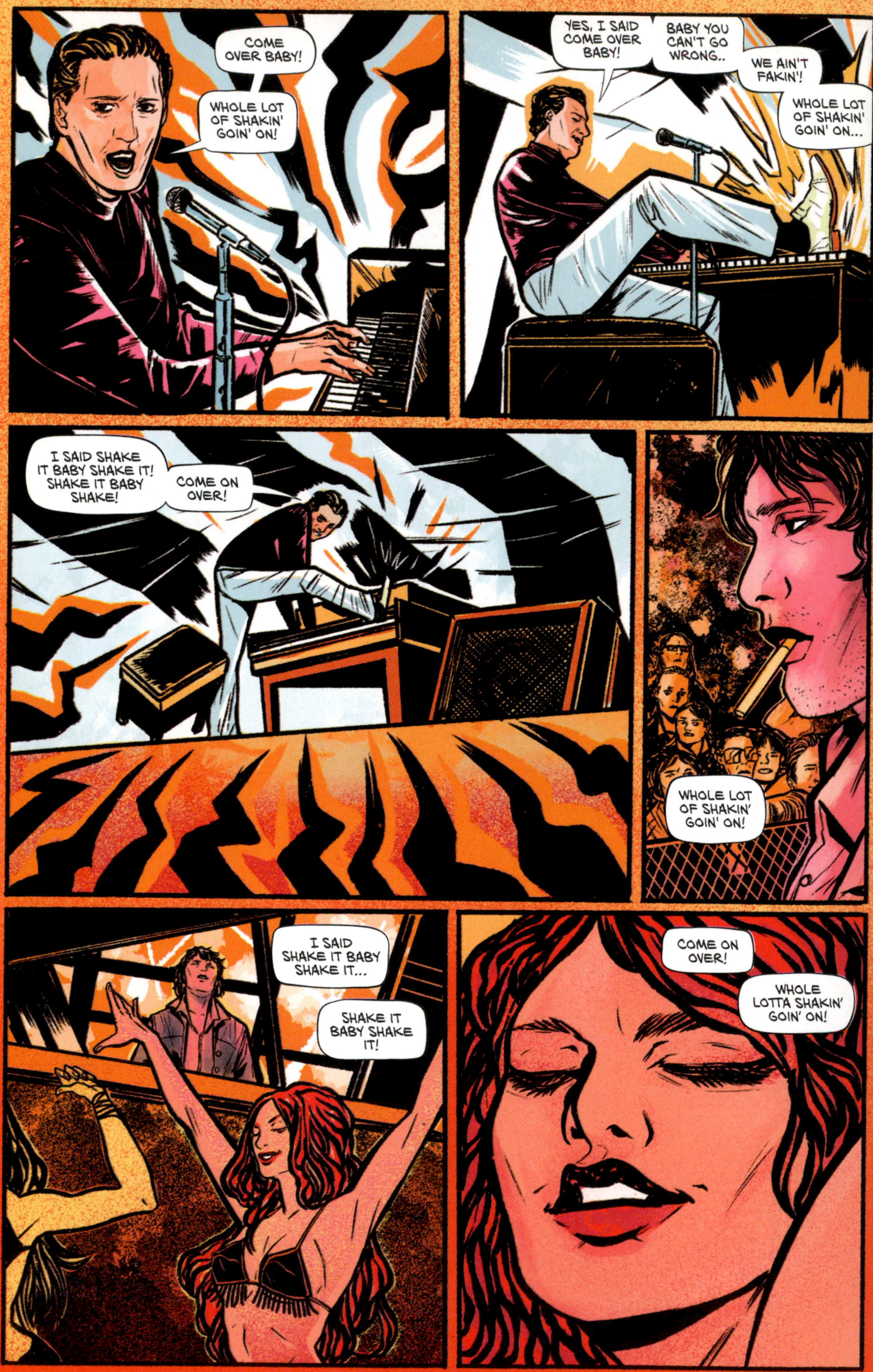
COME OVER BABY!
WHOLE LOT OF SHAKIN' GOIN' ON!
YES, I SAID COME OVER BABY!
BABY YOU CAN'T GO WRONG..
WE AIN'T FAKIN'!
WHOLE LOT OF SHAKIN' GOIN' ON...
I SAID SHAKE IT BABY SHAKE IT! SHAKE IT BABY SHAKE!
COME ON OVER!
WHOLE LOT OF SHAKIN' GOIN' ON!
I SAID SHAKE IT BABY SHAKE IT...
SHAKE IT BABY SHAKE IT!
COME ON OVER!
WHOLE LOTTA SHAKIN' GOIN' ON!

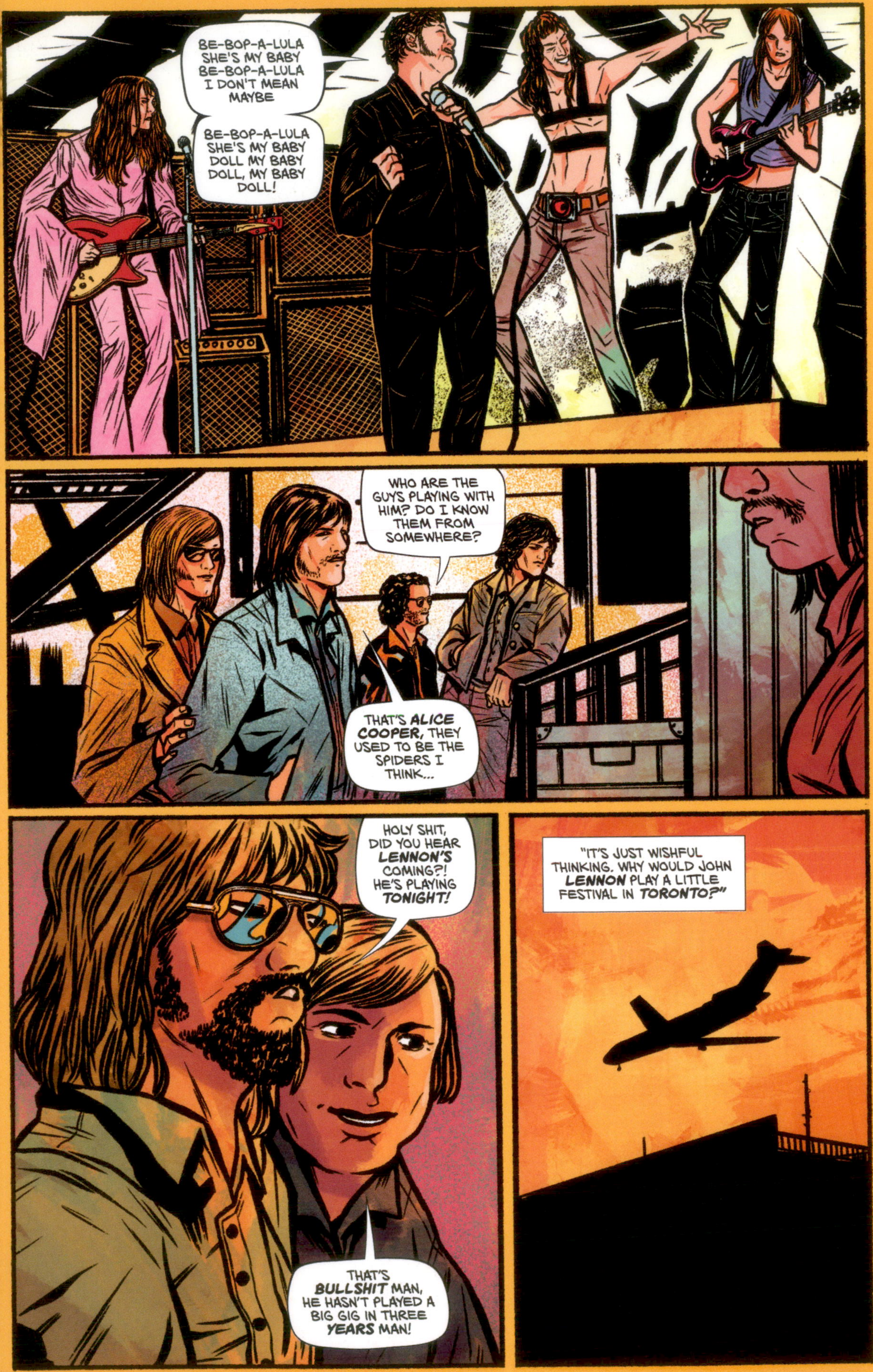
BE-BOP-A-LULA SHE'S MY BABY BE-BOP-A-LULA I DON'T MEAN MAYBE
BE-BOP-A-LULA SHE'S MY BABY DOLL MY BABY DOLL, MY BABY DOLL!
WHO ARE THE GUYS PLAYING WITH HIM? DO I KNOW THEM FROM SOMEWHERE?
THAT'S **ALICE COOPER,** THEY USED TO BE THE SPIDERS I THINK...
HOLY SHIT, DID YOU HEAR **LENNON'S** COMING?! HE'S PLAYING **TONIGHT!**
THAT'S **BULLSHIT** MAN, HE HASN'T PLAYED A BIG GIG IN THREE **YEARS** MAN!
"IT'S JUST WISHFUL THINKING. WHY WOULD JOHN **LENNON** PLAY A LITTLE FESTIVAL IN **TORONTO?"**

JOHN! THIS WAY JOHN! ANY WORDS FOR THE FANS JOHN?

WILL THE BEATLES PLAY AGAIN IN CANADA? JOHN!

WHAT AM I DOING *HERE*? I COULD HAVE GONE TO BRIGHTON!

OH, BLOODY 'ELL!

WHUDDD

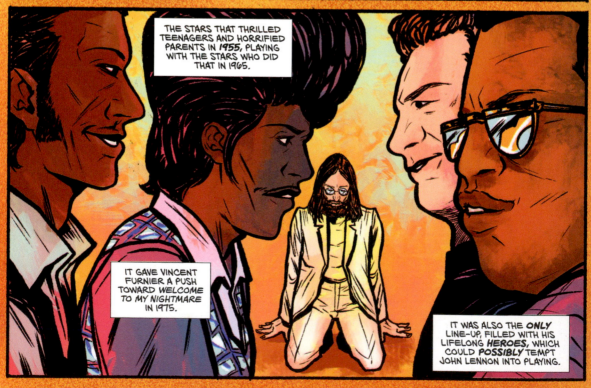

THE STARS THAT THRILLED TEENAGERS AND HORRIFIED PARENTS IN *1955*, PLAYING WITH THE STARS WHO DID THAT IN 1965.

IT GAVE VINCENT FURNIER A PUSH TOWARD *WELCOME TO MY NIGHTMARE* IN 1975.

IT WAS ALSO THE *ONLY* LINE-UP, FILLED WITH HIS LIFELONG *HEROES*, WHICH COULD *POSSIBLY* TEMPT JOHN LENNON INTO PLAYING.

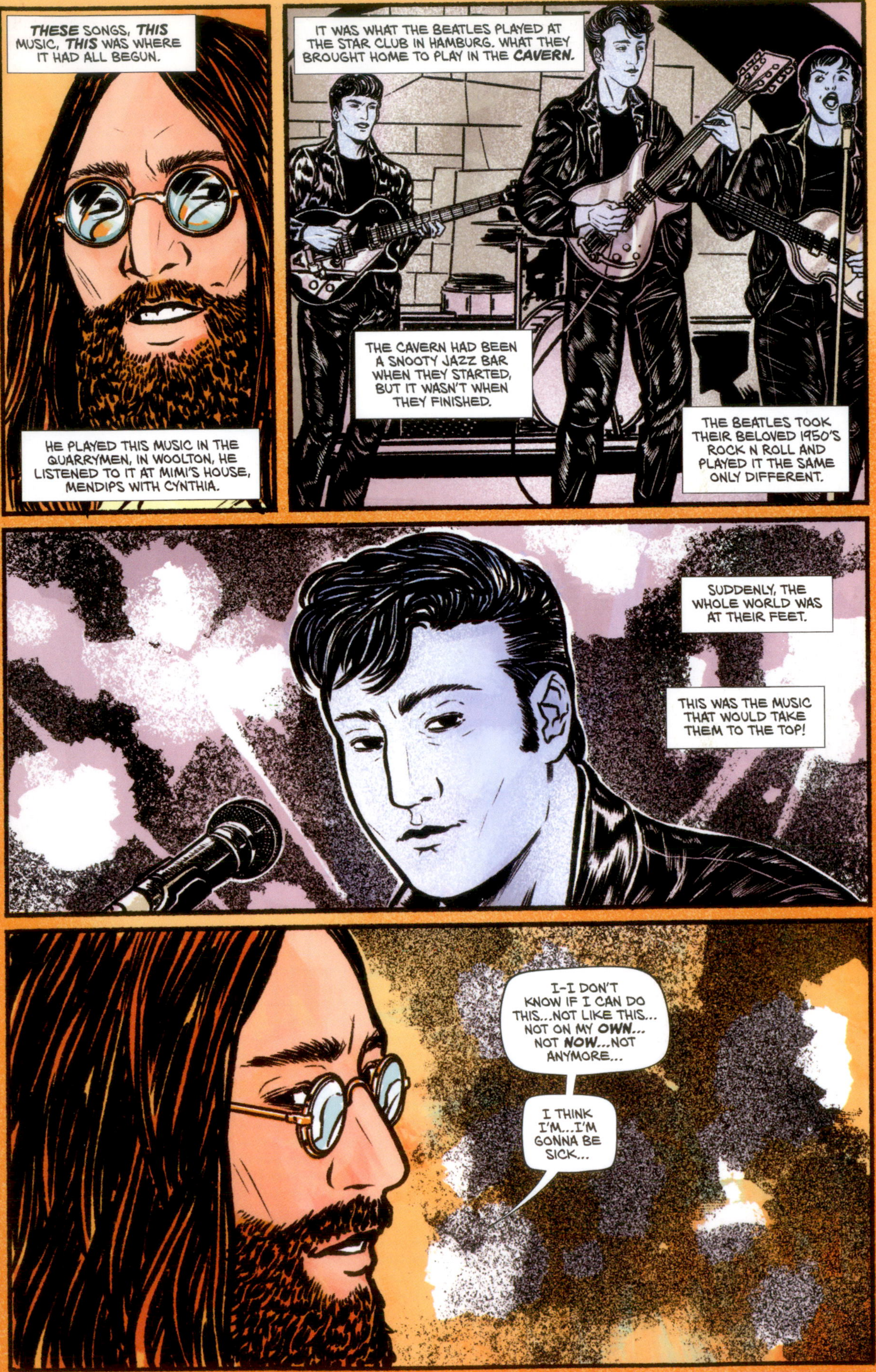
THESE SONGS, THIS MUSIC, THIS WAS WHERE IT HAD ALL BEGUN.
HE PLAYED THIS MUSIC IN THE QUARRYMEN, IN WOOLTON, HE LISTENED TO IT AT MIMI'S HOUSE, MENDIPS WITH CYNTHIA.
IT WAS WHAT THE BEATLES PLAYED AT THE STAR CLUB IN HAMBURG. WHAT THEY BROUGHT HOME TO PLAY IN THE CAVERN.
THE CAVERN HAD BEEN A SNOOTY JAZZ BAR WHEN THEY STARTED, BUT IT WASN'T WHEN THEY FINISHED.
THE BEATLES TOOK THEIR BELOVED 1950'S ROCK N ROLL AND PLAYED IT THE SAME ONLY DIFFERENT.
SUDDENLY, THE WHOLE WORLD WAS AT THEIR FEET.
THIS WAS THE MUSIC THAT WOULD TAKE THEM TO THE TOP!
I-I DON'T KNOW IF I CAN DO THIS...NOT LIKE THIS... NOT ON MY OWN... NOT NOW...NOT ANYMORE...
I THINK I'M...I'M GONNA BE SICK...

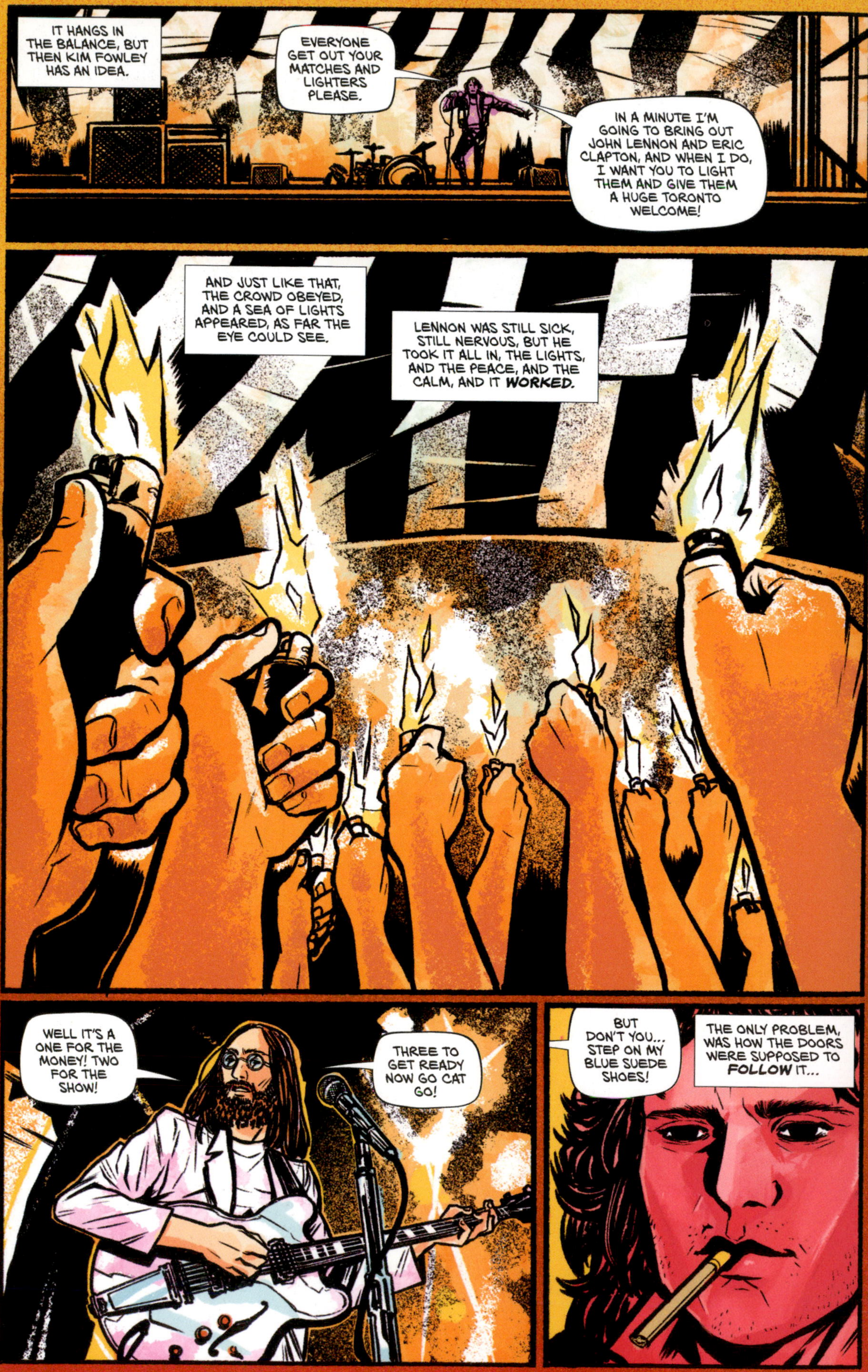
IT HANGS IN THE BALANCE, BUT THEN KIM FOWLEY HAS AN IDEA.
EVERYONE GET OUT YOUR MATCHES AND LIGHTERS PLEASE.
IN A MINUTE I'M GOING TO BRING OUT JOHN LENNON AND ERIC CLAPTON, AND WHEN I DO, I WANT YOU TO LIGHT THEM AND GIVE THEM A HUGE TORONTO WELCOME!
AND JUST LIKE THAT, THE CROWD OBEYED, AND A SEA OF LIGHTS APPEARED, AS FAR THE EYE COULD SEE.
LENNON WAS STILL SICK, STILL NERVOUS, BUT HE TOOK IT ALL IN, THE LIGHTS, AND THE PEACE, AND THE CALM, AND IT ***WORKED.***
WELL IT'S A ONE FOR THE MONEY! TWO FOR THE SHOW!
THREE TO GET READY NOW GO CAT GO!
BUT DON'T YOU... STEP ON MY BLUE SUEDE SHOES!
THE ONLY PROBLEM, WAS HOW THE DOORS WERE SUPPOSED TO ***FOLLOW*** IT...

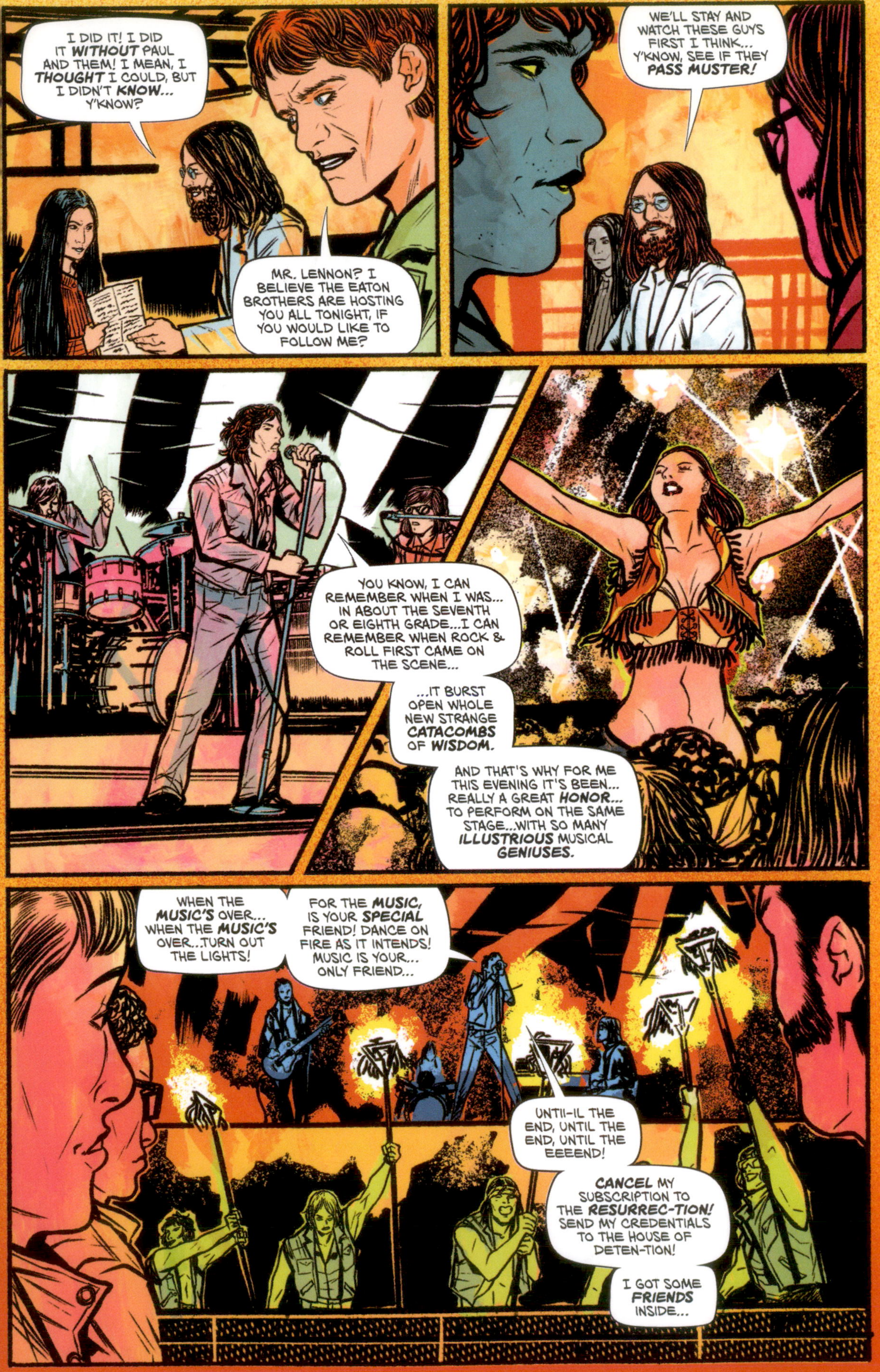
I DID IT! I DID IT WITHOUT PAUL AND THEM! I MEAN, I THOUGHT I COULD, BUT I DIDN'T KNOW... Y'KNOW?
MR. LENNON? I BELIEVE THE EATON BROTHERS ARE HOSTING YOU ALL TONIGHT, IF YOU WOULD LIKE TO FOLLOW ME?
WE'LL STAY AND WATCH THESE GUYS FIRST I THINK... Y'KNOW, SEE IF THEY PASS MUSTER!
YOU KNOW, I CAN REMEMBER WHEN I WAS... IN ABOUT THE SEVENTH OR EIGHTH GRADE...I CAN REMEMBER WHEN ROCK & ROLL FIRST CAME ON THE SCENE...
...IT BURST OPEN WHOLE NEW STRANGE CATACOMBS OF WISDOM.
AND THAT'S WHY FOR ME THIS EVENING IT'S BEEN... REALLY A GREAT HONOR... TO PERFORM ON THE SAME STAGE...WITH SO MANY ILLUSTRIOUS MUSICAL GENIUSES.
WHEN THE MUSIC'S OVER... WHEN THE MUSIC'S OVER...TURN OUT THE LIGHTS!
FOR THE MUSIC, IS YOUR SPECIAL FRIEND! DANCE ON FIRE AS IT INTENDS! MUSIC IS YOUR... ONLY FRIEND...
UNTII-IL THE END, UNTIL THE END, UNTIL THE EEEEND!
CANCEL MY SUBSCRIPTION TO THE RESURREC-TION! SEND MY CREDENTIALS TO THE HOUSE OF DETEN-TION!
I GOT SOME FRIENDS INSIDE...

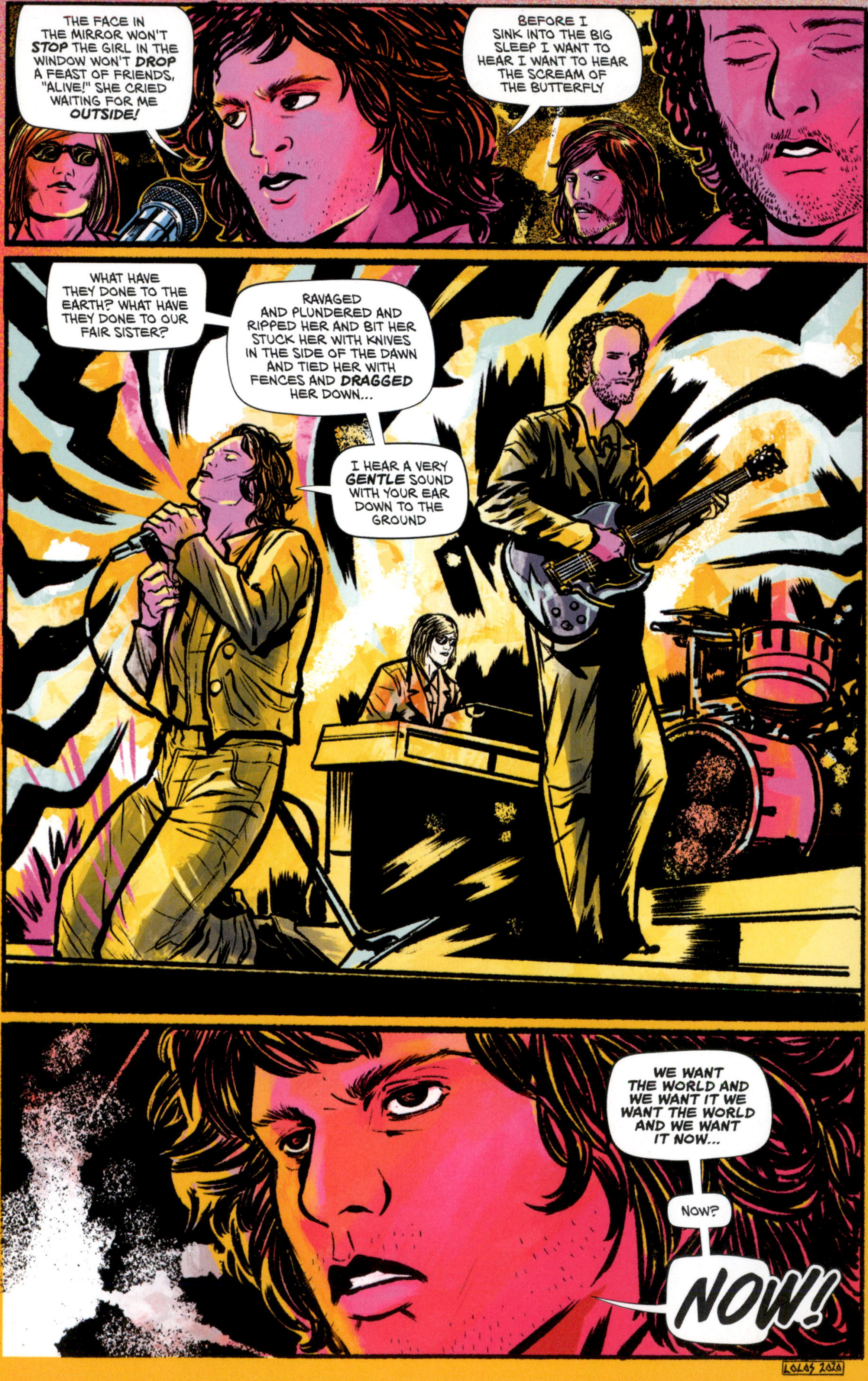
THE FACE IN THE MIRROR WON'T STOP THE GIRL IN THE WINDOW WON'T DROP A FEAST OF FRIENDS, "ALIVE!" SHE CRIED WAITING FOR ME OUTSIDE!
BEFORE I SINK INTO THE BIG SLEEP I WANT TO HEAR I WANT TO HEAR THE SCREAM OF THE BUTTERFLY
WHAT HAVE THEY DONE TO THE EARTH? WHAT HAVE THEY DONE TO OUR FAIR SISTER?
RAVAGED AND PLUNDERED AND RIPPED HER AND BIT HER STUCK HER WITH KNIVES IN THE SIDE OF THE DAWN AND TIED HER WITH FENCES AND DRAGGED HER DOWN...
I HEAR A VERY GENTLE SOUND WITH YOUR EAR DOWN TO THE GROUND
WE WANT THE WORLD AND WE WANT IT WE WANT THE WORLD AND WE WANT IT NOW...
NOW?
NOW!
LOLOS 2020

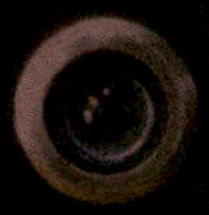

Indian Summer

Artist . . . Jill Thompson

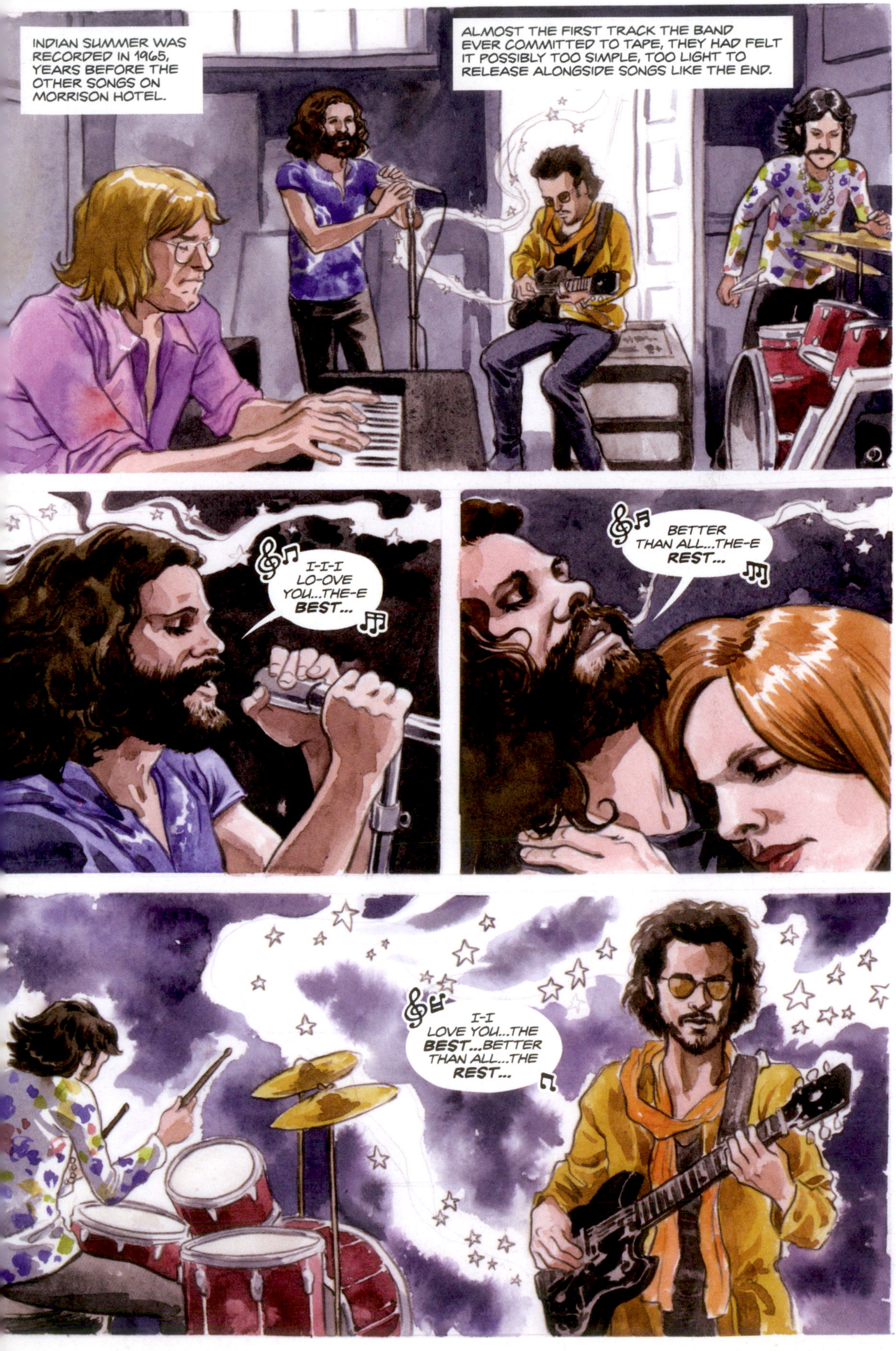
INDIAN SUMMER WAS RECORDED IN 1965, YEARS BEFORE THE OTHER SONGS ON MORRISON HOTEL.
ALMOST THE FIRST TRACK THE BAND EVER COMMITTED TO TAPE, THEY HAD FELT IT POSSIBLY TOO SIMPLE, TOO LIGHT TO RELEASE ALONGSIDE SONGS LIKE THE END.
I-I-I LO-OVE YOU...THE-E BEST...
BETTER THAN ALL...THE-E REST...
I-I LOVE YOU...THE BEST...BETTER THAN ALL...THE REST...

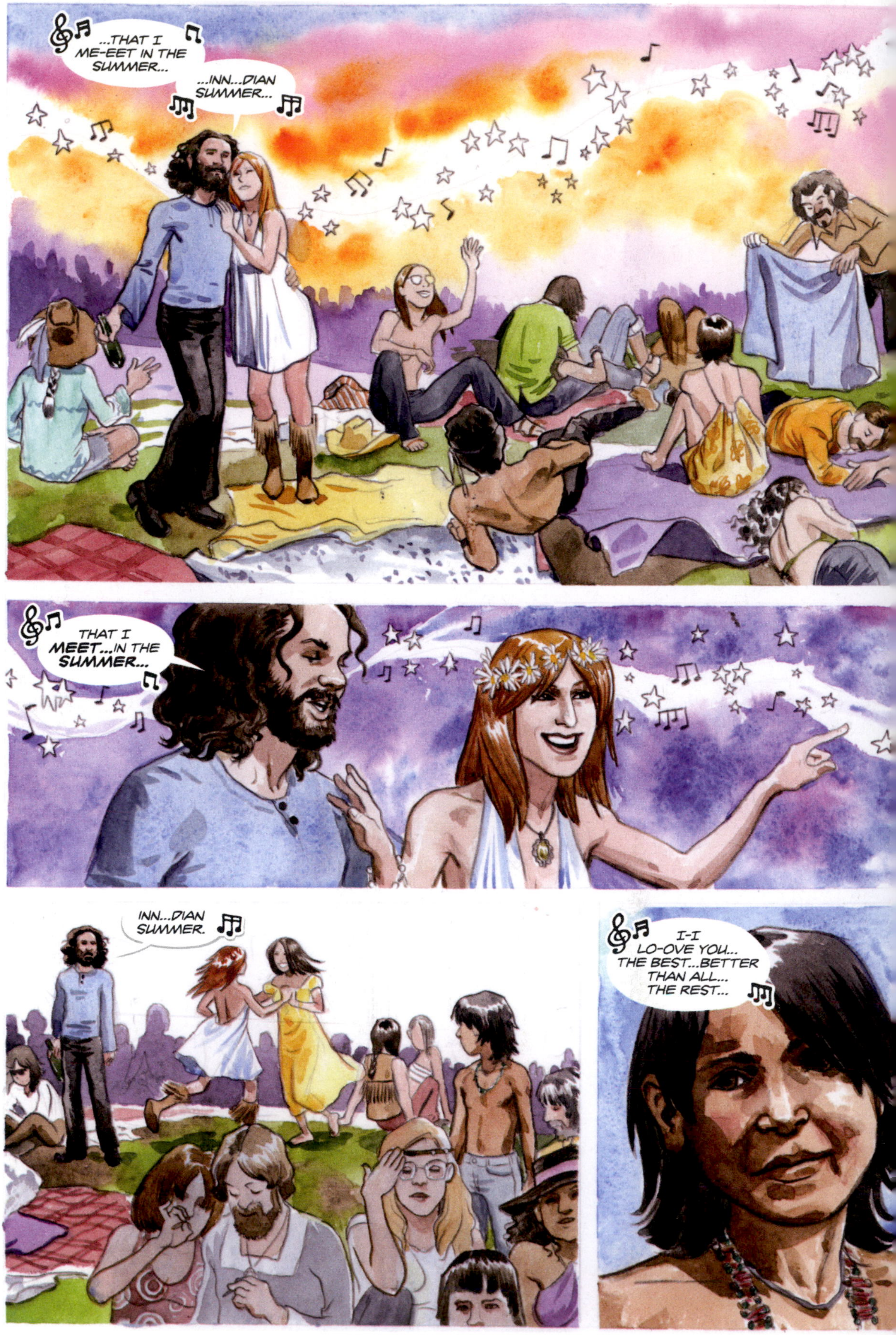
...THAT I ME-EET IN THE SUMMER...
...INN...DIAN SUMMER...
THAT I MEET...IN THE SUMMER...
INN...DIAN SUMMER.
I-I LO-OVE YOU... THE BEST...BETTER THAN ALL... THE REST...

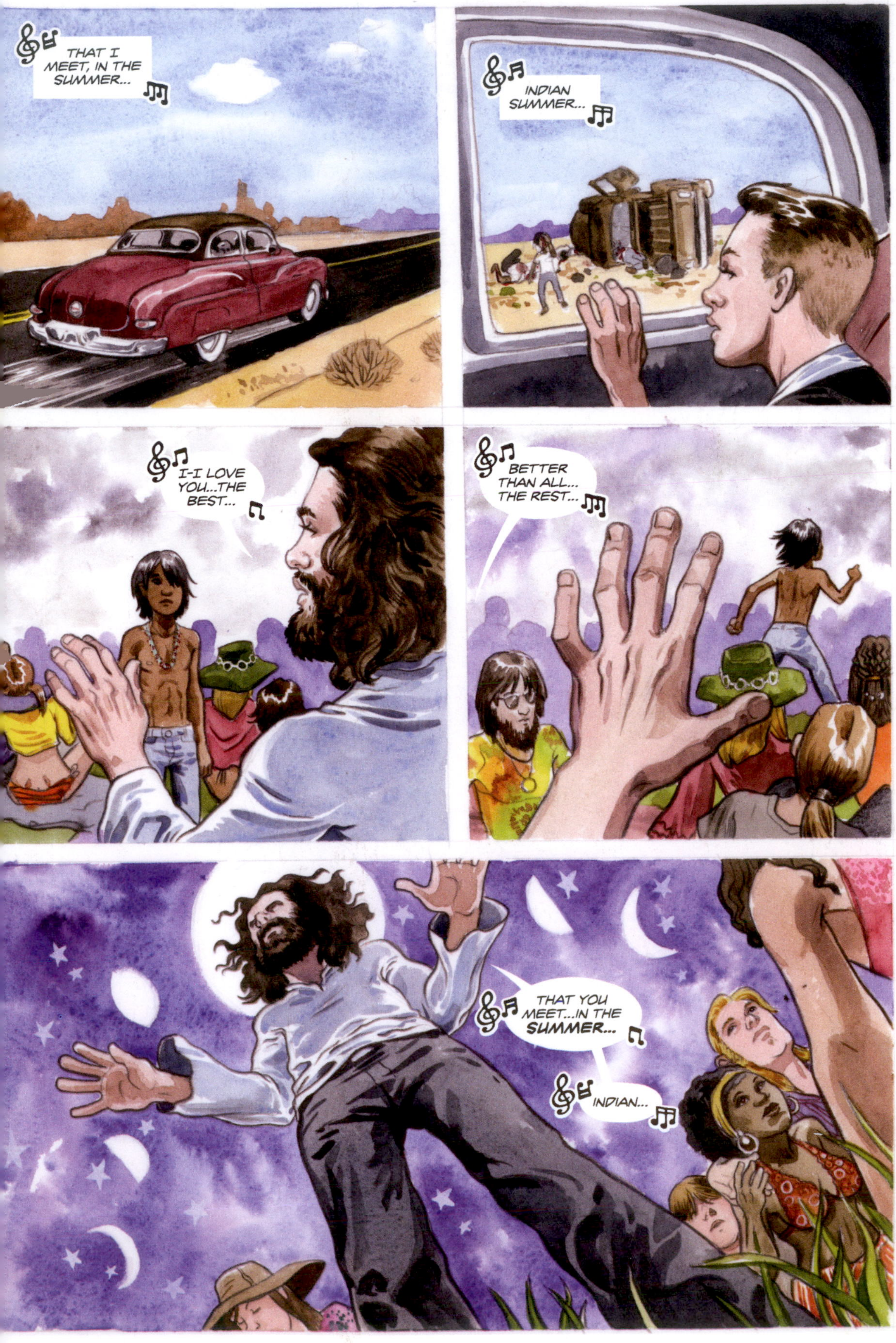
THAT I MEET, IN THE SUMMER...
INDIAN SUMMER...
I-I LOVE YOU...THE BEST...
BETTER THAN ALL... THE REST...
THAT YOU MEET...IN THE SUMMER...
INDIAN...

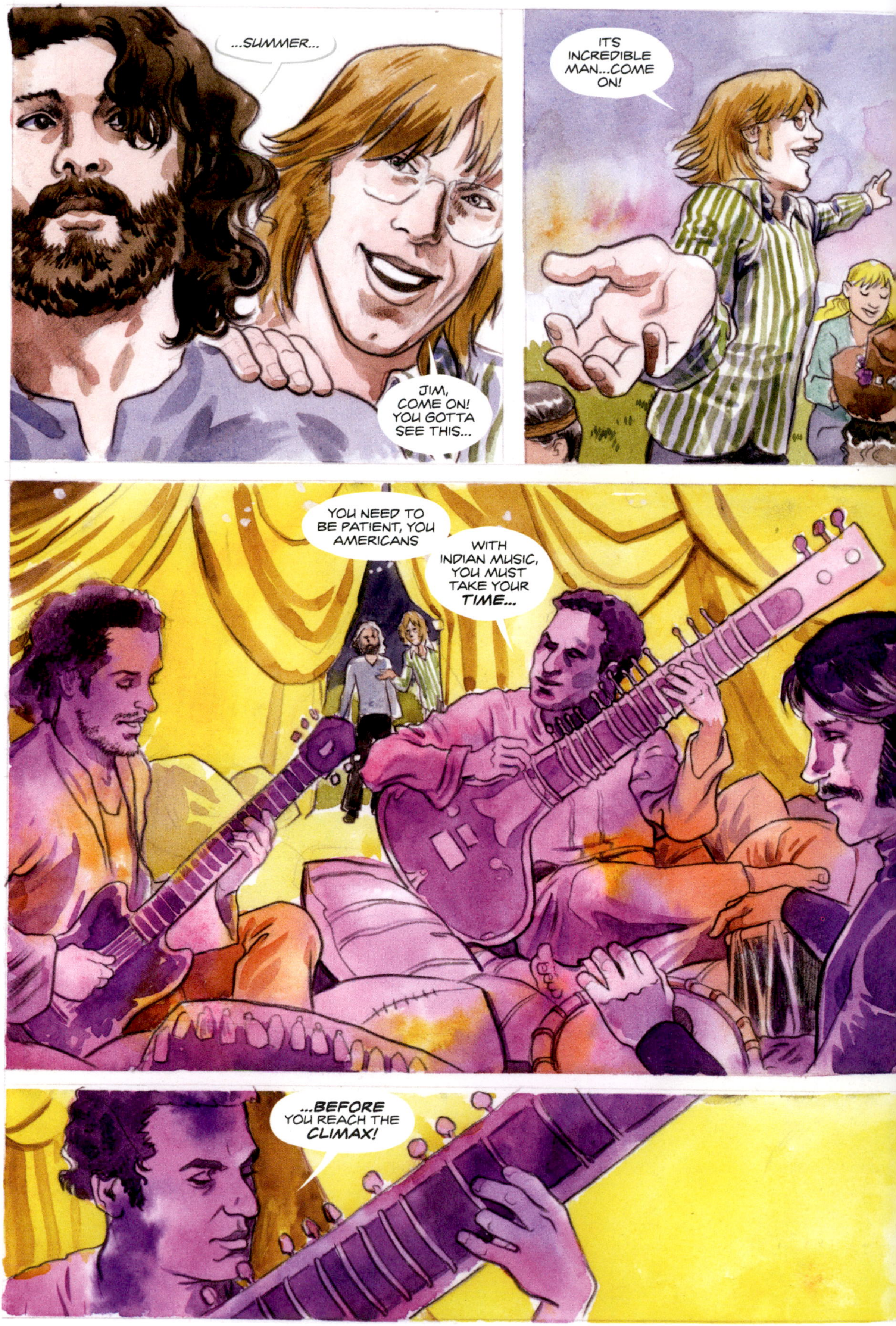
...SUMMER...
JIM, COME ON! YOU GOTTA SEE THIS...
ITS INCREDIBLE MAN...COME ON!
YOU NEED TO BE PATIENT, YOU AMERICANS
WITH INDIAN MUSIC, YOU MUST TAKE YOUR TIME...
...BEFORE YOU REACH THE CLIMAX!

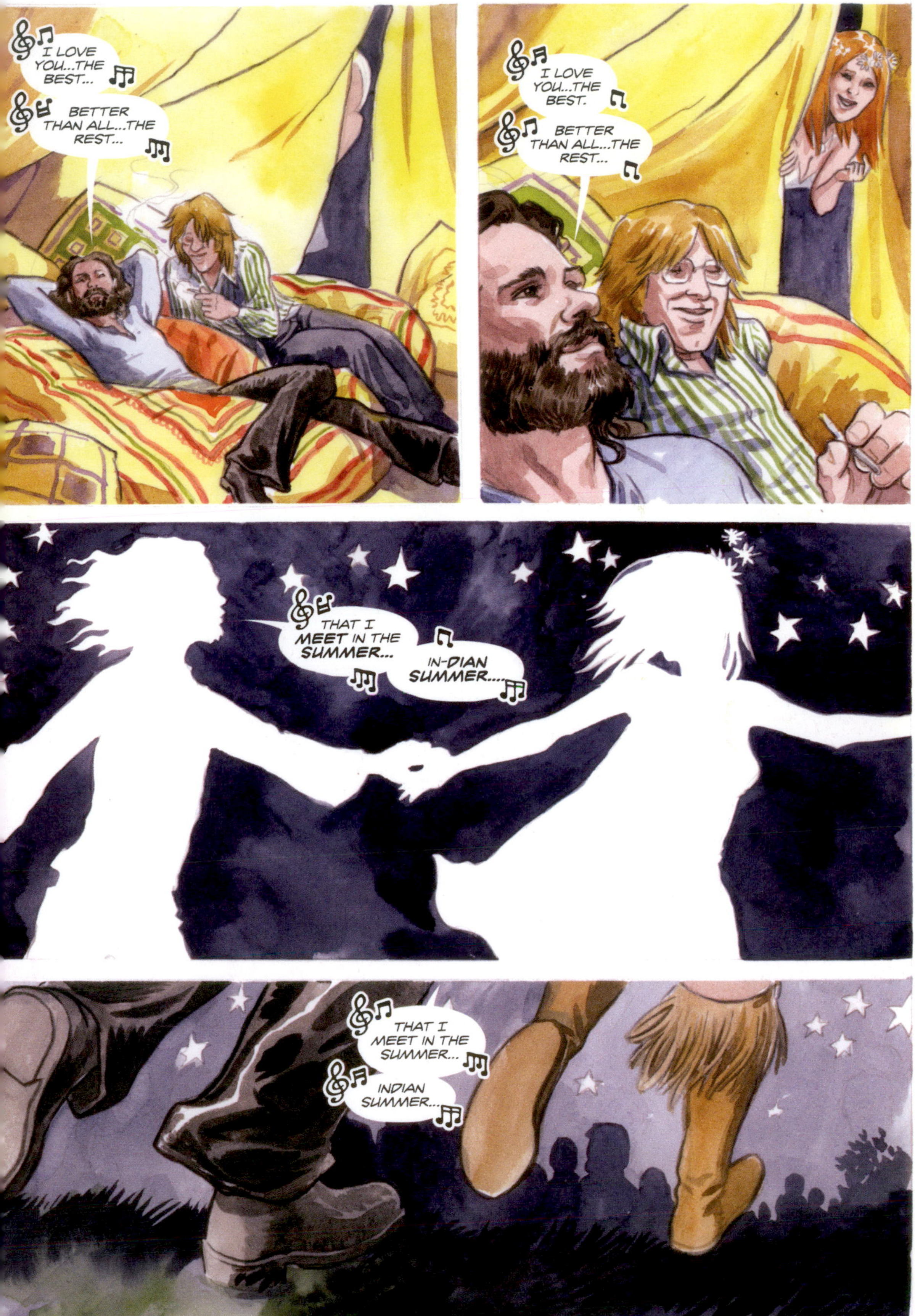
I LOVE YOU...THE BEST...
BETTER THAN ALL...THE REST...
I LOVE YOU...THE BEST.
BETTER THAN ALL...THE REST...
THAT I MEET IN THE SUMMER...
IN-DIAN SUMMER....
THAT I MEET IN THE SUMMER...
INDIAN SUMMER...

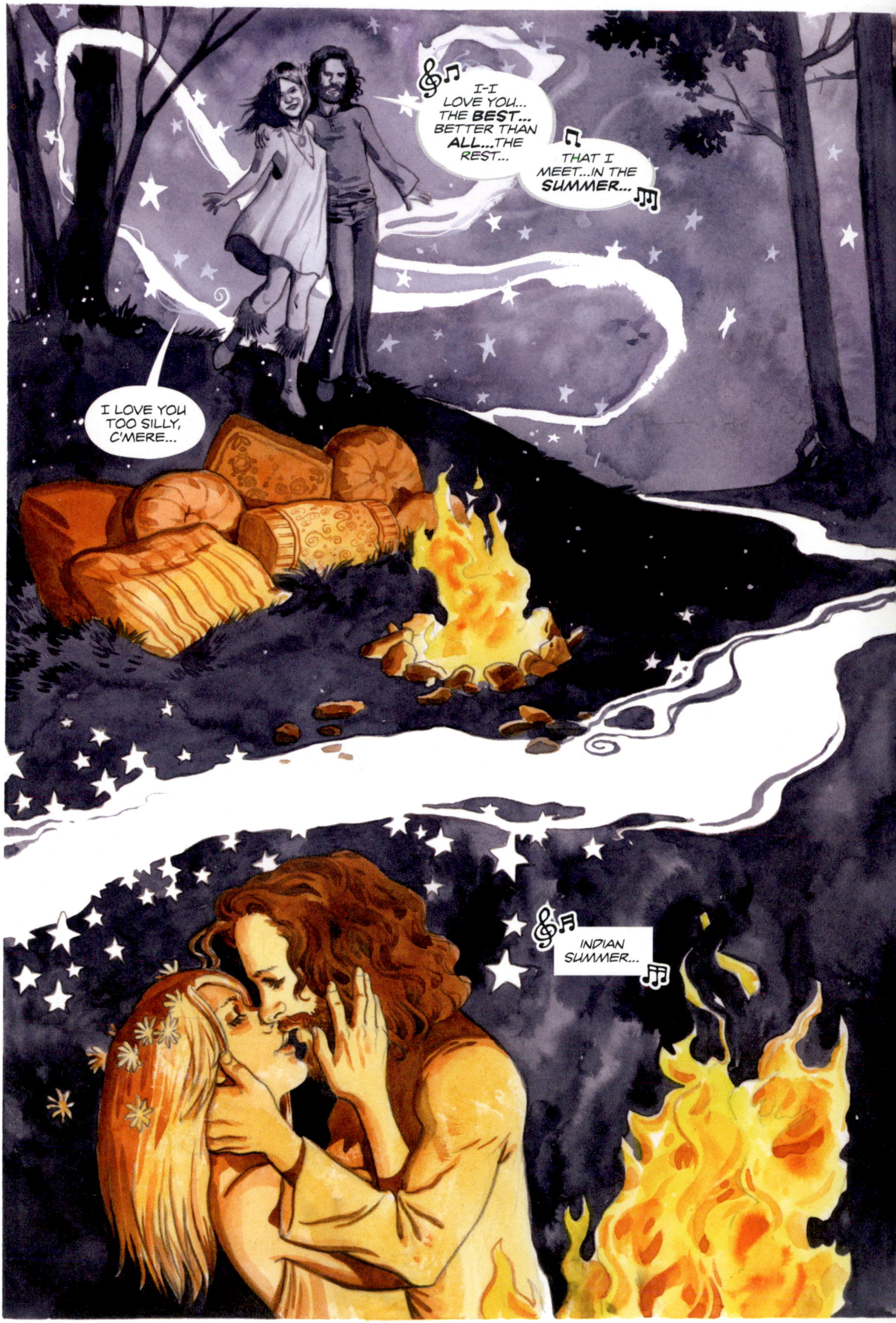
I-I LOVE YOU... THE BEST... BETTER THAN ALL...THE REST...
THAT I MEET...IN THE SUMMER...
I LOVE YOU TOO SILLY, C'MERE...
INDIAN SUMMER...

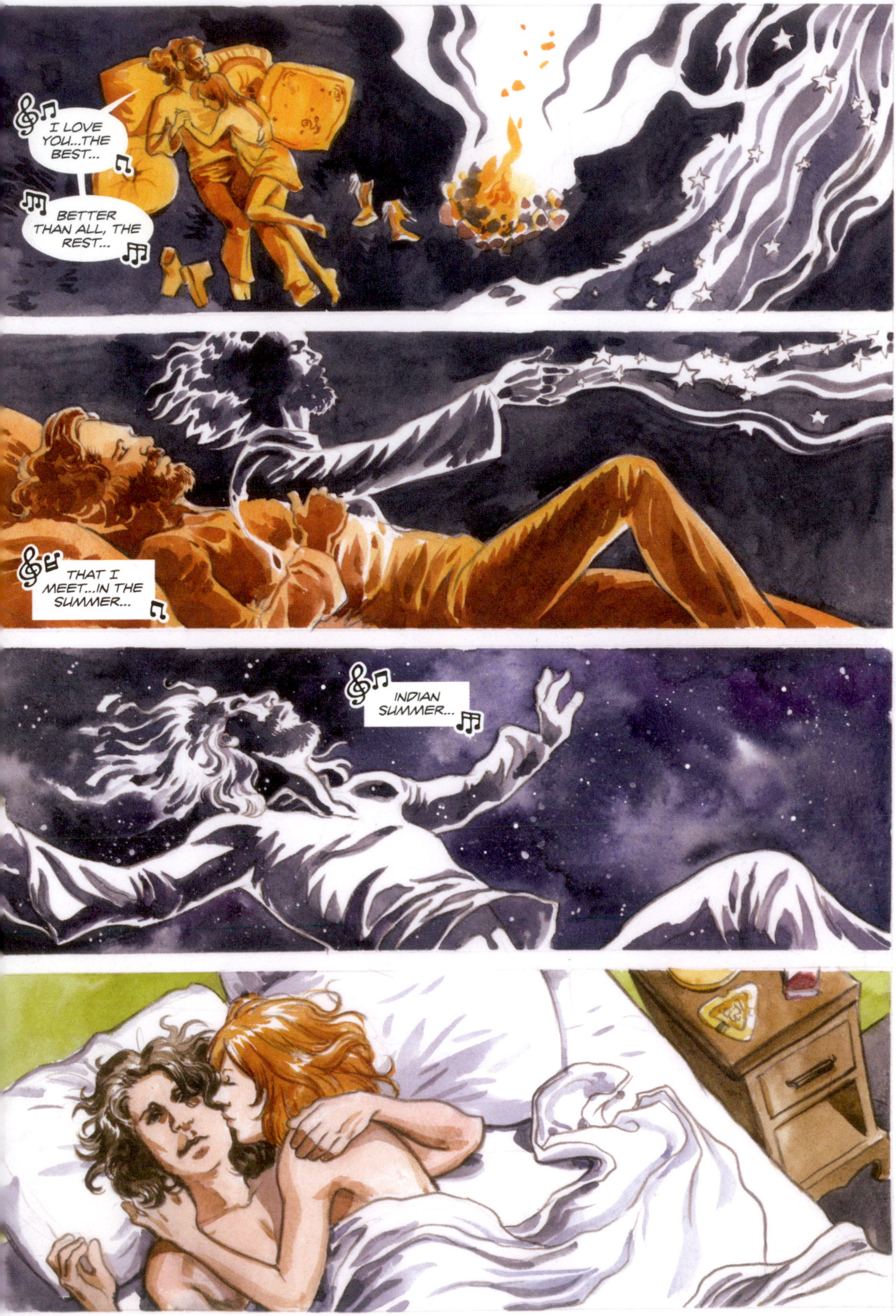
I LOVE YOU...THE BEST...
BETTER THAN ALL, THE REST...
THAT I MEET...IN THE SUMMER...
INDIAN SUMMER...

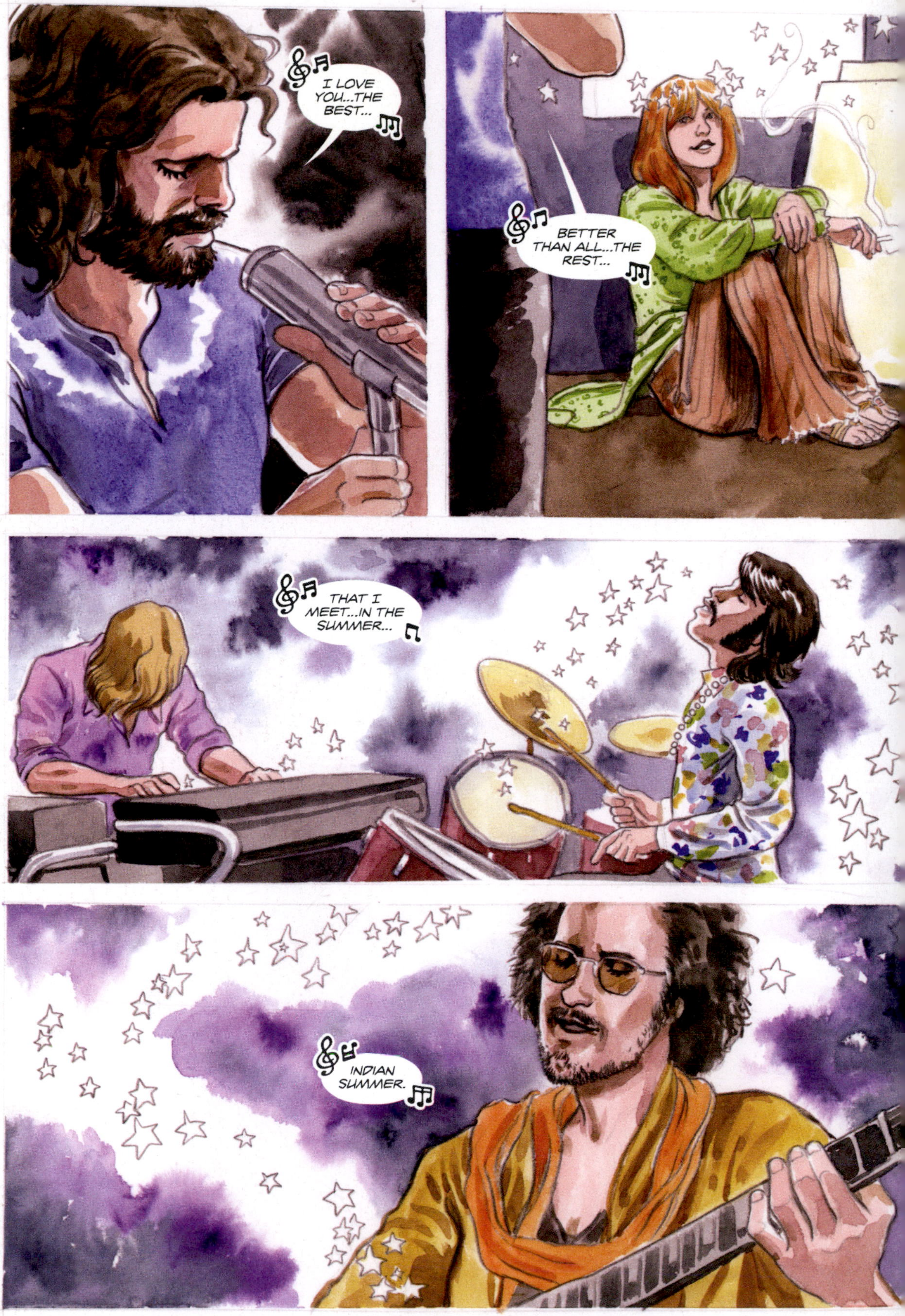
I LOVE YOU...THE BEST...
BETTER THAN ALL...THE REST...
THAT I MEET...IN THE SUMMER...
INDIAN SUMMER.

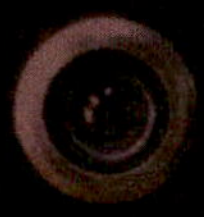

Maggie M'Gill

Artist . . . John K. Snyder III

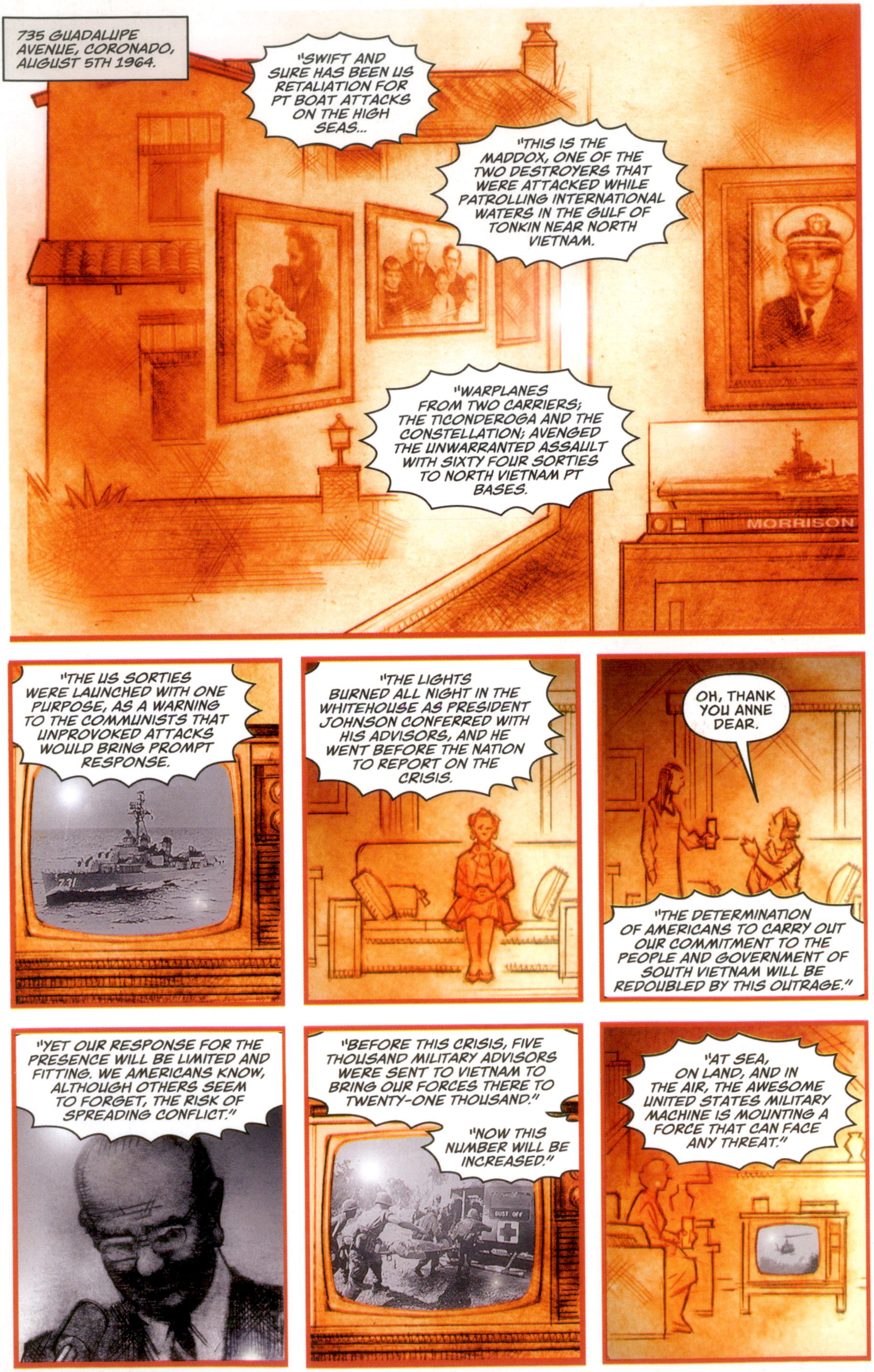
735 GUADALUPE AVENUE, CORONADO, AUGUST 5TH 1964.
"SWIFT AND SURE HAS BEEN US RETALIATION FOR PT BOAT ATTACKS ON THE HIGH SEAS...
"THIS IS THE MADDOX, ONE OF THE TWO DESTROYERS THAT WERE ATTACKED WHILE PATROLLING INTERNATIONAL WATERS IN THE GULF OF TONKIN NEAR NORTH VIETNAM.
"WARPLANES FROM TWO CARRIERS; THE TICONDEROGA AND THE CONSTELLATION; AVENGED THE UNWARRANTED ASSAULT WITH SIXTY FOUR SORTIES TO NORTH VIETNAM PT BASES.
MORRISON
"THE US SORTIES WERE LAUNCHED WITH ONE PURPOSE, AS A WARNING TO THE COMMUNISTS THAT UNPROVOKED ATTACKS WOULD BRING PROMPT RESPONSE.
731
"THE LIGHTS BURNED ALL NIGHT IN THE WHITEHOUSE AS PRESIDENT JOHNSON CONFERRED WITH HIS ADVISORS, AND HE WENT BEFORE THE NATION TO REPORT ON THE CRISIS.
OH, THANK YOU ANNE DEAR.
"THE DETERMINATION OF AMERICANS TO CARRY OUT OUR COMMITMENT TO THE PEOPLE AND GOVERNMENT OF SOUTH VIETNAM WILL BE REDOUBLED BY THIS OUTRAGE."
"YET OUR RESPONSE FOR THE PRESENCE WILL BE LIMITED AND FITTING. WE AMERICANS KNOW, ALTHOUGH OTHERS SEEM TO FORGET, THE RISK OF SPREADING CONFLICT."
"BEFORE THIS CRISIS, FIVE THOUSAND MILITARY ADVISORS WERE SENT TO VIETNAM TO BRING OUR FORCES THERE TO TWENTY-ONE THOUSAND."
"NOW THIS NUMBER WILL BE INCREASED."
"AT SEA, ON LAND, AND IN THE AIR, THE AWESOME UNITED STATES MILITARY MACHINE IS MOUNTING A FORCE THAT CAN FACE ANY THREAT."

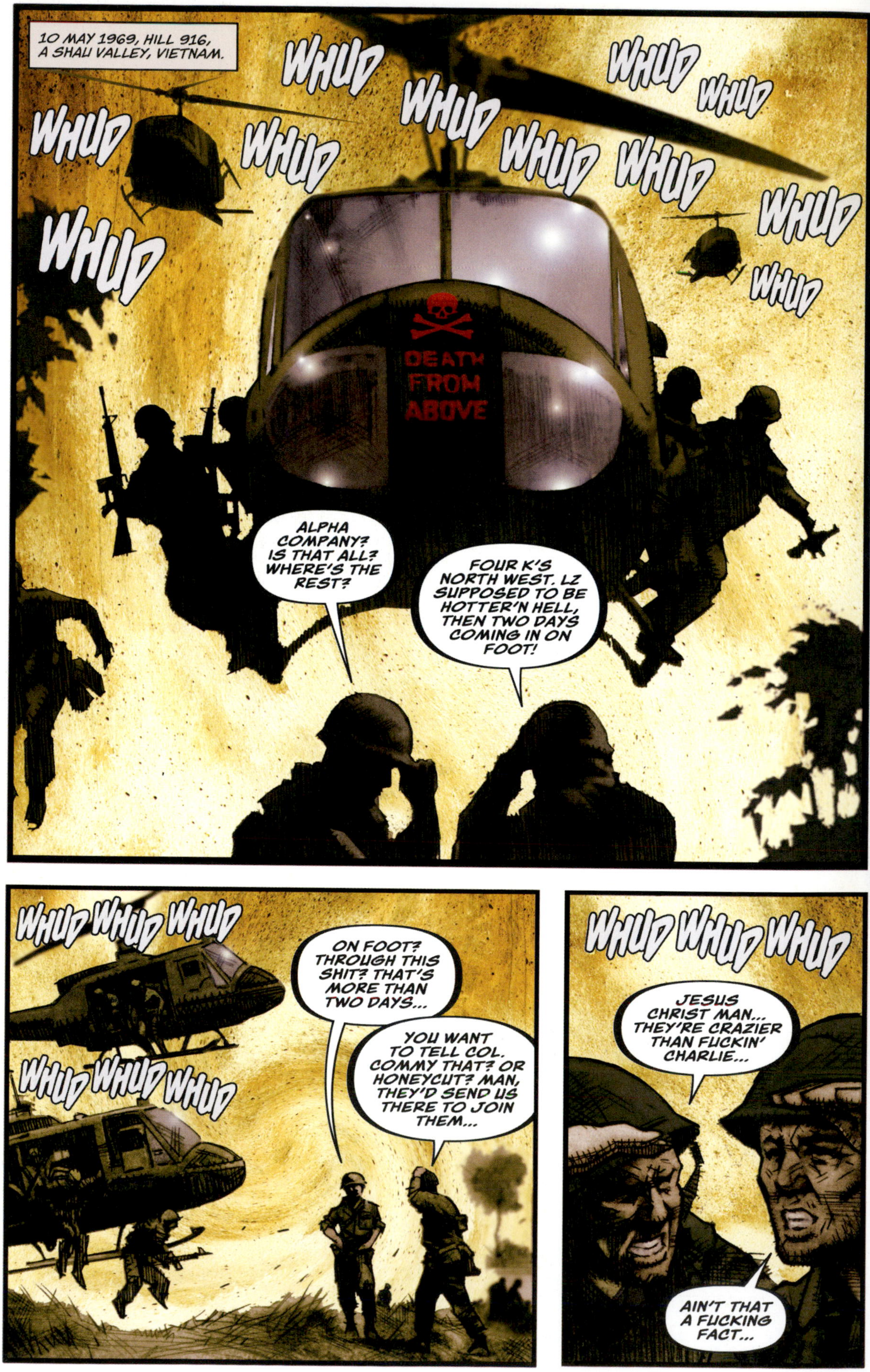
10 MAY 1969, HILL 916, A SHAU VALLEY, VIETNAM.
WHUD WHUD WHUD WHUD WHUD WHUD WHUD WHUD WHUD WHUD WHUD
ALPHA COMPANY? IS THAT ALL? WHERE'S THE REST?
FOUR K'S NORTH WEST. LZ SUPPOSED TO BE HOTTER'N HELL, THEN TWO DAYS COMING IN ON FOOT!
DEATH FROM ABOVE
WHUD WHUD WHUD
WHUD WHUD WHUD
ON FOOT? THROUGH THIS SHIT? THAT'S MORE THAN TWO DAYS...
YOU WANT TO TELL COL. COMMY THAT? OR HONEYCUT? MAN, THEY'D SEND US THERE TO JOIN THEM...
WHUD WHUD WHUD
JESUS CHRIST MAN... THEY'RE CRAZIER THAN FUCKIN' CHARLIE...
AIN'T THAT A FUCKING FACT...

HILL 916 WAS CHOSEN AS A DEFENDABLE LANDING ZONE CLOSE TO DONG AP BIA.

AMERICAN TROOPS WOULD TAKE THE RIDGE TO THE SOUTHWEST OF AP BIA. HILL 937.

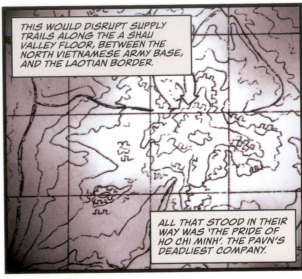

THIS WOULD DISRUPT SUPPLY TRAILS ALONG THE A SHAU VALLEY FLOOR, BETWEEN THE NORTH VIETNAMESE ARMY BASE, AND THE LAOTIAN BORDER.

ALL THAT STOOD IN THEIR WAY WAS 'THE PRIDE OF HO CHI MINH'. THE PAVN'S DEADLIEST COMPANY.

THIS IS IT FELLAS, A FOUR-K STROLL WITH A CASE OF COLD SUDS WAITING FOR US AT THE END OF IT.

VISIBILITY IS ZERO, SO WATCH YOUR SIX. CHARLIE KNOWS THIS PLACE LIKE THE BACK OF HIS HAND.

SINGLE FILE GENTLEMEN, STEP DAINTY NOW...

THIS IS THICK AS FUCK MAN, HOW FAR WE DONE? LIKE A HUNDRED YARDS? THAT CASE OF BEER BETTER BE ICY COLD...

JESUS DE ANGELO YOU SOUND LIKE MY SISTERS' KID! YOU WANNA PISS BREAK TOO?

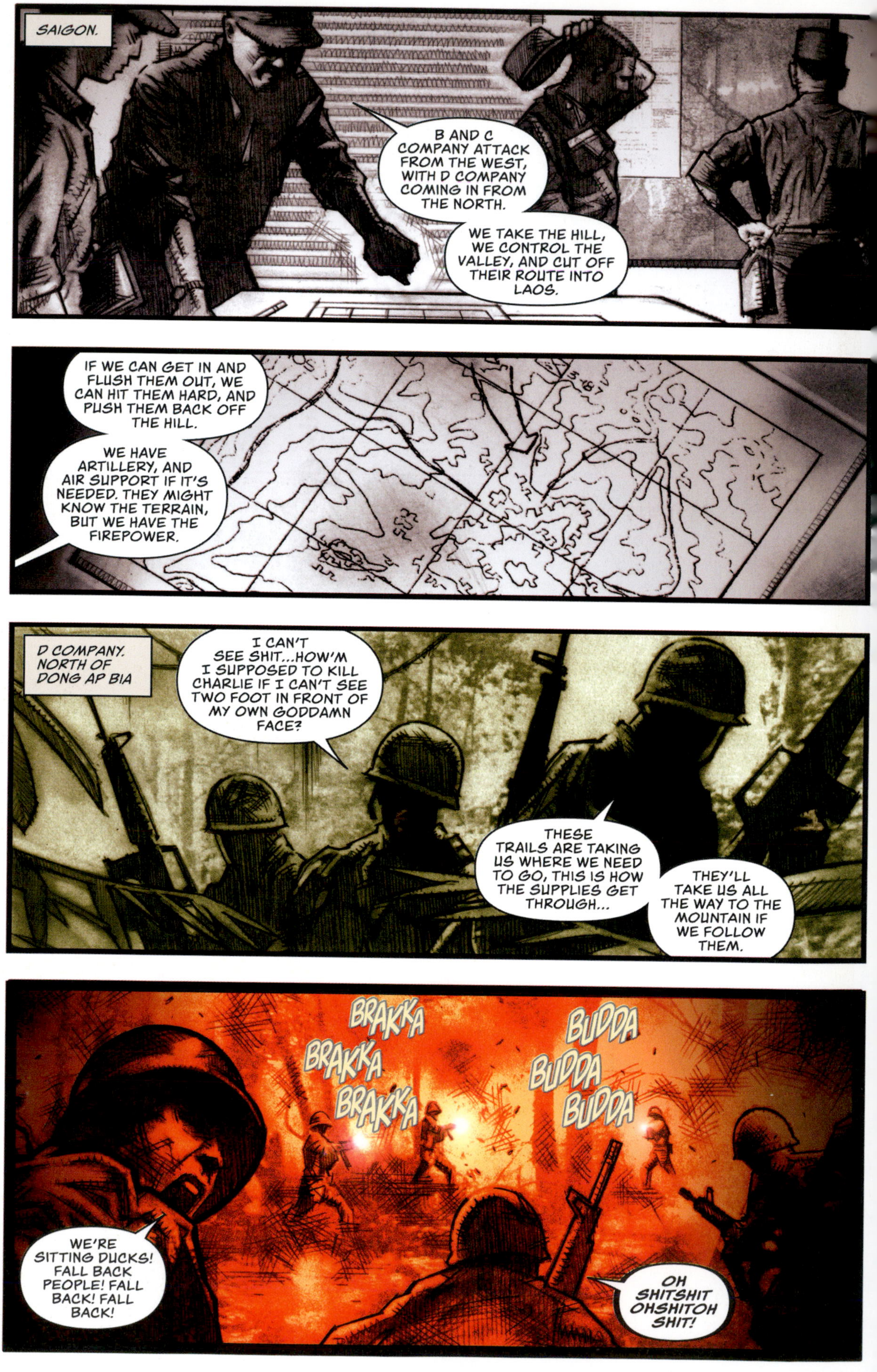
SAIGON.
B AND C COMPANY ATTACK FROM THE WEST, WITH D COMPANY COMING IN FROM THE NORTH.
WE TAKE THE HILL, WE CONTROL THE VALLEY, AND CUT OFF THEIR ROUTE INTO LAOS.
IF WE CAN GET IN AND FLUSH THEM OUT, WE CAN HIT THEM HARD, AND PUSH THEM BACK OFF THE HILL.
WE HAVE ARTILLERY, AND AIR SUPPORT IF IT'S NEEDED. THEY MIGHT KNOW THE TERRAIN, BUT WE HAVE THE FIREPOWER.
D COMPANY. NORTH OF DONG AP BIA
I CAN'T SEE SHIT...HOW'M I SUPPOSED TO KILL CHARLIE IF I CAN'T SEE TWO FOOT IN FRONT OF MY OWN GODDAMN FACE?
THESE TRAILS ARE TAKING US WHERE WE NEED TO GO, THIS IS HOW THE SUPPLIES GET THROUGH...
THEY'LL TAKE US ALL THE WAY TO THE MOUNTAIN IF WE FOLLOW THEM.
BRAKKA BRAKKA BRAKKA
BUDDA BUDDA BUDDA
WE'RE SITTING DUCKS! FALL BACK PEOPLE! FALL BACK! FALL BACK!
OH SHITSHIT OHSHITOH SHIT!

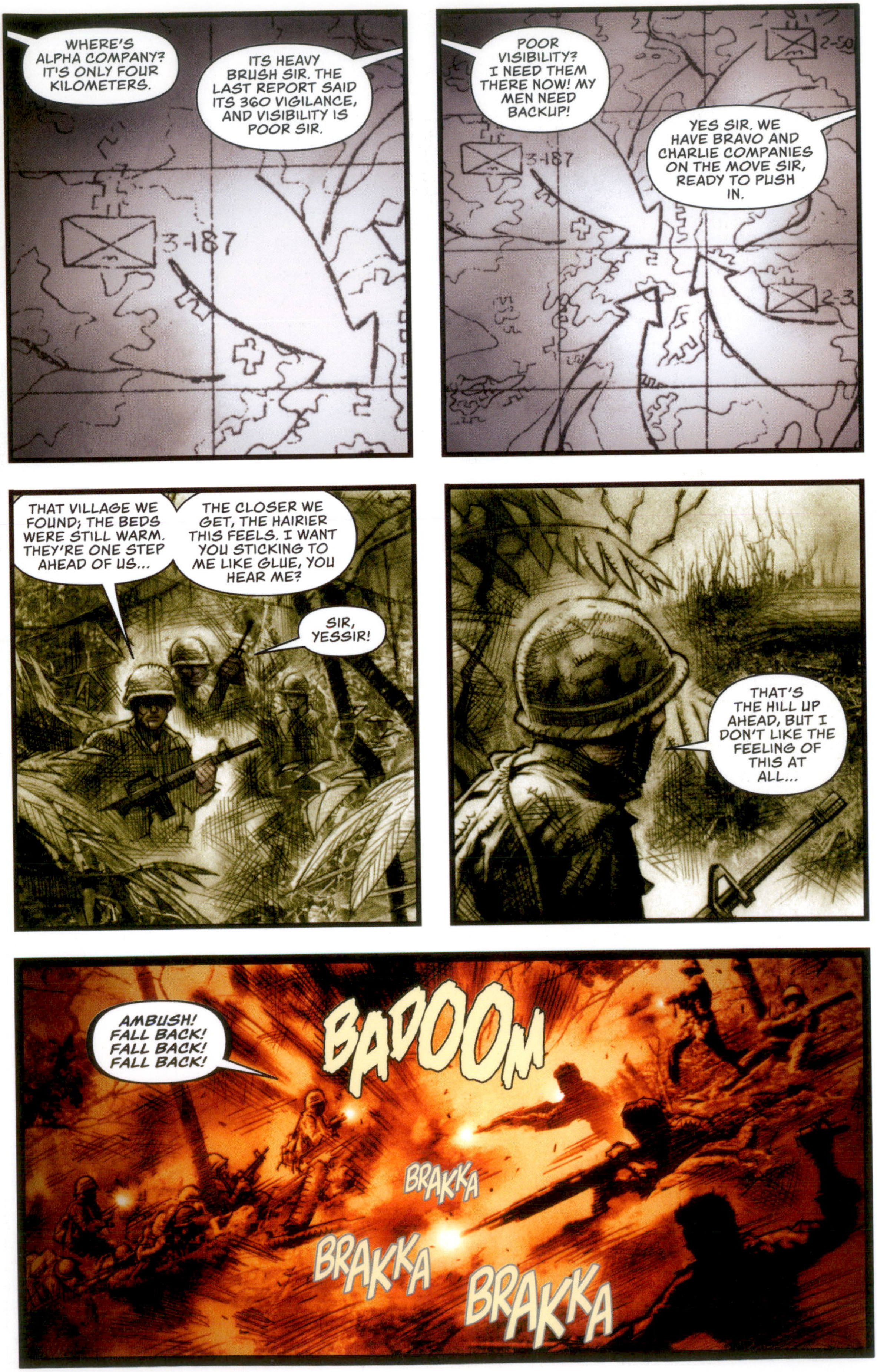
WHERE'S ALPHA COMPANY? IT'S ONLY FOUR KILOMETERS.
ITS HEAVY BRUSH SIR. THE LAST REPORT SAID ITS 360 VIGILANCE, AND VISIBILITY IS POOR SIR.
3-187
POOR VISIBILITY? I NEED THEM THERE NOW! MY MEN NEED BACKUP!
YES SIR. WE HAVE BRAVO AND CHARLIE COMPANIES ON THE MOVE SIR, READY TO PUSH IN.
3-187
THAT VILLAGE WE FOUND; THE BEDS WERE STILL WARM. THEY'RE ONE STEP AHEAD OF US...
THE CLOSER WE GET, THE HAIRIER THIS FEELS. I WANT YOU STICKING TO ME LIKE GLUE, YOU HEAR ME?
SIR, YESSIR!
THAT'S THE HILL UP AHEAD, BUT I DON'T LIKE THE FEELING OF THIS AT ALL...
AMBUSH! FALL BACK! FALL BACK! FALL BACK!
BADOOM
BRAKKA
BRAKKA
BRAKKA

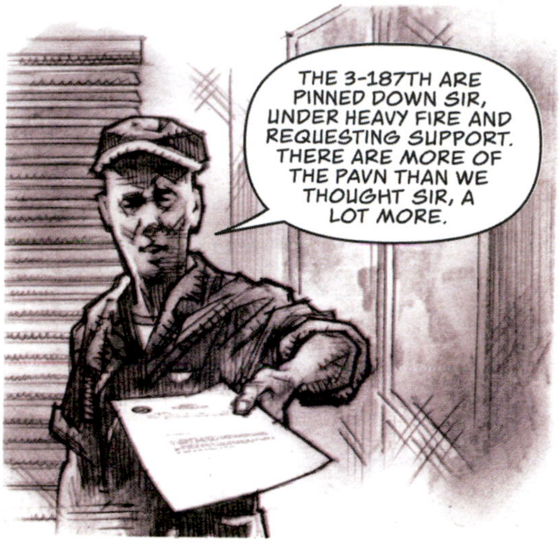
THE 3-187TH ARE PINNED DOWN SIR, UNDER HEAVY FIRE AND REQUESTING SUPPORT. THERE ARE MORE OF THE PAVN THAN WE THOUGHT SIR, A LOT MORE.

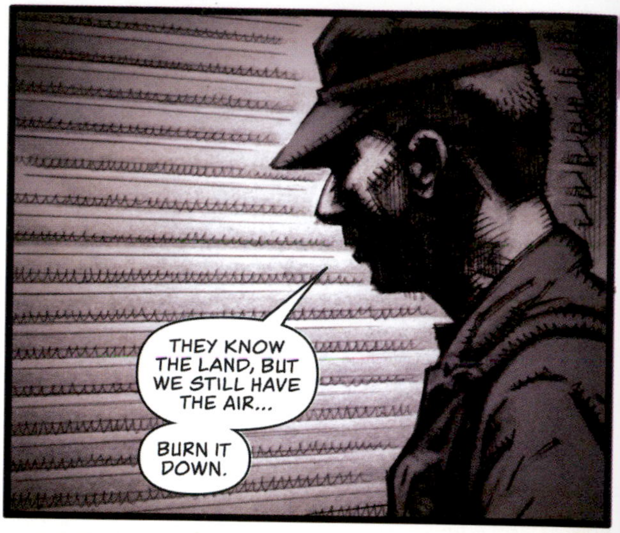
THEY KNOW THE LAND, BUT WE STILL HAVE THE AIR...
BURN IT DOWN.

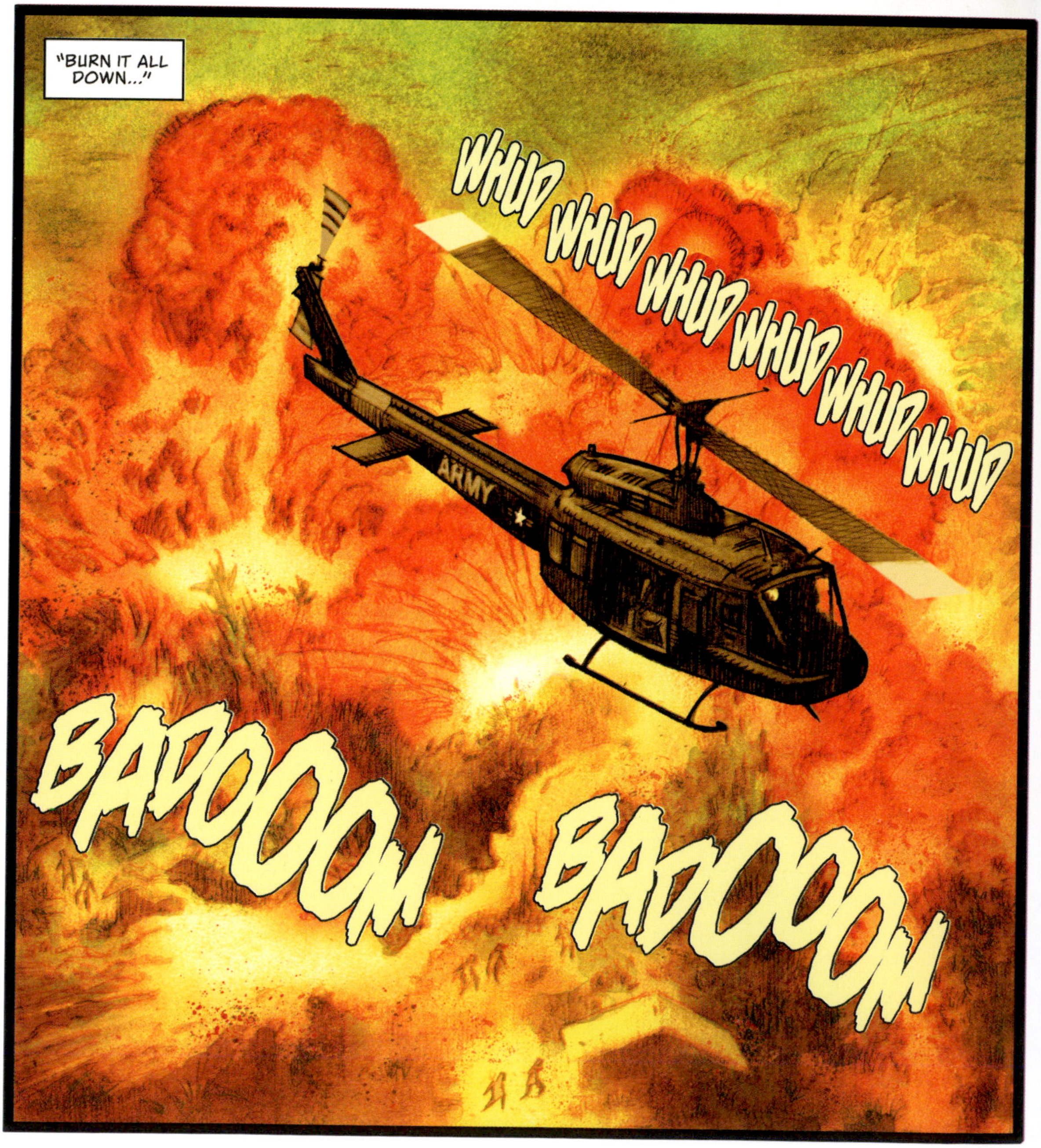
"BURN IT ALL DOWN..."
WHUD WHUD WHUD WHUD WHUD WHUD
ARMY
BADOOOM BADOOOM

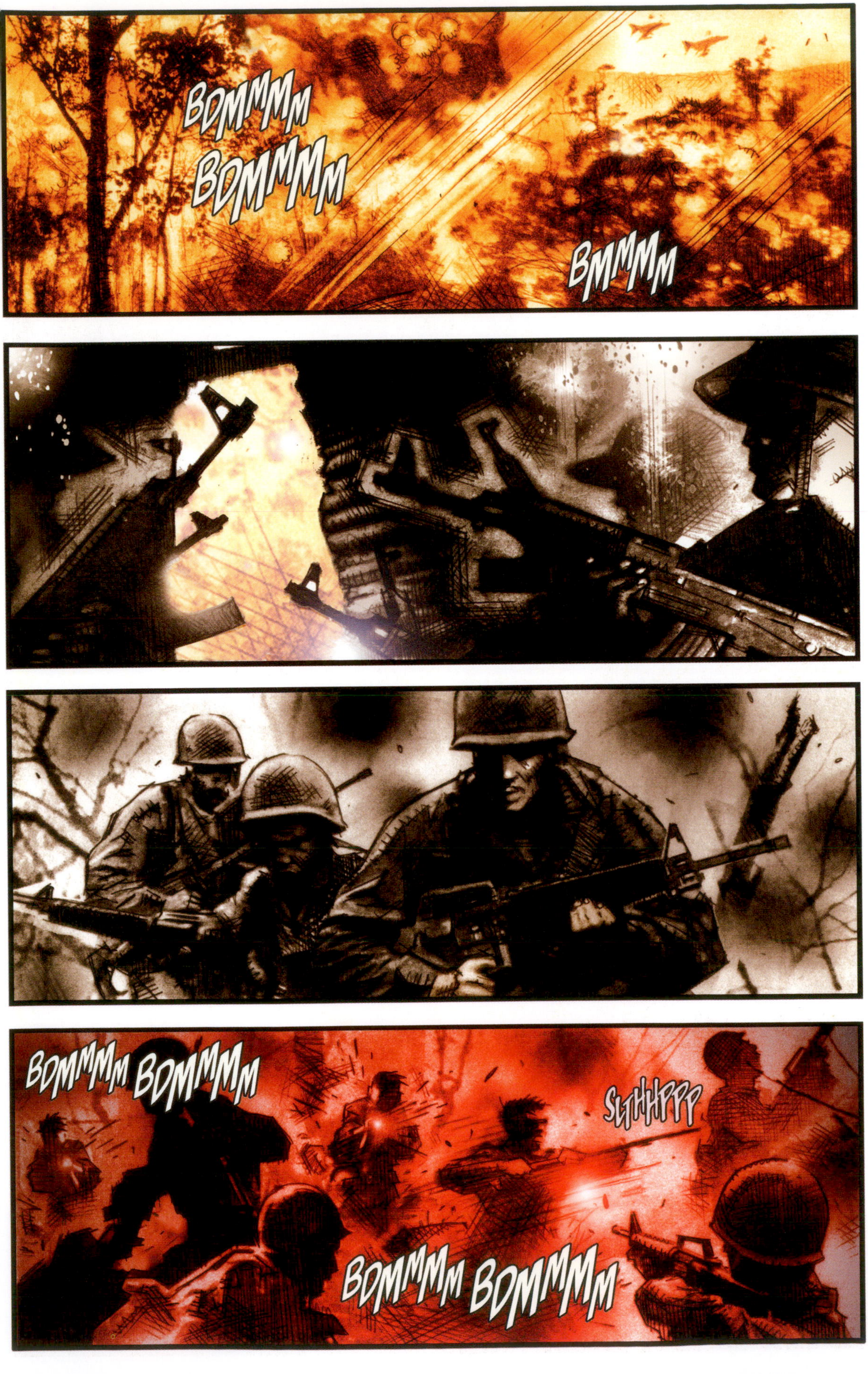
BOMMMM
BOMMMM
BMMMM
BOMMMM BOMMMM
SLTHHPPP
BOMMMM BOMMMM

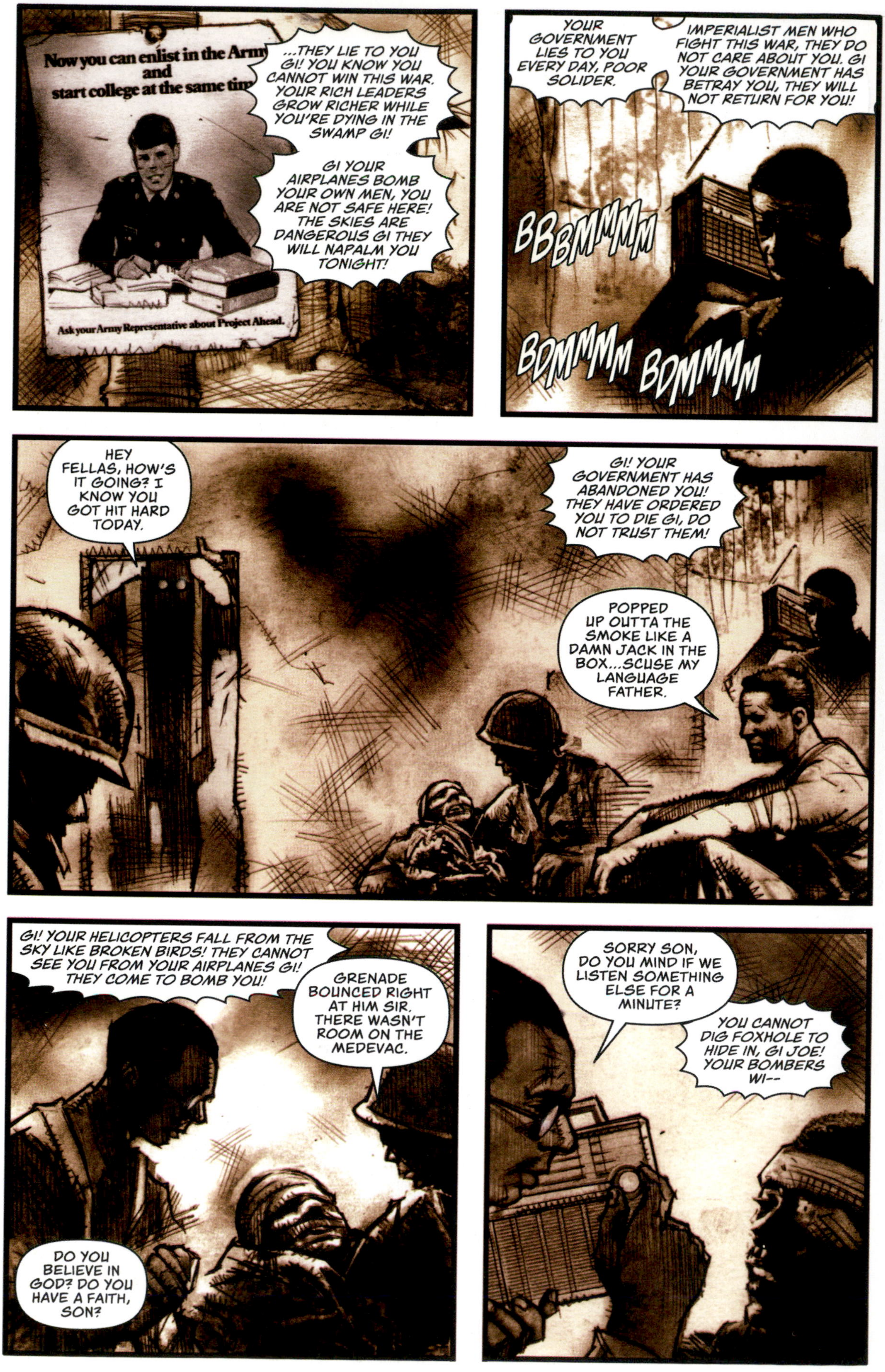
Now you can enlist in the Army and start college at the same time
Ask your Army Representative about Project Ahead.
...THEY LIE TO YOU GI! YOU KNOW YOU CANNOT WIN THIS WAR. YOUR RICH LEADERS GROW RICHER WHILE YOU'RE DYING IN THE SWAMP GI!
GI YOUR AIRPLANES BOMB YOUR OWN MEN, YOU ARE NOT SAFE HERE! THE SKIES ARE DANGEROUS GI THEY WILL NAPALM YOU TONIGHT!
YOUR GOVERNMENT LIES TO YOU EVERY DAY, POOR SOLIDER.
IMPERIALIST MEN WHO FIGHT THIS WAR, THEY DO NOT CARE ABOUT YOU. GI YOUR GOVERNMENT HAS BETRAY YOU, THEY WILL NOT RETURN FOR YOU!
BBBMMMM
BDMMMM BDMMMM
HEY FELLAS, HOW'S IT GOING? I KNOW YOU GOT HIT HARD TODAY.
GI! YOUR GOVERNMENT HAS ABANDONED YOU! THEY HAVE ORDERED YOU TO DIE GI, DO NOT TRUST THEM!
POPPED UP OUTTA THE SMOKE LIKE A DAMN JACK IN THE BOX...SCUSE MY LANGUAGE FATHER.
GI! YOUR HELICOPTERS FALL FROM THE SKY LIKE BROKEN BIRDS! THEY CANNOT SEE YOU FROM YOUR AIRPLANES GI! THEY COME TO BOMB YOU!
GRENADE BOUNCED RIGHT AT HIM SIR. THERE WASN'T ROOM ON THE MEDEVAC.
DO YOU BELIEVE IN GOD? DO YOU HAVE A FAITH, SON?
SORRY SON, DO YOU MIND IF WE LISTEN SOMETHING ELSE FOR A MINUTE?
YOU CANNOT DIG FOXHOLE TO HIDE IN, GI JOE! YOUR BOMBERS WI--

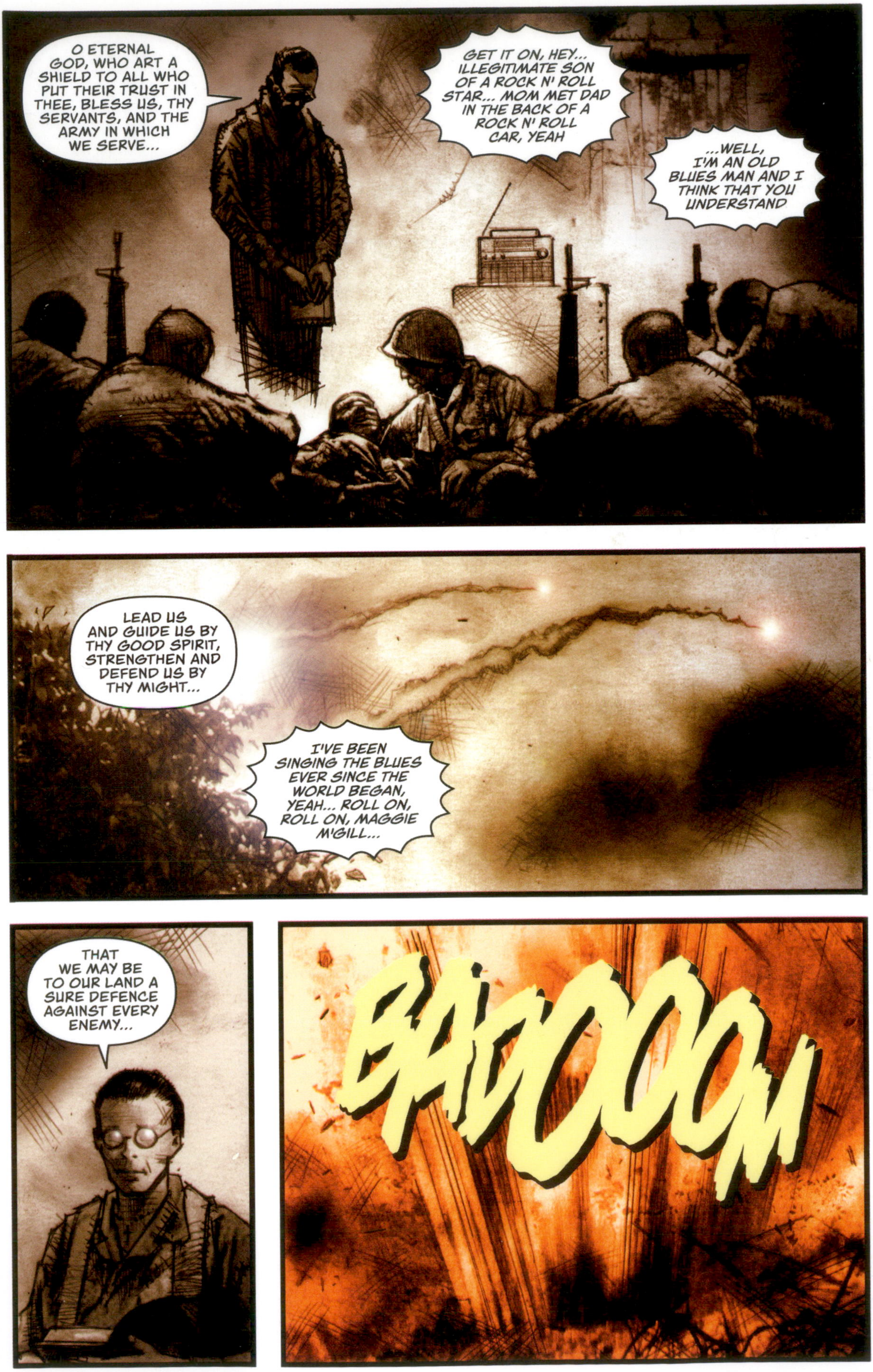
O ETERNAL GOD, WHO ART A SHIELD TO ALL WHO PUT THEIR TRUST IN THEE, BLESS US, THY SERVANTS, AND THE ARMY IN WHICH WE SERVE...
GET IT ON, HEY... ILLEGITIMATE SON OF A ROCK N' ROLL STAR... MOM MET DAD IN THE BACK OF A ROCK N' ROLL CAR, YEAH
...WELL, I'M AN OLD BLUES MAN AND I THINK THAT YOU UNDERSTAND
LEAD US AND GUIDE US BY THY GOOD SPIRIT, STRENGTHEN AND DEFEND US BY THY MIGHT...
I'VE BEEN SINGING THE BLUES EVER SINCE THE WORLD BEGAN, YEAH... ROLL ON, ROLL ON, MAGGIE M'GILL...
THAT WE MAY BE TO OUR LAND A SURE DEFENCE AGAINST EVERY ENEMY...
BADOOOM

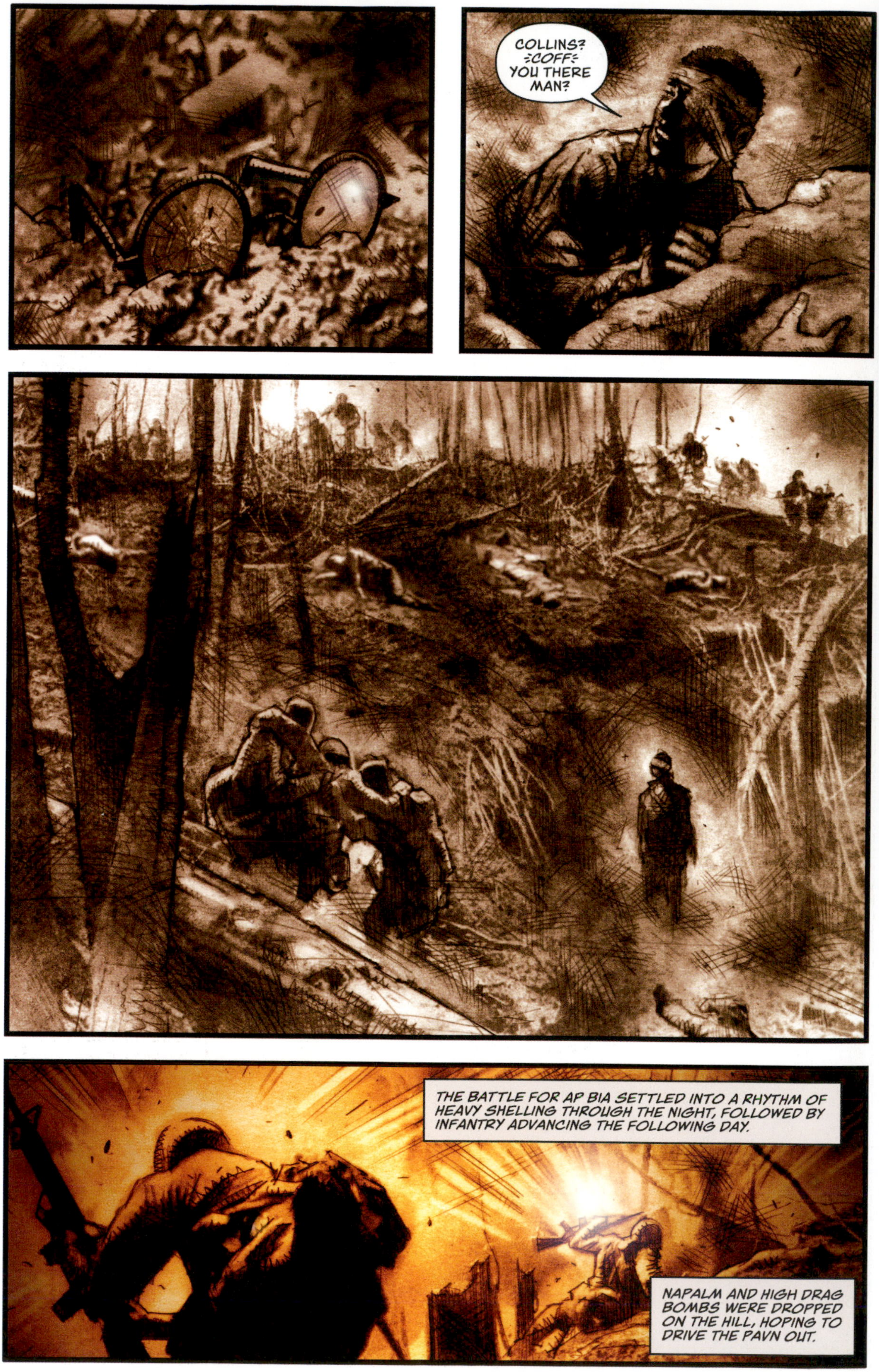
COLLINS?
:COFF:
YOU THERE
MAN?
THE BATTLE FOR AP BIA SETTLED INTO A RHYTHM OF HEAVY SHELLING THROUGH THE NIGHT, FOLLOWED BY INFANTRY ADVANCING THE FOLLOWING DAY.
NAPALM AND HIGH DRAG BOMBS WERE DROPPED ON THE HILL, HOPING TO DRIVE THE PAVN OUT.

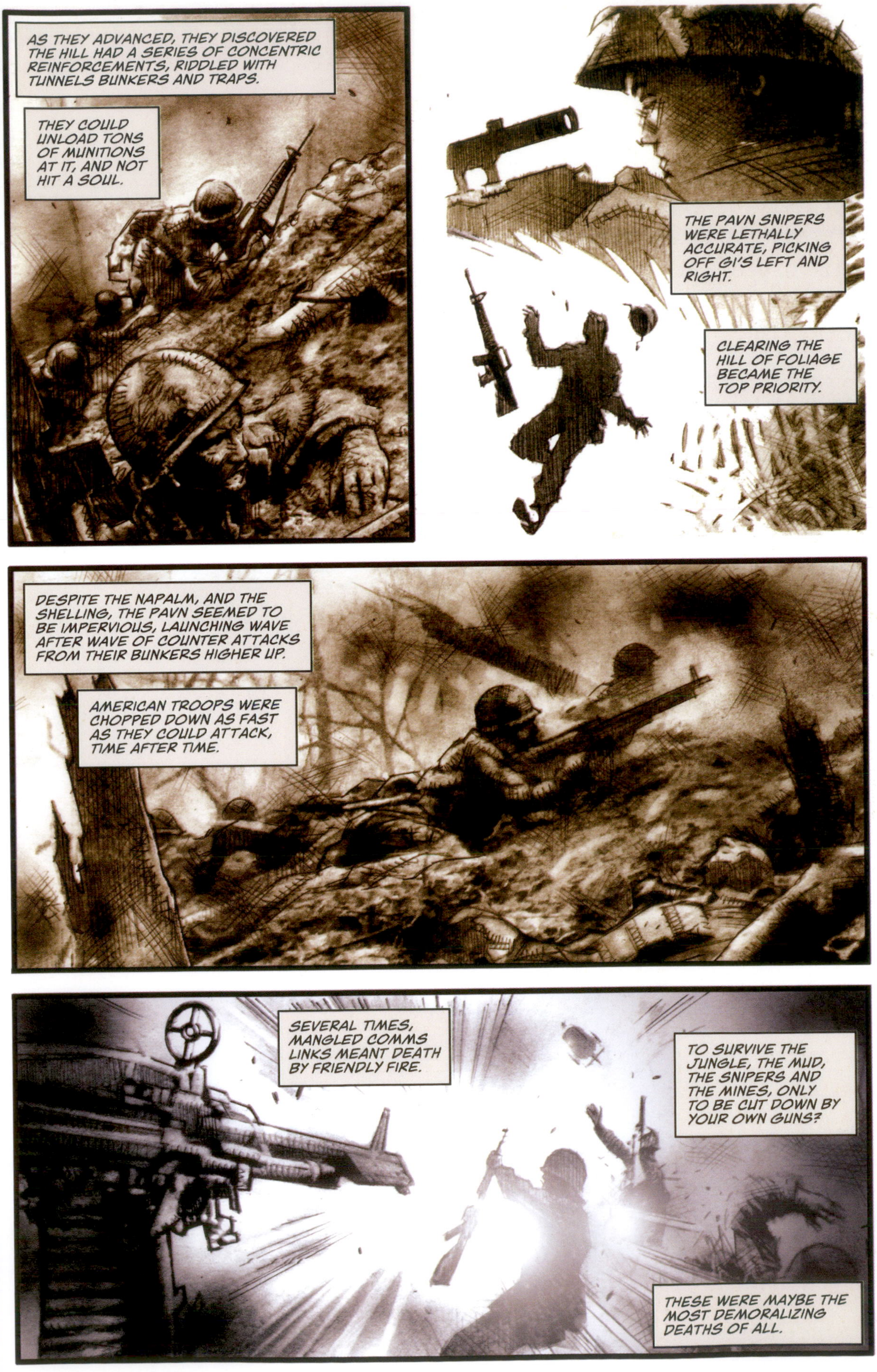
AS THEY ADVANCED, THEY DISCOVERED THE HILL HAD A SERIES OF CONCENTRIC REINFORCEMENTS, RIDDLED WITH TUNNELS BUNKERS AND TRAPS.
THEY COULD UNLOAD TONS OF MUNITIONS AT IT, AND NOT HIT A SOUL.
THE PAVN SNIPERS WERE LETHALLY ACCURATE, PICKING OFF GI'S LEFT AND RIGHT.
CLEARING THE HILL OF FOLIAGE BECAME THE TOP PRIORITY.
DESPITE THE NAPALM, AND THE SHELLING, THE PAVN SEEMED TO BE IMPERVIOUS, LAUNCHING WAVE AFTER WAVE OF COUNTER ATTACKS FROM THEIR BUNKERS HIGHER UP.
AMERICAN TROOPS WERE CHOPPED DOWN AS FAST AS THEY COULD ATTACK, TIME AFTER TIME.
SEVERAL TIMES, MANGLED COMMS LINKS MEANT DEATH BY FRIENDLY FIRE.
TO SURVIVE THE JUNGLE, THE MUD, THE SNIPERS AND THE MINES, ONLY TO BE CUT DOWN BY YOUR OWN GUNS?
THESE WERE MAYBE THE MOST DEMORALIZING DEATHS OF ALL.

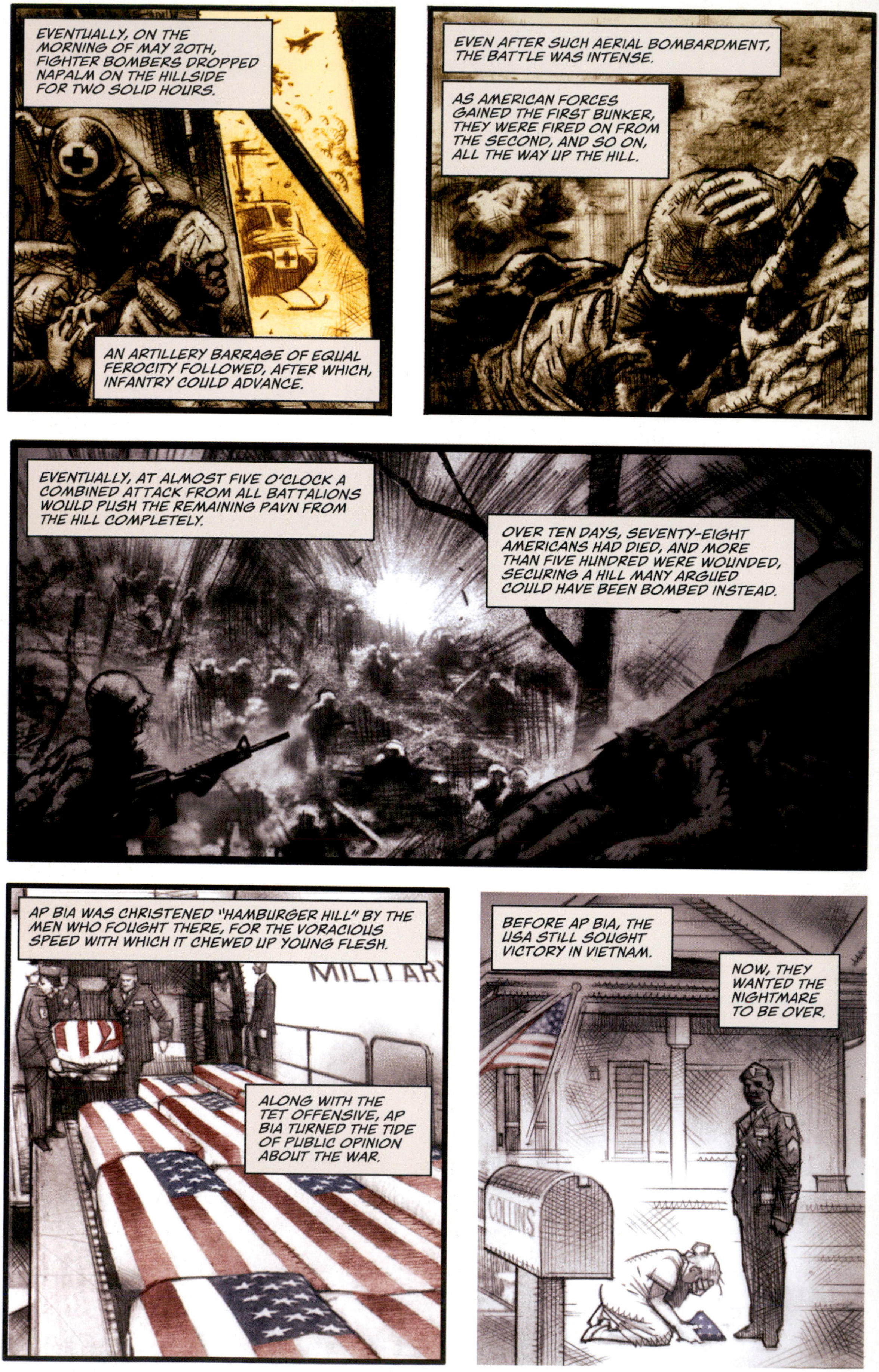
EVENTUALLY, ON THE MORNING OF MAY 20TH, FIGHTER BOMBERS DROPPED NAPALM ON THE HILLSIDE FOR TWO SOLID HOURS.
AN ARTILLERY BARRAGE OF EQUAL FEROCITY FOLLOWED, AFTER WHICH, INFANTRY COULD ADVANCE.
EVEN AFTER SUCH AERIAL BOMBARDMENT, THE BATTLE WAS INTENSE.
AS AMERICAN FORCES GAINED THE FIRST BUNKER, THEY WERE FIRED ON FROM THE SECOND, AND SO ON, ALL THE WAY UP THE HILL.
EVENTUALLY, AT ALMOST FIVE O'CLOCK A COMBINED ATTACK FROM ALL BATTALIONS WOULD PUSH THE REMAINING PAVN FROM THE HILL COMPLETELY.
OVER TEN DAYS, SEVENTY-EIGHT AMERICANS HAD DIED, AND MORE THAN FIVE HUNDRED WERE WOUNDED, SECURING A HILL MANY ARGUED COULD HAVE BEEN BOMBED INSTEAD.
AP BIA WAS CHRISTENED "HAMBURGER HILL" BY THE MEN WHO FOUGHT THERE, FOR THE VORACIOUS SPEED WITH WHICH IT CHEWED UP YOUNG FLESH.
MILITAR
ALONG WITH THE TET OFFENSIVE, AP BIA TURNED THE TIDE OF PUBLIC OPINION ABOUT THE WAR.
BEFORE AP BIA, THE USA STILL SOUGHT VICTORY IN VIETNAM.
NOW, THEY WANTED THE NIGHTMARE TO BE OVER.
COLLINS

Outro

Artist........Tony Parker
Colorist...Aladdin Collar

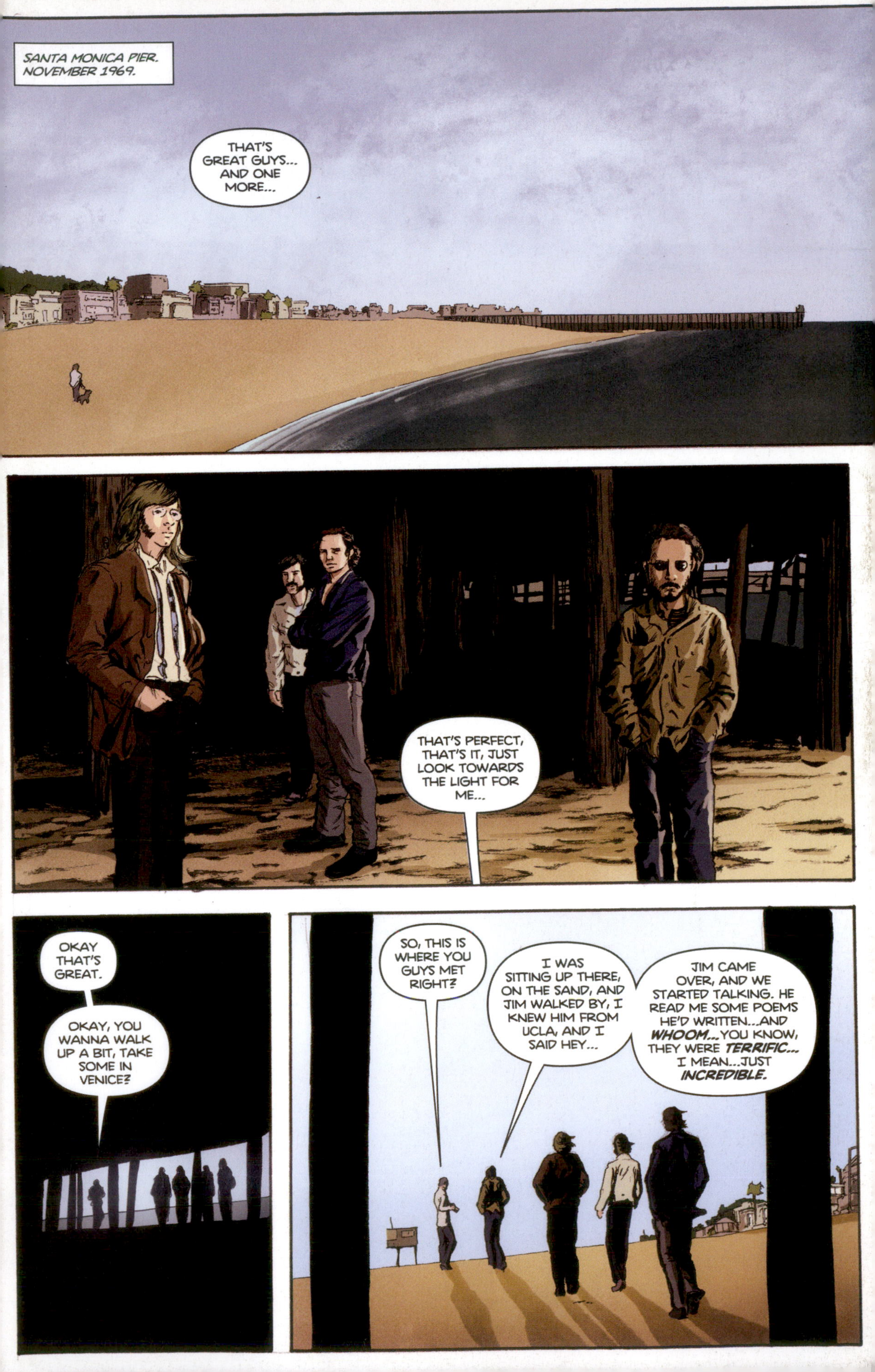
SANTA MONICA PIER.
NOVEMBER 1969.
THAT'S GREAT GUYS... AND ONE MORE...
THAT'S PERFECT, THAT'S IT, JUST LOOK TOWARDS THE LIGHT FOR ME...
OKAY THAT'S GREAT.
OKAY, YOU WANNA WALK UP A BIT, TAKE SOME IN VENICE?
SO, THIS IS WHERE YOU GUYS MET RIGHT?
I WAS SITTING UP THERE, ON THE SAND, AND JIM WALKED BY, I KNEW HIM FROM UCLA, AND I SAID HEY...
JIM CAME OVER, AND WE STARTED TALKING. HE READ ME SOME POEMS HE'D WRITTEN...AND WHOOM... YOU KNOW, THEY WERE TERRIFIC... I MEAN...JUST INCREDIBLE.

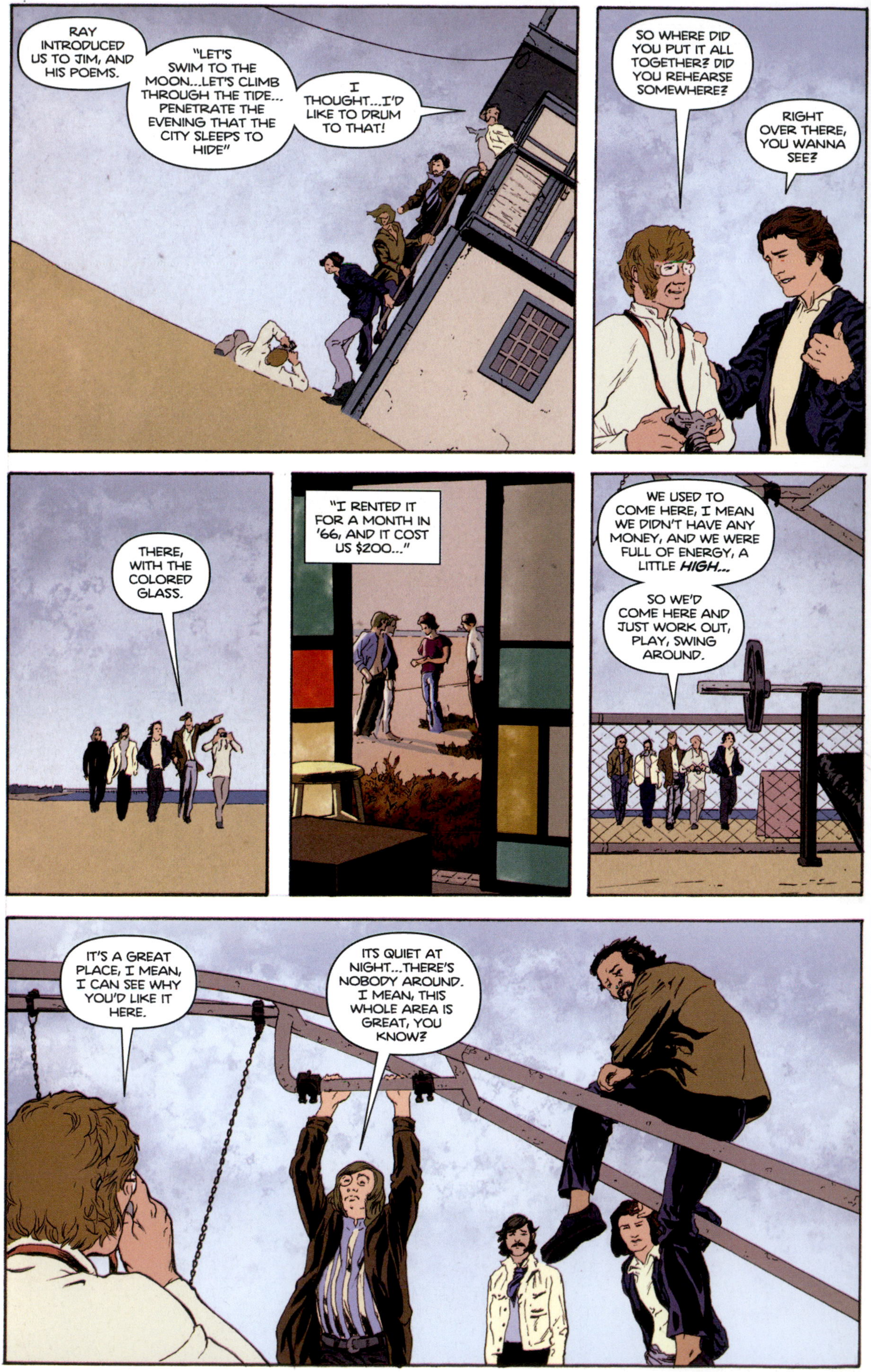
RAY INTRODUCED US TO JIM, AND HIS POEMS.
"LET'S SWIM TO THE MOON...LET'S CLIMB THROUGH THE TIDE... PENETRATE THE EVENING THAT THE CITY SLEEPS TO HIDE"
I THOUGHT...I'D LIKE TO DRUM TO THAT!
SO WHERE DID YOU PUT IT ALL TOGETHER? DID YOU REHEARSE SOMEWHERE?
RIGHT OVER THERE, YOU WANNA SEE?
THERE, WITH THE COLORED GLASS.
"I RENTED IT FOR A MONTH IN '66, AND IT COST US $200..."
WE USED TO COME HERE, I MEAN WE DIDN'T HAVE ANY MONEY, AND WE WERE FULL OF ENERGY, A LITTLE *HIGH...*
SO WE'D COME HERE AND JUST WORK OUT, PLAY, SWING AROUND.
IT'S A GREAT PLACE, I MEAN, I CAN SEE WHY YOU'D LIKE IT HERE.
ITS QUIET AT NIGHT...THERE'S NOBODY AROUND. I MEAN, THIS WHOLE AREA IS GREAT, YOU KNOW?

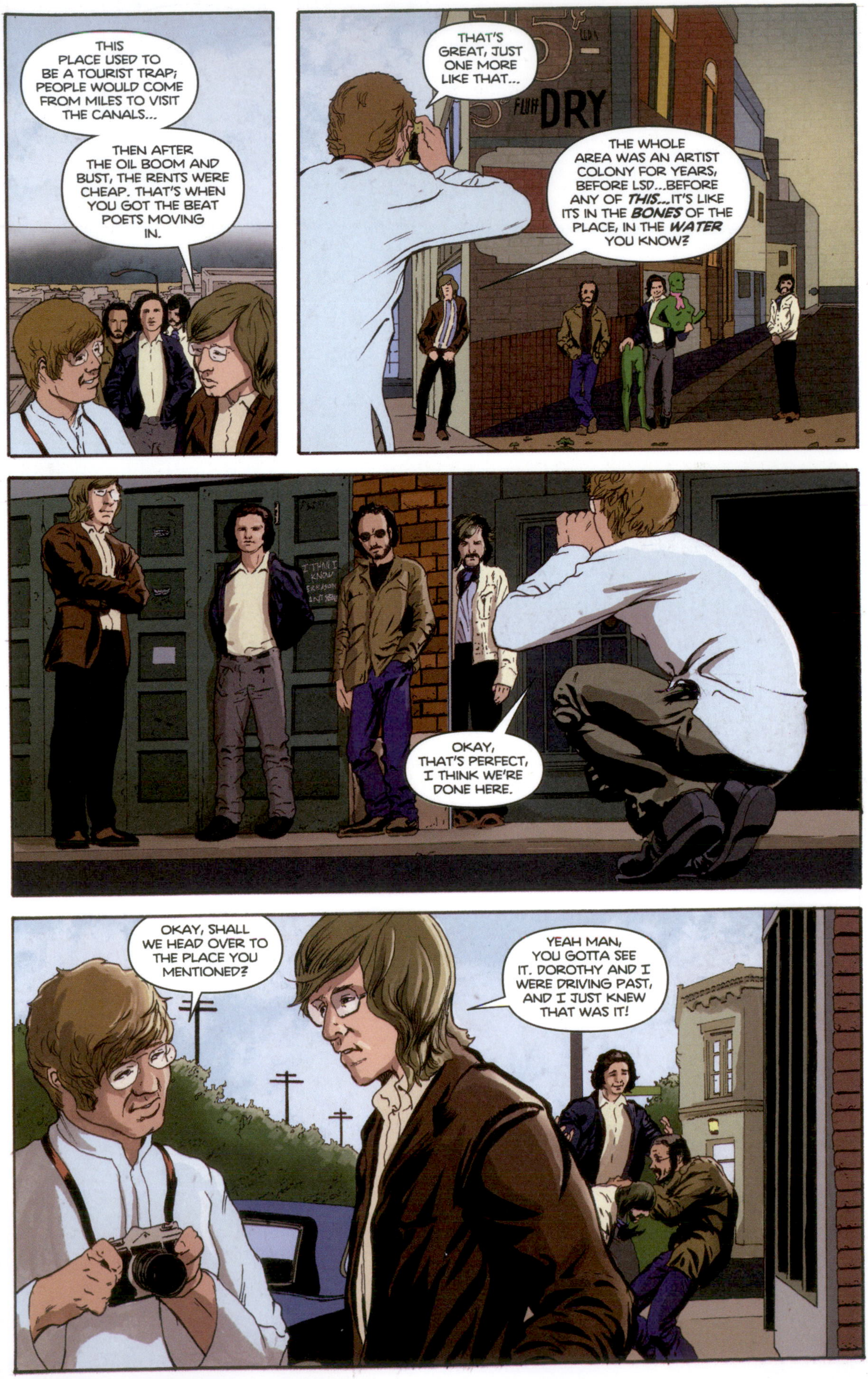

THIS PLACE USED TO BE A TOURIST TRAP; PEOPLE WOULD COME FROM MILES TO VISIT THE CANALS...
THEN AFTER THE OIL BOOM AND BUST, THE RENTS WERE CHEAP. THAT'S WHEN YOU GOT THE BEAT POETS MOVING IN.
THAT'S GREAT, JUST ONE MORE LIKE THAT...
DRY
THE WHOLE AREA WAS AN ARTIST COLONY FOR YEARS, BEFORE LSD...BEFORE ANY OF *THIS*...IT'S LIKE ITS IN THE *BONES* OF THE PLACE, IN THE *WATER* YOU KNOW?
OKAY, THAT'S PERFECT, I THINK WE'RE DONE HERE.
OKAY, SHALL WE HEAD OVER TO THE PLACE YOU MENTIONED?
YEAH MAN, YOU GOTTA SEE IT. DOROTHY AND I WERE DRIVING PAST, AND I JUST KNEW THAT WAS IT!

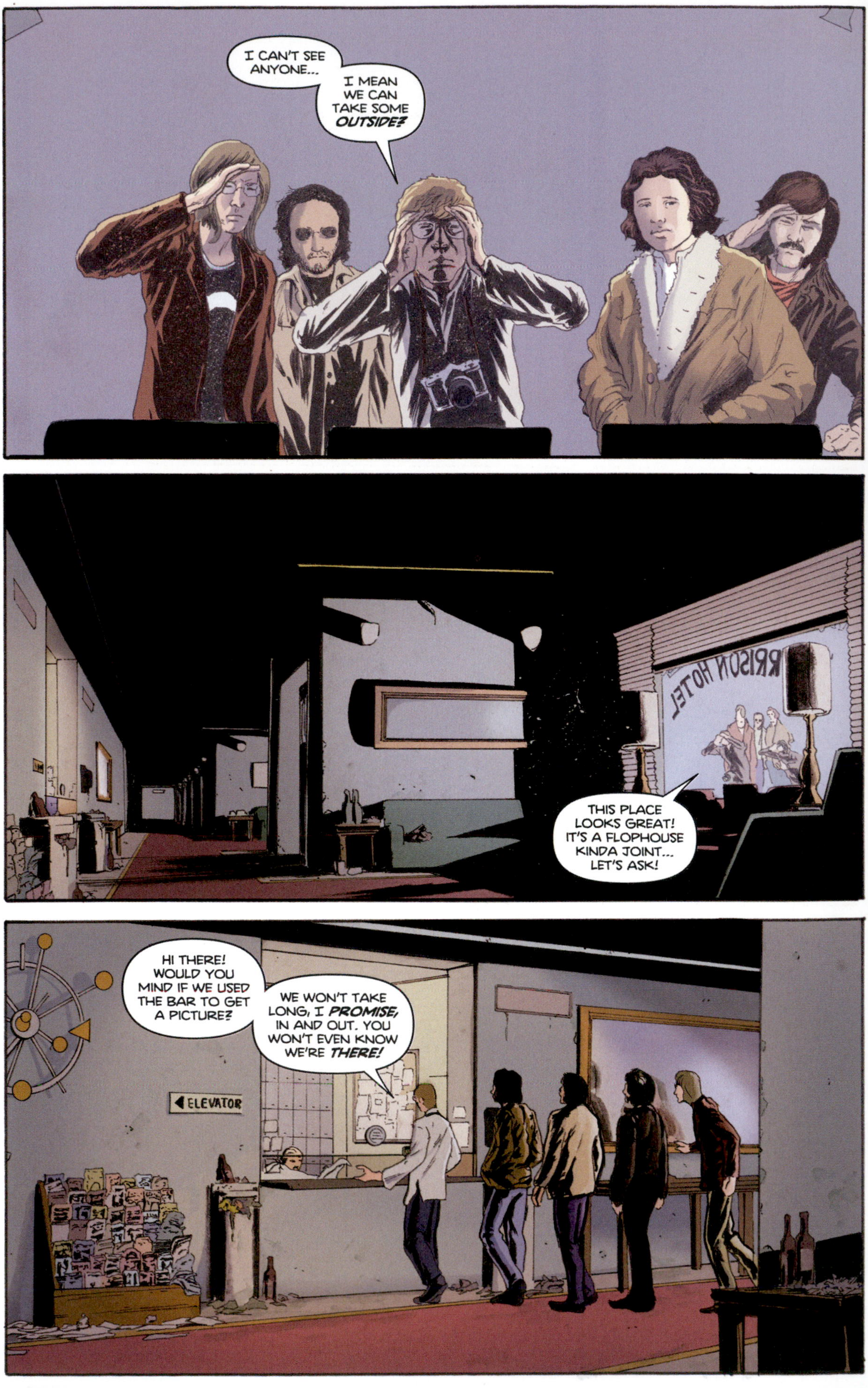

I CAN'T SEE ANYONE...
I MEAN WE CAN TAKE SOME *OUTSIDE?*
THIS PLACE LOOKS GREAT! IT'S A FLOPHOUSE KINDA JOINT... LET'S ASK!
HI THERE! WOULD YOU MIND IF WE USED THE BAR TO GET A PICTURE?
WE WON'T TAKE LONG, I *PROMISE,* IN AND OUT. YOU WON'T EVEN KNOW WE'RE *THERE!*
ELEVATOR

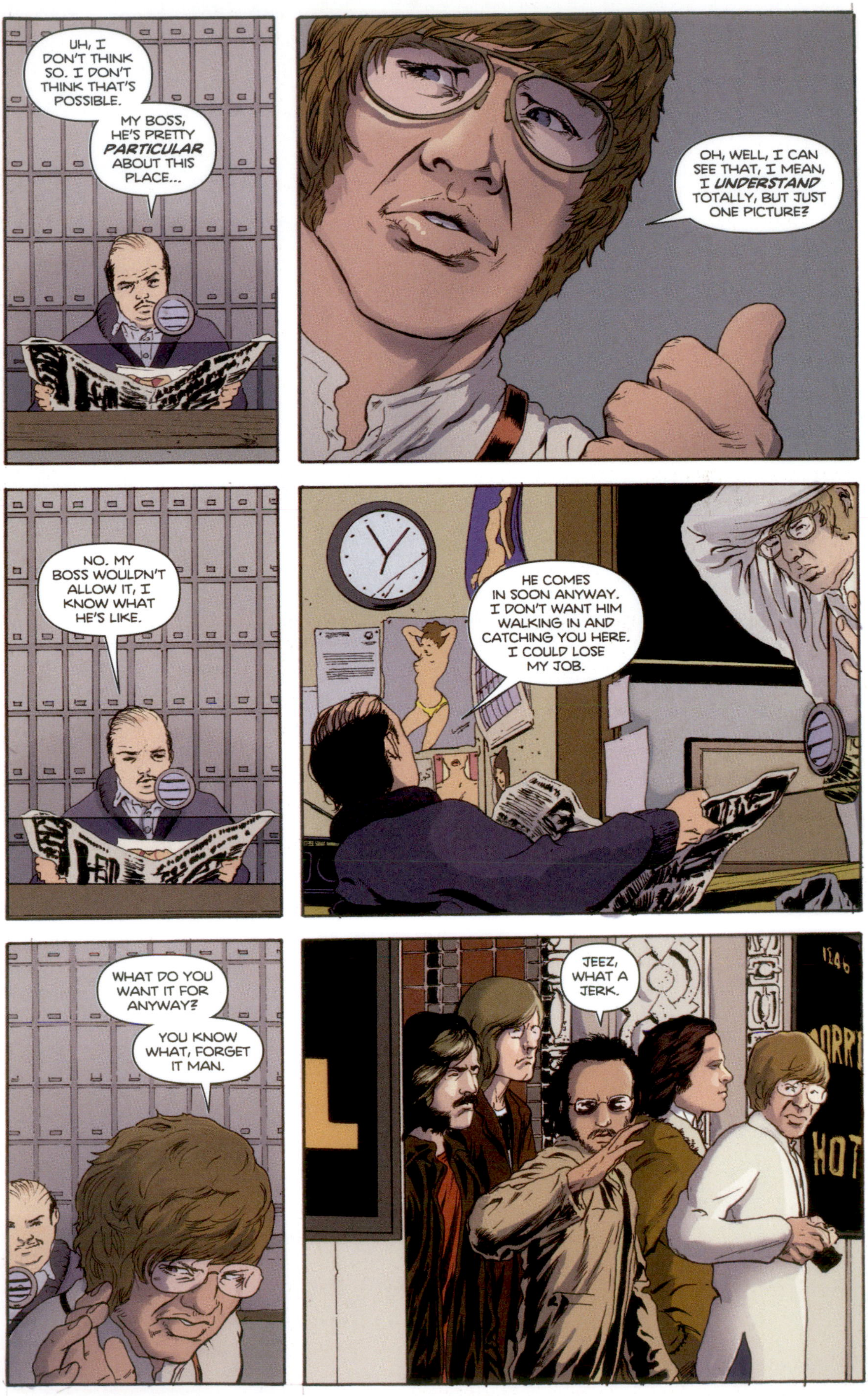
UH, I DON'T THINK SO. I DON'T THINK THAT'S POSSIBLE.
MY BOSS, HE'S PRETTY PARTICULAR ABOUT THIS PLACE...
OH, WELL, I CAN SEE THAT, I MEAN, I UNDERSTAND TOTALLY, BUT JUST ONE PICTURE?
NO. MY BOSS WOULDN'T ALLOW IT, I KNOW WHAT HE'S LIKE.
HE COMES IN SOON ANYWAY. I DON'T WANT HIM WALKING IN AND CATCHING YOU HERE. I COULD LOSE MY JOB.
WHAT DO YOU WANT IT FOR ANYWAY?
YOU KNOW WHAT, FORGET IT MAN.
JEEZ, WHAT A JERK.

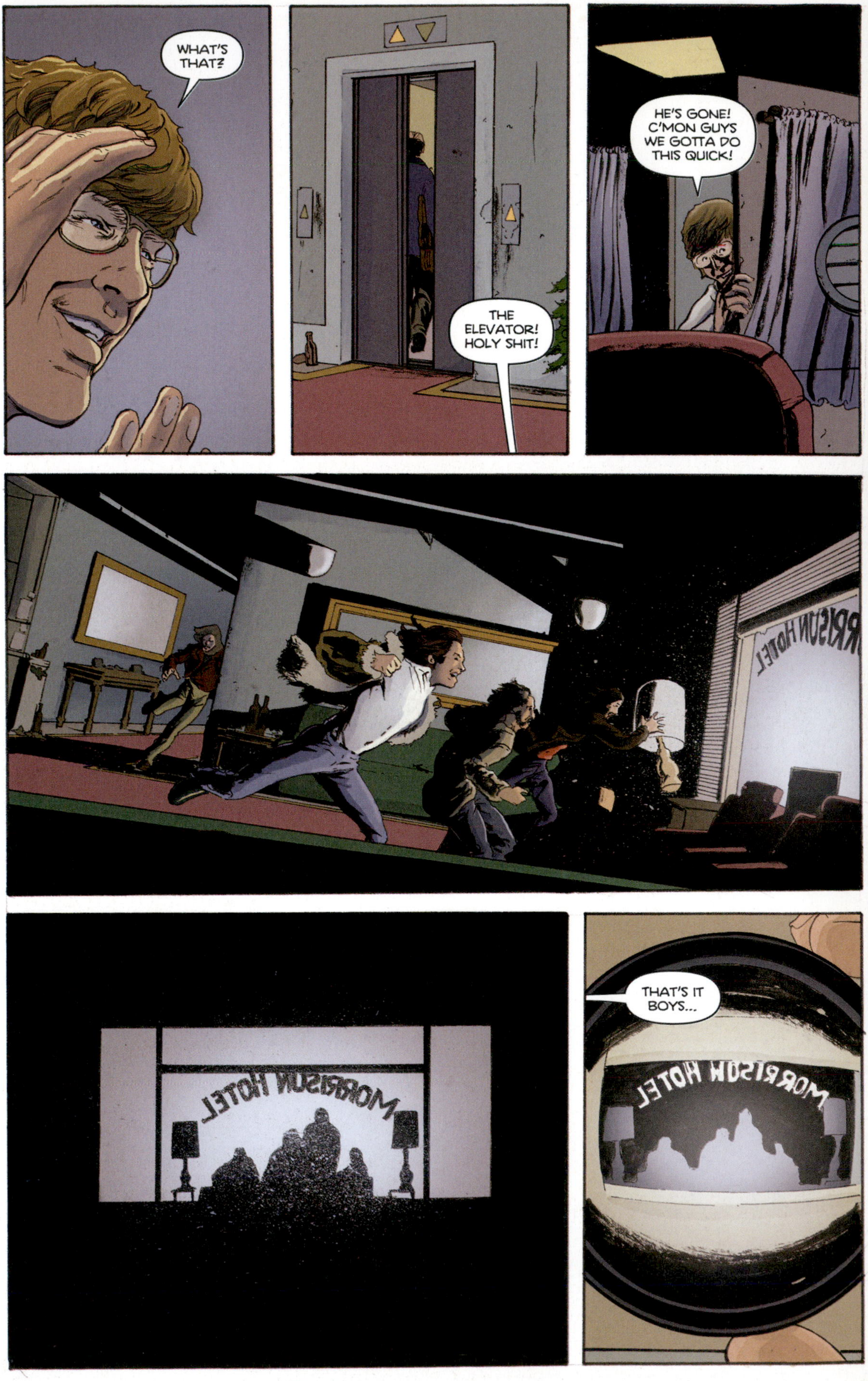
WHAT'S THAT?
THE ELEVATOR! HOLY SHIT!
HE'S GONE! C'MON GUYS WE GOTTA DO THIS QUICK!
MORRISON HOTEL
MORRISON HOTEL
THAT'S IT BOYS...
MORRISON HOTEL

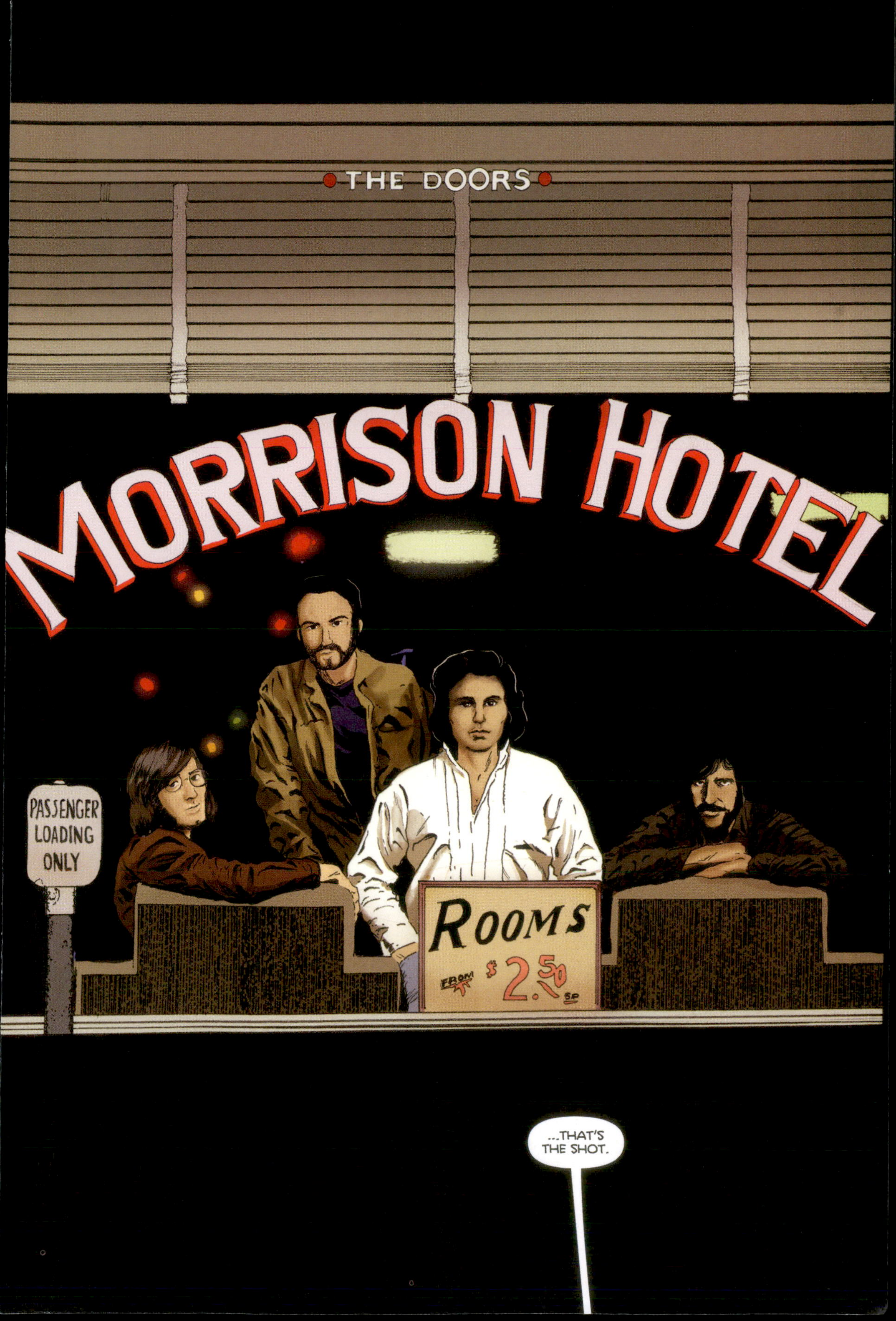
THE DOORS
MORRISON HOTEL
PASSENGER LOADING ONLY
ROOMS
FROM $2.50
...THAT'S THE SHOT.

HA, THAT WAS GREAT! WOW...

HEY, SHALL WE GET A BEER? THERE'S A PLACE I KNOW...

...IT'S CALLED THE HARD ROCK CAFÉ...

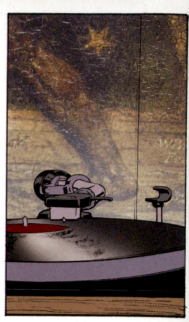

SO? WHAT DID YOU THINK?

FFFFFFFFFFF

WAS IT WHAT YOU IMAGINED?

NO! I MEAN, YEAH, IT *WAS* BUT...I TOTALLY GET WHAT YOU MEAN...IT WAS A *TRIP!*

I MEAN, I KNOW WE ONLY JUST FINISHED LISTENING TO IT...

I WANT TO LISTEN TO IT AGAIN. I WANT TO SPEND MORE TIME *THERE*, YOU KNOW?

WELL, THERE YOU GO. YOU CAN DO THAT. JUST DON'T SCRATCH IT...OKAY?

MORRISON HOTEL

YOU SURE? I MEAN, THANKS! I WON'T!

The End

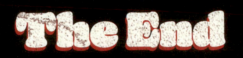